love is not enough

Love Is Not Enough

the treatment of
emotionally disturbed children

BY BRUNO BETTELHEIM

THE FREE PRESS
A Division of Macmillan Publishing Co., Inc.
New York

Collier Macmillan Publishers
London

99397

306 . 855

BET

The Free Press
A Division of Macmillan Publishing Co., Inc.
866 Third Avenue, New York, N.Y. 10022

Collier-Macmillan Canada Ltd.

Printed in the United States of America

printing number
11   12   13   14   15   16   17   18   19   20

To Ralph W. Tyler

preface

A REPORT such as this on the day-to-day life at an institution for the treatment of emotionally disturbed children represents the combined efforts of all staff members involved. Therapeutic efforts, taken singly or added up, cannot easily achieve what is done through the integrated efforts of a total staff; but the condition for such work is a pattern of group living that is harmoniously concerted without any single voice losing its independent character. If variety within a unity is what makes for a work of art, as Kant saw, so the individual uniqueness, the "variety" of all persons who live and work together in the institution, must be preserved within the unity of living if any success is to be achieved.

The author's contribution to this work was the elaboration and implementing of what he felt was best in present day thinking on the education and treatment of emotionally disturbed children, and its application to the particular tasks of the institution. His aim was to bring these ideas to fruition in the setting of the School but, while he provided much of the basic frame of reference within which the work of the School unfolds, it became alive through and was deeply influenced by the contributions of all staff members. With gratitude and humility he wishes to acknowledge that it was the community of all of them which alone made the School, and hence this book, possible. In this sense it would be unjust if he were to single out particular staff members and mention them here, although one exception must surely be made: Dr. Emmy Sylvester, psychiatrist for the School during the years covered in this book, has contributed so much to the development of its philosophy and the shaping of its practice that to her is due special acknowledgment. She has influenced the actions and the viewpoints of staff members so extensively that it would be difficult to acknowledge each of her contributions specifically.

As principal of the School, the author was responsible for the over-all planning and directing of staff efforts, and in this book, for the selection and interpretation of material drawn from the records. To the various staff members belongs full recognition for their work in setting theory into practice, and their reports as participant observers are individually credited in footnotes accompanying the text. Ruth Soffer's untiring help in editing the book is also gratefully acknowledged.

Beyond those dealing directly with the children are the many other staff members who contribute invaluably to the work of the School, including the workers in the office as well as the maids, the cooks, and the janitors. Even more than an army, a treatment institution for children must advance on its stomach. Without a pleasantly filled stomach, even the most assiduous efforts will fail. After that, the unending labour of cleaning the dormitories and bathrooms which need recleaning shortly after they have been done, taxes the patience of maids who cannot even enjoy the reward of following the children on their way to recovery. Everything that gets dirty or disorderly must immediately be cleaned or made orderly again because the children cannot resist the temptations that inhere in disorder. For the same reason, anything broken has to be fixed as soon as possible, because it is an invitation to more breakage. Fixing broken windows (thirty-two has thus far been the maximum for one day—but permitting that rampage made it the turning point of a child's life) and innumerable broken toys in addition to all their other work asks for very special janitors; and so on ad infinitum for the work of all staff members and not only the professional staff.

Throughout the book the names of the various children will appear in different contexts. If the many statements made by any one child do not always seem to accord with one another, it should be realized that the events they were part of may have been separated by perhaps two or even three years, a period during which significant and often radical changes may have occurred in the child's behaviour and outlook on life, if not in his basic personality structure.

For obvious reasons none of the children are called by their real names. The events related in the book were not always selected on the basis of their significance for a particular child, but as often because they are typical for what might occur during any day at the school.

The collection of the material and the preparation of this book were materially aided by a research grant from the National Institute of Mental Health, United States Public Health Service (Research Grant MH-R/81). The present report forms part of a larger investigation on the "Institutional Treatment of Emotionally Disturbed Children," a study made possible by this grant.

Last but certainly not least, the author wishes to express his gratitude to the University of Chicago which makes possible this unique experiment in therapeutic living, and particularly to the Dean of its Division of Social Sciences, Ralph W. Tyler. To him this book is dedicated in friendship and as a token of appreciation for the personal encouragement, the interest, and the practical wisdom which still guide the experiment to whatever success it achieves.

the photographer:
myron h. davis

MR. MYRON H. DAVIS spent two weeks at the School, first in getting acquainted with the children and then just being with them through the normal daily round of events. He, too, became a "participant observer" before he took these photographs. In order to do that, Mr. Davis attached himself mainly to one dormitory group, which will explain why many of the pictures were taken in one dormitory, and mostly of the same group of children.

Only those children were photographed who expressed a spontaneous desire to have their pictures taken.

That the children, in a short space of two weeks, fully accepted Mr. Davis, took him into their confidence and ceased to consider him a stranger, that they were able to go on with their lives as if he were part of the School, all this and much more speaks for Mr. Davis' tact, and for his fine understanding of children.

To the casual observer, much in these pictures will seem not at all different from a series of pictures showing normal children enjoying normal activities. And in a way, this is some measure of the success we achieve in arranging at least the external life of these children to make it similar to that of all others. Since our children are inwardly so chaotic, we must organize the daily recurring activities in such a way that children can quiet down, get some control over their emotions and learn how to master the tasks of living despite their great emotional difficulties. The rest, Mr. Davis' pictures will tell.

contents

list of illustrations

love is not enough

introduction

IN RECENT times, a great deal of the research findings and popular writings in the field of child psychology, child rearing, and psychotherapy have been placing undue stress on such general problems as nursing and education to cleanliness, as if the core of the matter were how often a child is fed or when, exactly, his education to cleanliness is begun or achieved. Certainly we are going through a healthy reaction against antiquated, authoritarian methods of child rearing, and the imposing of rigid schedules that run contrary to a child's desires. But today parents are also told to give love to their children, as if anybody can give what he does not possess, or as if a mother who loves her child needs to be told to do so.

Things only become complicated if we ask what exactly we mean when we talk about "love." Is it really just cuddling and the much discussed "parental approval," or is it a less dramatic willingness to go to some trouble in answering the child's spoken or unspoken needs? Through this book-length discussion of how we handle everyday happenings with the child as they occur, events large and small, we hope to show some of the things that are needed in addition to love in order to raise children successfully in our present day complex environment.

Modern living conditions have made it much more difficult for parents to create a setting in which both their own legitimate

needs and the needs of their children can be satisfied with relative ease. That is why love alone is not enough and must be supplemented by deliberate efforts on the part of the parent. Fortunately most parents love their children and conscientiously strive
to be good parents. But more and more of them become weary
of the struggle to arrange life sensibly for their children, while
modern pressures create more and more insensible experiences
which are added to the life of the child. More and more they are
exposed to crowded living quarters, to overstimulating and incomprehensible experiences through radio and television, and
have to face almost daily some new gadget they must learn to
master or avoid.

Many a tired-out parent finds himself giving up his effort to
turn off the radio or the screen or to put dangerous or breakable
things out of the child's reach. More and more he finds himself
taking the easier way out, since it undoubtedly takes more effort
and ingenuity, for example, to put breakable things out of the
child's reach than to say no! no! to him, or to slap his hands. But
the first requires some minimum of planning by the parent, while
the second creates inconveniences mainly for the child. Even impressing on him the importance of daddy's books he will eventually interpret to mean that dead and replaceable objects were
more important to his parents than his irreplaceable feeling that
it's a good thing to try to explore the world around him—at least
as far as the world is within his reach.

Again, it seems simple to fence a child in behind gates, with
the excuse that he must be protected from hurting himself on
the hot kitchen stove. But with only a little imagination it should
be possible to fence off the kitchen stove and thus enlarge the
realm in which the child may explore safely; not to speak of the
short-sighted (but again well-meaning) parents who consider it
their duty to be active in promoting civic improvements at large,
but who would little interest themselves in a campaign to have
gas ranges so redesigned that the toddler cannot reach its knobs.

The result is that frequent and often angry "nos" convince the
child that finding things out for himself is dangerous and disap-

proved of by parents; that this is a world full of incomprehensible dangers where the safe thing to do is to do nothing, or only what parents explicitly permit. Often, too, the child is convinced in the end that to try to find out for oneself is something bad. And this, often in homes where enlightened parents feel it their duty to see that the child is given adequate sex information (which is desirable), is even permitted to explore this affair on his own. Exploration of sex, yes, but of the kitchen stove, no.

Thus, while the frequent admonition to "love one's child" is well-meant, it falls short of its purpose when the parent applies it without the appropriate or genuine emotions. We have known many children who have resented their parents' going through the prescribed motions of "loving" them because they felt it was not genuine. The mother who indulges her child to show the neighbours how good a mother she is will often hurt the child just as much as if she were only indifferent. The child will not understand that his mother may be acting on her fears or anxieties ("The ideal mother never gets irritated as I am so often"). He will sense only that he is being used, in one way or another, and indulgence received to impress others is no indulgence at all; actually, it is painful for him because he is misused for the mother's extraneous purposes.

I am aware that these and other observations about parents, both here and throughout the book, may sound unduly harsh to the reader, or critical without relief. I must emphasize, therefore, that my examples are drawn from the rearing of emotionally disturbed children. They are meant to serve the conscientious parent toward a better understanding of the reactions of the normal child, just as the study of diseases promotes our understanding of the normal functioning of the body.

It is not my intention in these pages to draw any conclusions as to what educators or parents should do, or avoid doing, in their everyday dealings with a particular normal child. It is hoped that such implications will be drawn by the reader on the basis of his own experiences and the particular setting and emotions in which the lives of the children he is concerned with proceed.

On the other hand, one of the major contributions we can make at an institution such as ours is to study the impact—good or bad—on the individual, of his everyday normal activities, the emotions created in and around them, and how these are related to the human contacts those activities involve. In the course of our efforts at helping children to overcome their difficulties we can see very clearly how because these activities are only "routine" for adults they are too often taken for granted and their importance neglected. But for children these are often the central activities of their lives. We can also observe how the personal contacts experienced around them influence the formation and also the distortion of the human personality, often much more so than do personal contacts in other situations. The deviate, often exaggerated behaviour we observe in the children when they are eating, washing, playing, learning, or going to bed are prototypes of behaviour which comprise, in their totality, the whole range of experience of all normal children.

As a matter of fact, it was these very experiences which led, in our children, to personality disturbances. Therefore, by showing how we handle those situations in dealing with severely damaged children, it may become clear to the reader how their mishandling brought about the disturbances we must now try to rectify.

On this level, our efforts at the School [1] have much broader implications than the helping of some thirty-four emotionally disturbed children, important as that is in itself. As we find how to help the children to solve those problems which prevented them from succeeding in life, as their distress becomes relieved while living at the School, and as we observe their improvement, we gain a better understanding of where in our society things go astray in the rearing of children. Hence, the widest and most important implications of our work are to be found in what we might call preventive psychology, or preventive mental hygiene.

[1] The full name of the School is: The University of Chicago Sonia Shankman Orthogenic School. It is one of the University's experimental or laboratory schools, and will hereinafter be referred to, in brief, as "the School."

In learning to understand behaviour, the study of abnormal psychology has taught us a great deal about the functioning of the normal mind, and functions not easily recognized in studying the normal individual have become clear in the exaggerations and distortions of abnormal behaviour. The theories of psychoanalysis and dynamic psychology which have given the School its underlying frame of reference were themselves mainly dependent on the study of neurotic patients, beginning with hysteric ones. In the behaviour of such persons psychological phenomena were so exaggerated in form that one could study them better and then come to recognize the same problems in normal persons where they existed less intensely. In a similar sense, the exaggerated way in which our children react to considerable shortcomings in their upbringing and to the impact of specific aspects of modern urban living should bring into relief the less serious and hence less obvious mistakes that are made in the rearing of many normal children.

As if the rearing of children in contemporary society, with its ill defined values and mores were not difficult enough, the pressures under which most parents live often defeat even the best intentioned efforts. Thus it is not even enough to do the right thing at the right moment, it must also be done with emotions that belong to the act. Again and again in our work we have found that what counted was not so much the hard facts as the feelings and attitudes that went with them.

Superficially, for example, the mother who does not scold her child for wetting his bed seems more permissive than the one who scolds him severely. Yet if the permissive mother also kicks up a fuss about the labour of washing the sheets, her child may suffer even greater guilt feelings than the one who is scolded for wetting himself. Permissiveness in itself may thus be useless or even harmful if it is more academic than felt.

Again, if the mother is ambitious to have a child who develops better and faster than others, in order to prove to herself and to others that she is really successful as a mother, she can easily stick to the rules and still get her way. The pushing for achievement will simply be displaced from a strictness in toilet training —now taboo with enlightened parents—to a less obvious area.

One such mother recently told me with pride that she would not dream of beginning to toilet-train her eighteen-month-old son. She said she could wait for that until he could indicate spontaneously that he was ready to make regular use of the toilet. On the other hand, this mother kept a list of the words in his vocabulary and had calculated that he was learning two new words every day—a record she was bent on his keeping up or improving. The new words were discussed early and often in the home, and were the main substance of letters from the mother to her parents and in-laws.

In this case, the pressure for one type of achievement—education to cleanliness—was replaced by the pressure for a much more difficult achievement—verbalization. The mother could allow herself much greater pressure with respect to her son's intellectual progress, since her leniency about toilet training had established her clearly as permissive, not only in her own mind but also before all her enlightened friends. Yet in a way this boy was worse off than if his mother had imposed a too early toilet training. Because the sequence of development was here reversed: the ability to verbalize extensively preceded toilet training instead of coming after it; sphincter control, for which he was by and large ready, was delayed, and verbalization, for which he was by no means yet ready, was pushed.

It is not difficult to assume that this child felt under much greater pressure as things were, and was hence a lot more tense than he might have been, had the mother just settled for an early toilet training. The pressure for conformity to his mother's demands would have been great in either case, but it would at least have been steered toward a goal more in line with the boy's actual state of maturity.

For these reasons it would be misleading of us to make specific recommendations either here or in other cases. They could only create the impression that the externals of the situation were what counted instead of the particular child with his particular development and relationships. Again and again we have found it to be minor details more than any particular way that a child was taught to be clean which then aroused emotions in him leading to difficulties later on.

It is less the adult's actions than the way the child tries to interpret or explain his observations to himself which may interfere with his normal development, much more so than the facts of his training which may have been rigid or permissive. In our work, for example, we have found it to be pretty immaterial how much we permit a child to dirty himself, when compared with the importance of the emotional involvement (on his and our part) that accompanies his actions, or how adequately our actions—either permissive or restraining—were made readily understandable to the child. But here an example might better illustrate.

Since cleanliness is so important in our society, the taboos against dirt are very strong. For the same reason it is a problem area well known to anyone interested in therapeutic work with children. Hence many beginners are quick to offer the children the supposedly simple pleasure of getting dirty. But when adults are not too sure about it within themselves they try, in their actions, to rely on what they know about problem children in general, rather than trust to their spontaneous insight into a particular child's needs at the moment.

A child who has formerly been over-clean but has already been started on his way toward the breakdown of his defenses may hesitate about getting himself dirty if he is playing with wet sand, while at the same time wanting to do so. Unable to solve this conflict, he will probably look to the adult for guidance. But suppose, in this case, that the adult has not entirely solved the conflict between his own childish desire to mess with dirt and the demands for personal cleanliness that we make in our society. He will then find himself either defensive about the need to be clean, or defensive about the child's "right" to get dirty. But since he is working in a modern therapeutic institution, he will be convinced it would be better for the child if he were encouraged to dirty himself. So there is little doubt that his overt attitude will be one of permissiveness toward the child about dirt. Yet because of his own unsettled conflict, this conscious behaviour will be flavoured by unconscious tendencies.

For example, he may verbalize encouragement, but may unconsciously recognize that he must swallow a personal repugnance, and this may express itself in a too eager encouragement or a too eager joining of the child in his messing with sand. The child, in a personal conflict between his desire to get dirty and his wish to live up to his parents' demands, will feel that the adult, too, is in conflict no matter what he says out loud. This will tend to make the child more, rather than less doubtful, and in any case make him suspicious of the adult who speaks one way and seems to feel quite another.

In other instances the adult may be influenced in part by a conscious or unconscious aversion toward dirtiness. He may still say encouraging things out of therapeutic conviction, but in doing so, his inner hesitation may reflect itself in a more distant behaviour toward the child than he would normally show in connection with other activities. In activities that are less closely connected with his own unresolved problems, he would easily join in or withdraw as the situation and the needs of the child might require. But this freedom and spontaneity are lacking if he acts on the basis of therapeutic conviction rather than spur-of-the-moment direction in line with his true inclinations. Any child, but particularly the emotionally disturbed child, is apt to respond less to the adult's overt behaviour than to what he senses is different about it when compared with that person's more usual behaviour.

Only the adult whose integration is such that he is relatively indifferent to messiness will react to the child's conflict in terms of the child's needs. Adults who are conflicted themselves about dirtiness or cleanliness will react in terms of preconceived notions about what is therapeutic, or on the basis of their own unresolved conflicts. If the child's anxiety about getting himself dirty grows too great, the adult who is relatively free of conflicts about cleanliness will encourage him to leave the tempting situation. And this he will manage in such a way that the child can do so without threat to his pride and without any leftover fears about entering such a situation later on. On the other hand, with the child whose defenses are already so weak that he can indulge in such activities without guilt or a loss of self-respect, such an adult will offer encouragement and will do so in ways that will allow the child to feel he is not following suggestions but acting out of independent choice.

It would be unrealistic to think that any person can be free of conflict about all, or almost all of those infantile (instinctual) activities that are heavily tabooed in our society. Some adults may be able to take messiness or dirtiness in children without a qualm, but may find it quite another story (despite their theoretical knowledge) when it comes to children's masturbation. Others may be free of inner conflicts about obscenity and exhibitionism in children but may be full of conflicts about such expressions of orality as wolfish eating or thumbsucking, or about physical aggression, and so on. The best we can hope for is that the adult himself will recognize which areas of behaviour he is still not at peace about, and that on the basis of such insight he will try to stay away from the children when they are doing things that unsettle him. While the children are thus occupied, he should leave them to be handled by a person who is not apt to be disturbed by this type of behaviour.

In a treatment institution such as the School it becomes a major task of the supervisor or administrator to assess correctly which staff members are least in conflict about particular problem areas and to guide them to concentrate on these areas and leave the others to be handled by the ones better able to do so. In our School at least four adults—one teacher and two or three counselors, to whom another therapist must often be added— have intimate contact with each group of children. This permits us to select the staff members assigned to any one group so that the children have at least one (and often more) adult available who is free of conflict about particular areas of behaviour in which the child will need help or support.

In addition to these adults who take major responsibility for a group, there are also many others (the nurse, the shop teachers, the coach, etc.) who are available to the children. And again, each of these adults has at least one problem area about which he has little or no conflict, and which makes it that much easier to protect the child from having to engage in an activity with a person who is conflicted about it. When I speak of a person as being conflicted about a particular aspect of living, or behaviour, I include not only feelings of ambivalence about the activity tabooed, but also—if there is such a thing—non-ambivalent rejection or an over attachment to this type of behaviour.

In other respects, too, the well-integrated adult just by being himself and by accepting his adult responsibilities (as well as his prerogatives)—by being without conflict about his adulthood, for example—can be helpful to the child where the conflicted adult may create emotional difficulties precisely through his wanting to help the child.

For example, due to complex modern living many a well-meaning parent is literally unable to spend enough time with his child. If, in addition, such an adult is none too sure of his emotional attitude to his child, he may then try to deny or make up for the lack of time (or emotional attachment) by conscious efforts to win the child's affection. Often enough we find that a father, wanting to become, or remain, a companion to his son, goes so far as to deprive him of the protection and security which only a father can provide. By acting the playmate to his son he deprives him of an adult image in whose semblance the child may one day form his own personality; by being childish himself he convinces his son that he cannot control or protect him.

In order to give the child back his security, which depends on the fact that adults can protect, and if necessary control him, all the adult at the School has to do is be himself and act in line with his age. By doing just that, he provides an image for the children to emulate. At the same time he restores the child's security which derives from his being cared for by a strong and effective adult.

To cite an example, one day Stuart, one of our seven-year-old boys, was playing in the park and managed to provoke a group of children (whom he did not know) into ganging up on him. His counselor protected him from the onslaught, but as they walked away, Stuart seemed very pleased and remarked how lucky he was that his counselor could protect him. His father, he said, would never have been able to do it. Then he went on to relate how he used to wrestle with his father, and how he usually succeeded in beating him at least six times out of seven. He continued that his father was not as good a wrestler as he was, that while he nearly always managed to pin his father's shoulders down, his father was so weak that even the few times he won he could hardly ever pin both of Stuart's shoulders down.[2] (Stuart was puny for his age; his father had been a navy officer and had only recently left active service with decorations for valour.)

Three months at the School were sufficient to permit Stuart to state freely that it was anything but reassuring to be able to think himself superior to his father, that the real advantage for a child was to be able to believe that adults are superior to himself and therefore well able to protect him. One day at this time he told the same counselor how he could sing all kinds of cowboy songs, and added, "I'm very good at it, that's the trouble." His counselor asked why that was a "trouble" and he answered: "My father isn't very good at it, that's the trouble."

From admitting that he was better than his father in singing, and that this troubled him, it was a long way (more than six months) before he could state that the reason he had to push

[2] Participant observer: Calvin Axford.

It goes without saying, however, that in a family setting which is on the whole stable and satisfying, in which the child has little reason to doubt a parent's strength or protective ability, this kind of incident is harmless enough and interpreted as no more than what it is: fun and play.

himself so hard was because he felt he had to look out for himself, since his parents couldn't seem to do it for him. This insecurity, combined with other factors, was enough of a motive for him to develop an intelligence that expressed itself in an I. Q. of 153, to the detriment of his ability to function as a human being in any social context; he was unable to sit still for a moment, unable to play with other children who one and all rejected him violently. His actually superior intellectual achievement had combined with his feeling of superiority toward his parents to support megalomanic actions that threw him out of all contact with reality.

Besides our direct work with the children enrolled in it, and the broader study of preventive psychology, the other main purpose of the School is to offer training for future workers in the field. Obviously the School cannot well provide training for future administrators of children's institutions, for child therapists and educators, or for other allied workers, unless it achieves some success with the treatment procedures it develops.

This is not to imply that we have now accumulated a body of absolute knowledge which will solve all the problems confronting us. On the contrary, we feel we are working in a relatively new field in which not even the basic assumptions underlying our efforts are definitely established, not to speak of their application to everyday practice. Much more knowledge is needed in this field, and at best, we can hope to add to it. Hence in a report such as this one our purpose is less to tell others how to go about helping these emotionally disturbed children who need our services so much, and more to stimulate others to test our methods, to refine those which they find useful, to discard others which are found wanting, and in general to help in determining the particular advantages and shortcomings of our various methods and procedures.

In presenting the work of the School, two basic approaches would have been equally useful. In one, a child is followed step by step through the process of his rehabilitation, and at each point the reader is shown the meaning of the step and its bene- ficial—or detrimental—impact on the particular child at the par- ticular moment.[3] The second approach, and the one followed in this book, is that of showing how the everyday activities of the children can be used in a purposeful way, how they can be made carriers of personal relations and of the experience of mastering tasks that were previously avoided, or those in which the child usually experienced defeat.

This latter approach was selected because it seems to show up more clearly the particular anxieties that may be aroused in a child by certain activities and the way they are handled by adults. It shows, too, the particular shadings of contact that the child will respond to in his every day activities, and how the individual flavour of the personal relationship at such moments can as easily be used in furthering mental health and emotional well-being, as it can start the child off on his way to failure and despair.

Later on, in giving composite pictures of how the emotional problems of children may be handled (when they wake in the morning, for example) we shall try to present what we consider to be an adequate handling of a specific problem situation. In doing so, we do not mean to imply that we are always a match for our tasks, because unfortunately we make mistakes. It seemed pointless, however, to burden the reader with an enumeration of our failures, and if we concentrate on presenting a more positive picture in this book, it must not be taken to mean that we never make errors. Nevertheless, when we make them, we try to learn what we can from them and set them to good use. At least as many good relations have been established by admitting our mis- takes to the child, by apologizing to him, and by our genuine effort to make up for them, as were established by correct han- dling in the first place. Again, that we also err bridges over the gap between us and the child. And that we find it easy to admit

[3] An example of this approach may be found in the case report on Harry. (See Publications on the School, no. 9. A volume of such case histories is in preparation.)

and correct our own shortcomings encourages the child to think that to correct his behaviour may not be as difficult as he thought, and need not entail loss of status, as he feared.

Before taking the reader through a day at the School and before we can show what makes living there beneficial for the child, a few general facts about the School might be helpful. The School is a residential institution for children of normal or better than normal intelligence. All the children who live there are free of physical disorder, but suffer from severe emotional disturbances that have proved (or are expected to prove) beyond the reach of the common therapeutic techniques.[4] Many of them, prior to enrollment, underwent various types of treatment such as child analysis, psychotherapy in child guidance clinics or with private physicians, but responded little or not at all to treatment efforts. Most children remain at the School on an average of two years or more. We can accommodate thirty-four children ranging in age between six and fourteen, and disturbances range all the way from delinquency or a functional inability to read, to childhood schizophrenia—if that term may be used.

Names, as such, are not too significant, yet some remarks on why we call it a *school* rather than a *home* may highlight a few pertinent facts. Though negative comparisons are notoriously unsuccessful, the idea of the children's home is so widespread that the basic philosophy of the School may be clarified by contrasting it with that of a children's home or a treatment center.

"Children's homes" try to re-create, if not a home atmosphere, at least a home setting. And usually they succeed in doing so, since in the majority of real homes the convenience of adults takes precedence over the child's interest, while in others, the child is forced into a mold called "what children like to do."

Lately, it is true, some homes have been geared mainly to the rhythm and interests of the children, as though there were no mature adults present. Only such homes are no longer fit for

[4] For indications on the placement of such children in an institution such as the School, see Publications on the School, nos. 3 and 6.

emotional health, but wonderlands in which parent figures act like mad hatters and permit Alice to regulate her parents' lives. The resultant insecurity is great, since the protectors a child needs are absent, and the child is properly confused about the working of this world and his own power and importance. Such regimes have sometimes brought a child to our School.

Most children's homes pride themselves on how successfully their house-parents take the place of true parents. Yet it is common knowledge that the difficulties of almost all emotionally disturbed children have originated in the relationship to a parent. It is therefore unrealistic to expect them to be able to form successful relationships to parent substitutes after so short a time. But since no other types of relationships are available, the child depends for satisfaction of his needs on conformity with the established pattern. He recognizes what is useful to him and pretends a child-parent relationship. The result is a pseudo-relationship which rules out any later formation of a true one.

The attitude of such homes might best be described by saying that their philosophy states (though never explicitly): Because the relationship to a parent is the one which the child was utterly unable to manage, it is the best starting point for his readjustment (every adult's insight into the complexity of his own relations to his parents notwithstanding).

A school for emotionally disturbed children, on the contrary, should start the child's readjustment by offering him the simplest and not the most complex of all personal relationships. It might also be mentioned that in our emotionally starved society, the need for immediate affectionate responses from children on the part of many adults who choose to work as house-parents in homes for children is often much greater than vice versa. Children who enter such institutions are much more apt to see adults as the source of conveniences rather than to seek their love which, biogenetically, is the result of having received ample satisfactions.

Therefore the newcomer in the School is not expected to seek and find parental figures and to relate to them. Instead, he is offered casual acquaintance with various people who provide him with whatever he needs, including respect for his need for privacy and non-interference. If he succeeds in relating to them, well and good; if not, little damage has been done since they need not become important to him.

With the exception of love at first sight, an adult's immediate love for a child can only be due to emotional starvation and keeps the child from one of the most maturing experiences—that of a slowly developing, mutually satisfying personal relationship. Immediate loving or mothering of a child implies the obligation to return such love, a response which is beyond the disturbed child's emotional capacity at first and results only in feelings of worthlessness and guilt.

True, over a period of several months, some particular figure in the total setting of the School is usually accepted by the child in a parental role. But this occurs only after his own experiences have taught him to want such a relationship, after his adjustment has made him ready for it, and after he has slowly convinced himself that he can handle it successfully. But such progress is made only very slowly.

Offering satisfaction in the ways in which a good mother may indulge her small child will finally lead even an older child to form ties similar to those he might originally have formed to a good parent. Then, and only then, is the child ready to form a relationship to a mother or a mother figure. This is now possible precisely because the figure has been selected by the child, according to his own inclinations and out of a number of possible choices.

Nothing is more dangerous for the child's readjustment than meeting a person who arrogates to herself a mother role, who has studied the Rights of Infants and concluded that rights are something that must be forced upon the individual. If unlimited response to his needs is immediately forced upon a child by a parent figure, instead of being offered casually, often his starvation (either emotional or otherwise) does not permit him to reject it, although it can only be had at unacceptable terms. This forces him into infant-like dependency.

On entering such a situation the first experience of the child is one of conflict between his desire, on the one hand, for receiving candy or being rocked and babied, and his opposing self-respect which makes such satisfaction acceptable only after his status has been well established, and the selection of the person from whom he is willing to accept satisfaction has been made autonomously.

Although emotions a child originally felt about his parents are continually being transferred to staff members, this always happens in diluted form. To some degree, too, the behaviour of adults at the School serves to counteract the anxiety a child felt about these very emotions. The difference between a counselor at the School and a child's mother gives the child a feeling of security at the School because he is safe there from his mother's interference, while the mother is safe from the possible consequences of his hostility.

After nearly five months at the School, Emily expressed all this as she began to communicate some of her feelings. In talking to the psychiatrist she was comparing her regular counselors, particularly her counselor Joan and a new substitute counselor whom we shall call Marilyn. Emily had brought with her to this interview a candy stick which she now unwrapped, saying it was a present from Joan. Then she added, "She becares me." When asked what this meant, she answered, "She becares me, she doesn't love me." Asked what love meant, Emily answered, "Love means to hug me and kiss me and carry me and put me down." After a pause she added, "Parents do it. Counselors becare you. They give you clothes and candy. Joan becares me. Marilyn loves me. My parents don't becare me, they're not counselors."

In these and similar remarks Emily expressed some of the reasons for her autistic withdrawal at home, but also, in a way, why it became possible for her to come out of her shell at the School and make some contacts with others. Parents, according to her, love and hug you and put you down—and from other remarks Emily made, one might add, not as the child wants things but as it pleases the parent. Counselors at the School take care of the child when the child shows a need and without the child having to give something in return. That is what Emily meant by "becaring" a child.

The new and inexperienced substitute counselor, she felt, came too close to her for comfort, imposed emotions on Emily (who was not ready for them) by cuddling her and carrying her around. This close contact, which she called love, was more than she could accept at the time and it overpowered her physically and emotionally. She was ready to be "becared," to take advantage of the care given her, but as yet she could only do so as long as no one expected her to love in return.

Experience at the School shows that of all possible relationships, the one to parental figures is formed last. This notwithstanding the fact that for one particular child or another, the same counselor may have represented first a slavey or a "sucker," good only to be taken advantage of, then a hated older sibling, and finally a much desired older friend.

The difficulty in forming parental relationships, and the time element involved in their formation, was nicely demonstrated by the statement of one eight-year-old after having been at the School for eighteen months. Speaking of me, he told his counselor: "First I had no use for him, I didn't even know when he was around. Then, about a year ago, I was terribly scared of him; when he even looked at me, I shivered. Now I like him a lot and I don't like it if he goes on one of his trips." [5]

This child, whose relationship to his father was one of the most disturbing elements in his previous life, was able to take significant steps in integration during his initial stay at the School because he was not forced to cope with those emotional problems which an attachment to a parental figure might have revived. During the second period of his adjustment, his guilt feelings were so great that forcing him into closeness to a father figure would have overpowered him with fear and guilt. Only

[5] Participant observer: Ronnie Dryovage.

in the latter phases of his adjustment was he able to master parental relations realistically and to take advantage of the added protection and security which only they can provide. But even then he could express his feelings only to the figure of an older sibling.

After so much has been said about how unsuitable it is for a treatment center to be organized along the lines of a home, it should be stressed that such institutions are very adequate for children whose ability to form ties to parental figures has remained unimpaired. Such children are soon able to transfer to them the positive ties they had once formed to their parents. But then there is no need for them to be placed in a special school for emotionally disturbed children.

Fortunately for our work, it is beneficial for the child to mix with other children who suffer from different types of disturbances, provided, of course, that the children are grouped carefully, and that their group life is so manipulated as to be effective in helping the child overcome his difficulties. For example, the extremely withdrawn child who sees the world in his own frame of reference cannot recognize that the acting-out child, let us say the delinquent, is suffering from anxieties as deep as his own. He thinks, instead, that the delinquent lives a free and easy life and may even have envied the truant his imagined freedom before he himself came to the School.

He never dared to behave like the delinquent because he was too afraid of what he viewed as the terrible consequences of such a life. But once he is living at the School, he can see for himself that the delinquent's greater ease in going after what he wants, or in letting off steam, does not lead to any disastrous results, and the fears that once kept him withdrawn from an active life, or from expressing his emotions, can slowly dissolve. Then the example of the delinquent becomes an incentive to greater freedom, but again, of course, only when carefully handled. The runaway child, on the other hand, envies the withdrawn child his apparent ability to enjoy quiet rest and peace, and eventually this becomes an incentive to try to live for himself what seems a more peaceful way of life.

Just as our actions and emotions alone are what convey to the child our general philosophy and our particular intentions, so our philosophy would reveal itself best if we could recount in detail what transpires at the School from one day to the next. But even a book length report such as this one must at best remain sketchy and inadequate.

In brief, it may be said that our approach is mainly psychoanalytic. Specifically it follows the direction first indicated by Aichhorn in the institutional treatment of delinquents, with those changes suggested by our progress in knowledge since those early efforts at rehabilitating children. In addition, we are strongly influenced by the educational philosophy of John Dewey.

Beyond that, the philosophy of the School, as it emerges from staff interaction, is obviously influenced by the thinking of many workers in the field. The efforts at helping emotionally disturbed children we are about to describe would not have been possible if we had not drawn heavily on the experience of all those who preceded us. Yet in our work it is not necessarily the research which bears most directly on therapeutic action from which one always learns most, nor is learning confined to reports one agrees with. Also included must be those reports which raise grave doubts in one's mind and are often more of a stimulant to vigorous experiment than those one agrees with entirely. For this reason, it is almost impossible to do justice to all sources in citing the works that have affected us.

But much more than to any specific works, we are indebted to the writings of Sigmund and Anna Freud, John Dewey, August Aichhorn, and all those other great educators from Comenius and Pestalozzi to the Buhlers, Montessori, and Piaget, who have helped us to understand children—and above all to understand ourselves.

And now, before presenting and discussing the observations of the various participant observers, it should be mentioned that while all staff members agree on the philosophy underlying our treatment efforts, this very philosophy requires that each staff member carry it out wholly in terms of his own personality. Nothing indeed would be more deadly than our all doing alike, and it would certainly make meaningless the variety and distinctness of personal relations on which all of our efforts are based.

Since personal relations are the essence of our work, the people who create and maintain them, more than anything else, are "the School." Varied as their training may be—some have degrees in anthropology, education, human development, in medicine, nursing, psychology, social work, and sociology—they function not as representatives of their particular professions, but as persons who are receiving or have received the necessary training to help emotionally disturbed children in a particular setting such as ours. Most of them served an apprenticeship at the School.

Just as the children have to cope with the tasks that are set by the particular world of the School, so staff members, too, have to integrate themselves in this cosmos before they can make any attempt to help children to do so. For them, too, this is a process that takes considerable time and effort. They, too, have to learn to become part of a purposeful unity and also what may seem still more difficult—to preserve, at the same time, their personal uniqueness. In a word, they must learn to become more themselves and not less so.

Just as the children must undergo a process of integration, so the staff members, too, must forever be integrating experiences the children subject them to, and the reactions those experiences evoke. Thus, basically, all staff members are apprenticed to all others at the School, and if the learning process is painful at times it is always rewarding. But only if they constantly feel they are learning to understand better, to act more spontaneously and at the same time more rationally, can staff members present to the children an example, not of integration achieved—if there is such a state—but of an ever higher integration that is gained in a slow, step by step process.

And finally, since staff members retain their distinct individuality, it is possible for the children to select freely from a variety of personalities those which appeal to them most in the forming of constructive relationships.

1

the children

THERE is no such thing as a typical child, and selecting any one of them to serve as a first example is even more difficult when writing about an institution that prides itself on considering each child as a distinct individual. But if one child must serve as an introduction, then the problems we faced with Lucille are as good as any others.

Lucille was not yet six when she entered the School. Her life history included placements in two children's homes—one of them a treatment institution—and three foster homes, none of which were able to cope with her or her problems. Between placements there were always times when she lived with her unmarried mother who was highly unbalanced. All the treatment efforts that were made in her behalf at two psychiatric clinics also failed to improve her disturbance. Among other things, psychiatric examination revealed schizophrenic tendencies, extreme hyperactivity and disorders of thinking. The symptoms which were most troublesome in her various placements were her uncontrollable temper tantrums and her sex delinquency. Before she was five years old she was already approaching strange men on the street, demanding attention from them, being extremely provocative toward them sexually, and making efforts to fondle them.

When I first saw her she approached me on all fours and was

barking like a puppy. Then she jumped at me, and tried first to bite and then to touch me in the genital region. Any conversation with her then was impossible because she immediately escaped into delusional talk. Later, when we began to understand her life experiences and her reactions to them, we realized that in playing the provocative puppy she was not acting out any phantasy play, but was repeating a scene she had enacted many times before in reality, often with pleasurable results for herself. Actually, she was trying realistically to please and amuse me as she had once amused a series of "fathers" she had "attracted" to the mother by her novel performances.

These fathers would usually begin by feeding her candy and handling her while she sat on her mother's lap, and then push her off when they were ready to take over. A frequent observation of the sex act formed her most impressive life experience and much later, when we could quiet her down enough to play with her, it became apparent, for example, that playing house (to her knowledge) meant the following sequence of events: the mother feeds the baby, who is then thrown into a corner while male and female puppets jump violently upon one another.[1]

For a child suffering from an anxiety neurosis, such play might have been a sadistic interpretation of the sex act, the repetition of a primal scene she had experienced as extremely upsetting, because it showed parents in a relationship so different from the usual one. In Lucille's case, however, the play represented not the most unusual part of her knowledge of how parents live with one another, but all she knew in the world of the relations between parents. Hers was a true and not a distorted picture of her parents' behaviour, or of those who took the place of parents in her life. An immediate "working through" of these traumatic experiences would have led to nothing since nothing was buried beyond them.

For Lucille, there was a long process of learning about normal human relationships that had to come before any efforts could be made to help her place her experiences in a more normal con-

[1] Participant observer: Florence White.

text. She had to learn first of all about what normal adult relationships to one another (and to a child) should be like, before she was ready to work through her childhood recollections, which she had neither repressed nor conceived of as unusual.

As a matter of fact, the greatest difficulties of the majority of our children have not come about through repressive or defensive mechanisms that interfere with the normal process of living. Although some also suffer from having had too much to repress, and although all of them have worked out pathological defenses for themselves, the most important reason for their inability to get along in the world is their having failed to organize their personalities from the very beginning. It is not that they have deviately organized personalities, but that their personalities are not sufficiently organized. In most cases, their living experiences have failed to coalesce and stayed fragmentary to such a degree that no more than the rudiments of personalities have developed.

Some children show such a total lack of repression that they are hardly socialized at all. Others have failed so completely in their defensive efforts that they have given up entirely trying to get along in this world; they have withdrawn from it totally, including an unwillingness to speak, or to eat. Hence our main task is to bring some intelligible order into chaos. The reorganization of disjointed personalities is secondary, and by comparison a much simpler task, but it comes only much later, if at all.

In helping to bring order into the child's personality we rely mainly on his desire to get along in a world that provides him with ample satisfaction of all, or almost all, of his needs and not only the ones that are commonly accepted by adults as legitimate. We feel that before anything else a child has to be utterly convinced that—contrary to his past experiences—this world can be a pleasant one, before he can feel any impulse to get along in it. Once such a desire has sprung up and has really become part of his personality, then and only then can we also expect him to accept and to come to terms with the less pleasant aspects of life.

This, incidentally, is the way the normal child learns, or should learn how to put up with displeasure. As an infant (and before birth) all his needs are presumably satisfied. But only after many months of experiencing the world as something relatively satisfying do we expect him to learn to control some of his behaviour, even if that seems an unpleasant task.

The satisfaction of a child's wants must become the means which will induce him to form a positive relation to the adults who provide for his well being. Then, to the satisfaction of the child's needs, is added the unique gratifying experience that only a genuine human relationship can offer. The relation to this person eventually challenges the child to change his personality at least in part in the image of the person or persons who are now so important to him. He identifies with them, as we say, and this identification is often the starting point for the organization of his personality. Those aspects of the adult's personality with which the child identifies then form the nucleus around which he organizes his talents, his interests, his desires and his temperament, all of which have until now been chaotic and undeveloped.

But the bringing of order into chaos must also be preceded by the experience of living in an orderly world. Living day in and day out among adults who provide the child with images of reasonable and orderly living becomes a challenge to him to take up their pattern, first in his external and then in his internal life. Nor must the idea of orderliness be imposed on him by force. It must be so presented that the child himself begins to realize that this way of life is more sensible and more to his advantage. Sooner or later then it will also help him to feel that it might be better for him to organize his inner life sensibly, too.

This is quite different from the analysis of the transference relationship which is the recognized tool of the prevalent schools of psychotherapy. This method, of course, presupposes the earlier existence of relationships that can be transferred. But since many of our children have never had the previous experience of a meaningful relation, we must rely at the School on real, honest-to-goodness relationships. For example, Lucille had experienced nothing in her previous life that was suitable as a basis for forming new relationships, nor any that had ever made life worth living for her. In order to rehabilitate her we had to provide her with the entirely new experience of satisfying human relationships. Only then could she evolve the frame of reference which led her to an understanding of the world around her and of her past experiences. In her case no obstacles to her understanding of the world had to be removed, other than those which originated in correctly interpreted past experiences. But these had not only been mostly upsetting, they had all been chaotic, and therefore so was her world. No child will try to understand or otherwise try to come to grips with a world that seems utterly senseless. First, the world had to begin to look pleasant and orderly to Lucille before she could feel any desire to become a pleasant person herself, and to organize her inner chaotic strivings. In many similar cases our task is to provide new experiences that will allow ordering of the actual world rather than doing away with misinterpretations of past experiences that interfere with the development of a correct world picture.

Since so many of our children have never before been a partner in a satisfying human relationship, they are unable, at first, to form personal relations of any kind. Even children who because of overpowering pressure have been forced into seeming submission and at first show "polite" behaviour, later reveal that the politeness was only a screen behind which lay a hatred of all other persons which kept them from forming relations. Later, as they felt the security of the School, this screen evaporated and their hatred appeared. Like Lucille, they barked or they growled at us, not in a seductive way but aggressively. They could only scream, but not talk.

Richard, an eleven-year-old, overanxious and compulsively clean boy, later told us: "My mother used to wash my mouth with soap when I used bad words, but along with the bad ones she washed away all the good words, too." Richard hardly spoke to us at all for many weeks. If he had to communicate he would scream at us and there were very few things he shouted that did not end with the repeated exclamation "kill, kill," most often "kill the Doctor" (meaning me). He called himself "the Killer," and instead of painting his name on his closet as other children do, he painted in huge red letters the word "Killer." During this time he held long growling conversations with his teddy bear whom he totally controlled, as he himself had been totally controlled in the past. This teddy bear he made the executor of all his hatred.[2] Although he quickly took ample advantage of the satisfactions we offered, it was many months before he was ready to talk to us, and many more before he was able to form even one meaningful human relation.

Children like Richard and Lucille, and nearly all other children who come to the School, do not know how to relate themselves to people because they have never acquired the techniques that are learned by the less disturbed child in the protected and simplified way of life that the family will normally provide for its infants. Few of our children are suffering from neuroses due to too great attachments to one or both parents, or to an inability to solve conflicts created by those allegiances, the typical neurotic conflicts of adults. Rather, they are children whose deviate development never gave them a chance to form consistent identifications in the first place. As a result, they have never formed a suitable set of images they could unify in their own minds and use as the model for an integrated personality.[3]

Primitive attachments will develop into simple identifications that are relatively free of ambivalence only after the child has learned to expect ample and predictable satisfaction of his needs. Ideally this development takes place at a time when other distracting relations and tasks are still absent. Normally, too, this unique concentration on the one relationship to the mother is the basis on which the child forms his personality in infancy. But the complexity of modern life, even when cut down to what is normally required of the eight- or the nine-year-old, provides far too many stimulants to permit them to concentrate safely on

[2] Participant observer: Patty Pickett.
[3] For a theoretical discussion of this type of case, see Publications on the School, nos. 2 and 3.

one central emotional and maturational task. Therefore, at the School, we try to provide the children with situations that are as simple, as uncomplicated and as protective as they can realistically be made for an eight- or a ten- or a twelve-year-old child.

In short, as regards the child's psychological reality, we try to create a setting that stimulates growth rather than stresses achievement, such as the setting in which the infant first learns to like and relate to the persons he knows. It is a setting which teaches the child to put greater value on emotional integration than on visible success in competition, and to shun an empty "popularity" in favour of one or a few intensive and emotionally meaningful relations. We prefer the development of a distinct and well-knit personality to any surface adjustment, even if the result is a person who cannot get along with "everybody." We are satisfied if the child learns to get along well with himself and a few favoured people, and otherwise successfully meets the task of becoming a useful citizen.

What is therefore most characteristic of the School is the fact that we try to create a total setting that includes all important activities of the children and permits them to concentrate on unifying their lives. In order to be able to do so we have to try to eliminate or to control certain other activities or experiences that we consider less important, or even a hindrance. In order to help the child to give up his delusional ways of approaching reality, and to give up his personal isolation in favour of human relations, we try first to reduce and later to eliminate all stimulants to solitary daydreaming, particularly the comics and the radio where the contents are mostly aggressive or fearful.

We try to wean the child away from "canned," mechanical stimulation and try to replace it by the experience of activities that lead to human contact and the conviction that the child can do things for himself. We encourage him not to rely on others but to prepare his own entertainment, an experience that stimulates the hope that eventually he will also be able to do something about his environment, to make it a better place for him to live in. Here it should not be overlooked that at the center of all staff members' attitudes toward their work is the desire to make life and the environment better for the child. That they succeed in doing so gives the child the feeling that it is possible to change things for the better, a feeling he has never had before. Eventually this feeling finds expression in the child's loss of interest in scary radio programs or scary movies, to which many of our children are addicted when they come.

Martin, a ten-year-old delinquent, very bright and manually very skillful, had spent the greater part of his life in the delusional world of his phantasies. As he escaped more and more from an unbearable world, he spent more and more time at the movies. But within two months after coming to the School the frequency of his visits decreased considerably. This was partly made possible by his learning to permit himself pleasures he really wanted much more, and partly by the guidance of his counselors who encouraged him to assert himself in various activities. A short time later when other boys of his group were discussing the possibility of going to a movie, he spontaneously declared he had no wish to go. "Why should I go to a movie?" he asked. "There I have to sit still and see unreal people do unreal things, while here I can do real things myself." [4]

But weaning children away from the radio and movies is only one of our many efforts to manipulate the child's environment so that its stimulus is mainly constructive and does not include too many experiences that lead to anxiety.[5] For this reason, we sometimes think of our work as environmental therapy rather than psychotherapy.[6] That is, we rely less on the isolated relationship to one person, or the working out of problems in a rela-

[4] Participant observer: Gayle Shulenberger.

[5] Of course we do not eliminate educational programs or any that are otherwise desirable. On the contrary, for teaching we rely very much on audio and visual material. A minimum of one educational movie program a week is part of the regular classroom activities, and all children who like them attend the movies at the Natural History Museum regularly on Saturday mornings, etc.

[6] For a further discussion of environmental, or "milieu therapy," see Publications on the School, nos. 2, 3, 5, 6 and 8.

tively secluded treatment room—or even the use of symbolic play material—and more on a variety of personal relationships between the children and the various staff members, and among the children themselves. We try to help the child to form genuine relationships to all those persons at the School who become important to him there. We also try to organize the child's total life activities so that gradually he becomes able to master more and more difficult tasks, and so that insight and experiences gained in the normal course of events may become steps toward his personal development. But this we can do only by creating a general setting in which all experiences are so dosed as to remain manageable by the child through efforts he can easily afford to make. We retain the dimensions of reality, but we present the tasks implied in successful living so that their mastery will strengthen the inadequate or damaged ego.

For example, success comes easier when it does not have to originate in being the victor in a hostile competition, but comes instead from winning respect for achievement in non-competitive activities—respect which a group is much readier to offer when they feel that the satisfaction of their most basic needs is assured and that they do not have to fight for it by showing they are "one up on the other guy." Similarly, going to class is less occasion for anxiety if there is no pressure to do so, if there are no failures in class and no report cards to take home, and if one can be sure that the teacher will know one is upset about something that happened in the morning and will make allowances for it—although always within bounds of what allowances can be made in a situation where others are studying.

Those children who truant from school because they fear the learning situation are not forced to attend classes; other children who are afraid mostly of competition are taught individually. And within the classroom situation, competition is at a minimum so that the set-up for academic failure is avoided.[7] Whether in class or out, an immediate discharge of the need for physical

[7] For a discussion of the educational work at the School in particular, see Publications on the School, no. 5.

movement is encouraged. Then there is less chance for new tensions to accumulate and both further defeat and additional reasons for explosive behaviour are eliminated. Slowly these factors and many others permit us to gain access to ever earlier, ever more hidden problems and to help the child solve them one at a time.

Our efforts are thus concentrated on making the child see everyday activities (particularly those around which his difficulties originated), as non-threatening. After that we must make them activities around which the child can gain, if not insight into his difficulties, at least mastery of those anxieties which have kept him until then from functioning adequately.

Anxieties that center around cleanliness or elimination are handled more directly and more easily with these children while they wash, or resent taking a bath, than by discussing their feelings in play sessions where the real experience can only be re-enacted with play dolls or toys. (Once a child has learned to play in a half orderly way with such breakable toys as plastic bathtubs or dolls, the most difficult task in his rehabilitation has been passed.) Therefore we try to deal with anxieties around cleanliness in the settings in which they arose; that is, in the bathroom and the toilet. By the same token, oral disturbances can be dealt with much more directly in the dining room than in the treatment room, and so on round the clock.

The feeding situations, the night fears, the inabilities to learn to be regular and clean were the very spots where parental efforts were misinterpreted, or too well understood (the rejecting parent who tries to hide his rejection behind punitively enforcing "what is best for the child"). These were the occasions on which tentatively formed relations to parents broke down. Therefore the help we give children around the mastering of these central, recurrent, and "routine," activities should permit doing away with the false interpretations and are therefore the settings in which events must again be experienced as satisfying. Once that is the case, these situations and activities must sooner or later become the starting point of a true personal relationship. Not only

PLATE 1. In the morning and at bedtime some children have to inspect their bodies (particularly their feet) before they can feel sure that things are in good order. There is no self-consciousness because other children go on unperturbed by one boy's concern with his body.

PLATE 2, FIGS. 1 and 2. Two of the six children in this class have given up in despair. They do not have to pretend to be attentive but can show openly how they feel, which makes it easy for the teacher to know where she is needed. True, she can only help one at a time, and while she helps the first child (*above*), the other one is left for a moment to his unhappiness. But when the first boy is ready to start out actively again with a different task, the teacher can concentrate on helping the other child (*below*) who is slowly lifting his head to meet life again.

PLATE 3, FIGS. 1 and 2. The investigation of nature (*above*) is often the child's first attempt at exploring the outside world after having been afraid for so long to acquire any knowledge. When the children become less afraid to understand what they can see, they go a step further and use the microscope (*below*) to see what has previously been invisible to them. Once they learn not to be afraid to see the invisible in nature, they can go on to try to learn to understand their invisible emotions.

PLATE 4. Most of our children are unable to form personal relations of any kind, because they have never known satisfying ones. They are afraid of adults, and can only be met on neutral ground. Here, the relation of teacher and pupil is not yet a you-and-me one. Despite the teacher's efforts to help, his pupil looks away from him—but together they study geography.

is this true of such obvious problem areas as the fear of dirt or resentment about having to wash oneself, but also of problems less obviously connected with any one time or situation. We do not, for example, always wait until the child brings his castration fears into what might be called a treatment situation, and then reflect with him about his anxieties; instead, we discuss it with him at strategic moments when the fear has revealed itself in his behaviour. In doing so, we make wide use of what Fritz Redl has described as the marginal interview, as will be demonstrated later and in varying contexts.[8]

A marginal interview, I might say here, is a conversation between the participant observer and one or more of the participants. It is interpretative in character but does not need to interfere with the momentary activity of the group or individual. The purpose may be to clear up an anxiety that interferes with the enjoyment or participation in an activity, or it may be to warn the child of an unavoidable outcome of his behaviour that he does not seem to foresee. The talk may simply help him to understand the reason for his actions, or explain a piece of behaviour in another person that he seems to have misunderstood, etc. One characteristic of this type of marginal conversation is that while it may change the course of events, or the child's view of them, it does not replace the action; the emphasis is rather on their continuing without unnecessary interference. It should clear the blocked channels of solitary activity or social interaction, but never take their place.

In this sense it is ego supporting, because it bolsters the ego in continuing the now more reality-correct activity. It does service for the child as in a better integrated child his own ego would serve him. As a matter of fact, in the most skillful handling of

[8] My long and close friendship with Fritz Redl has helped me immensely in developing the School's working philosophy and in setting it into practice. Our many conversations and our constant exchange of ideas have now created a situation in which I no longer know exactly where his ideas end and my own begin. Suffice it to say here that we at the School are deeply indebted to him not only for ideas but for much lively help and stimulation.

such marginal conversations the child will often alter his behaviour as if on the suggestions of his own ego—and will often
enjoy the feeling that he has figured things out for himself.

In general, when applying our theory to practice, our approach
is more concerned with strengthening the ego than with bringing
unconscious tendencies to light, although we must often do the
latter as well. This we try to do by supporting the ego in its efforts
to control instinctual desires and its strivings to master the problems of reality.

For example, just as the small child learns that conspicuous
masturbation in public is undesirable, so the child at the School
must be helped to reduce the frequency and openness of masturbation in line with the maximum of masturbation that society will accept. And he must be helped to do so without getting
the idea that masturbation is "bad," is something to be ashamed
or afraid of. In the case of our children it is thus neither a question of undoing the repression of masturbation, nor of suppress-
ing it, but of learning to behave in a socially acceptable way.

These remarks are not meant to imply that strengthening the
ego and making conscious the unconscious are contradictory; as
a matter of fact, in supporting the ego in its battle with the id
we must often bring to consciousness the nature and direction
of instinctual tendencies and show the child how much damage
might result if those tendencies were never to be checked. The
difference is thus one of emphasis, not of kind—an emphasis that
flows from the nature of our work. This strengthening of the
ego through experiences in which problems arising out of everyday occurrences are handled successfully, and this bringing to
awareness of unconscious tendencies as a step toward controlling
them, is the opposite only in method and not in essence of
classical psychoanalysis. Classical analysis, of course, concentrates
on bringing the unconscious into consciousness as a step in undoing restrictive repressions.[9] But the aim in both cases is still

[9] In a paper read at the 1949 meeting of the American Psychoanalytic
Society in Montreal, E. Kris suggested that we may here be dealing with
the phenomenon of "circular causation," an apt analysis which would resolve the seeming conflict between these two approaches.

the same, namely, the freeing of the individual and the opening of a way to a more satisfactory process of living.

Thus while we fully accept the Freudian theories of the structure of human personality and development, the method we use is conditioned by the problems that confront us. These problems are only occasionally a matter of too rigid inhibitions but more generally a question of incongruous development, of a misinterpretation of reality and a weak level of self-control.

2

first encounter

OF ALL days at the School, the first is the most important: for the child in forming an opinion of us
and the School, and for us in beginning those relations to him
which may later become stepping stones toward solving his
problems. Never again will the child be as anxious about the
School, and as little prepared to admit it. Never again will he be
as hopeful or as fearful about his life there, about the adults and
the other children, about the activities, and about how he will
stack up in the new order. But never again will he be quite so
apt to misinterpret what he experiences, to distrust and to fight
us. On the other hand, his behaviour may never again show us
so clearly what he is most frightened about, how distorted his
view of reality is, and how he tries to defend himself against real
problems and imaginary dangers.

Despite any of our efforts to the contrary, the child who is
faced with so difficult a situation is bound to feel anxious. He
has to make some kind of adjustment to a setting which is radically different from the one he has been accustomed to; he has
to change from living with a family to living in an institution—
a transition which is difficult enough even for the well-adjusted
adult. Even the child who may seem to have grown well acquainted with the School on a lengthy preliminary visit will respond very differently when he knows he is now at the School

"for good." Actually, the visit acquainted him only with the externals of the School and in all likelihood he feels it committed him to nothing. His emotions on knowing he has now come to the School to live there for a long time, even permanently, as some of them feel, are so radically different from what he felt during the earlier visit that he cannot but view everything—the setting, himself within it, the children, the adults—in a very different light. But since emotions are what make for the experience, and particularly with emotionally disturbed children, their experience on coming to the School "for good" is actually very different from what it was during the visit.

Our planning for the new child can at best mitigate his anxieties. But while our efforts, as such, may remain woefully inadequate, they do help him insofar as they leave him free to form some opinion about us and his possible life at the School. And here it is only our actions and attitudes that count. The less we talk, the more we allow the child to watch us without having to listen to our words, the more he will trust his own opinion.

In interpreting the School to the new child we rely more on the actual daily activities he can watch or take part in, and less on what we may think his acute problems are, or his major anxieties or delusions. Even if we knew for a fact what they were, it could only seem presumptuous on our part to show such superior knowledge instead of waiting until the child in his own good time should take us into his confidence. If we were to talk about his anxieties without waiting, we might only intimidate him into feeling we think him inadequate. Actually we aim at eventually giving the child the feeling that we believe that neither he alone nor we alone can solve his basic problems, but that he will be able to solve them with our help in a process of daily living together. Nevertheless, we wish to give the child the immediate feeling that we believe he is well able to manage the simple tasks of living, such as getting up and getting dressed, eating, washing, or spending his allowance. With these chores we help him only if and when he wants us to. Any other plan would be viewed by these children, on the basis of past experiences, not as help, but as an expression of distrust or a veiled wish to control them.

Many children, during their visit, or on their first day at the School, get a fairly true first impression of our intentions—not one that they necessarily trust, but one that they cannot help forming—from observing other children enjoying themselves, and even more from seeing that children at the School do many things freely that are frowned on by their parents or their consciences. They are also quick to notice that such behaviour is not merely suffered, but approved of by adults at the School.

We have always found it best to avoid any immediate or early efforts to discuss his pressing or central problems with the child or to try to help or assure him about them or our attitudes to them. Whatever his main difficulties are, be it his inability to learn or his delusions of grandeur or of persecution, his view of the world is too distorted to permit him to see our efforts in a true light; he would only distort them again in terms of his past experiences. It is always best to wait for the child to take the initiative in discussing what is most important to him. Every child who enters the School has had the experience that adults try to change him under the pretext of wanting to help. Since he feels that he acts as he must, or even thinks that his behaviour is the only reasonable or effective way to react to the world, he does not want to change, to be changed, or even to be helped. He does not think he needs help, and is least ready to accept it from adults, particularly not from adults who have been hand-picked by those he is most at odds with, namely the adults who have charge of him. That the School was selected by them is only one more good reason to distrust us.

In other respects, too, it is not always possible to provide the child with immediate proof, in the form of verbal or tangible experiences, that our attitudes are different from those of his parents or of the world of adults as he has known it. But it may be characteristic of our society, that there is one particular experience that has most often helped the new child to form the opinion that the School may be strikingly different from the world he was accustomed to, and that his fears and anxieties about life at the School may be unjustified. This is the experience that at the School his emotional needs take precedence over material considerations, and that we do not discount a child's feelings in a matter even when they clash with what are generally considered objective evaluations.

Often what specifically makes life at the School seem very "different" is our attitude toward money or material goods (allowances and their use, the freedom to waste food and materials, etc.), and the approval of infantile activities which are supposedly below the child's age level (playing with stuffed animals, thumbsucking, etc.). One boy, for example, picked up a sandwich at his first meal, bit into it and then put it down. Provocatively, he picked up another one, took a little bite, and put it down. And this he continued with another and another until he had bitten into eight altogether. By then he began to wonder if we might not, contrary to his expectations, be more interested in allowing him the freedom to behave in line with his emotional need to waste food, than we were in saving food or in enforcing good manners at the table.

Many children have also derived greater security from a discussion of their allowances (how much they will be given each week, the fact that it is given them to spend as they please without any strings attached; that it is allotted for their pleasure and not something to be saved, and so on) than they would have from any assurance extending beyond the concrete, particular issue. That the allowance is given to them without their having to account for it to anyone and not as a reward for good behaviour is more important to them at the moment than any assurance that their needs will be cared for, or that we will help them with their difficulties. At such a time they cannot recognize or admit that they have difficulties or need help, and thus our promises would seem pointless. For a long time they reject the idea that they need us, either because they are unaware of such needs, or because pride or anxiety does not permit them to admit the existence of their problems.

Often, too, it is the discovery that realistic situations are handled realistically at the School—that not all things are considered psychological problems—which makes the School acceptable to some children; that, and the realization that their everyday needs will be cared for and their emotional problems considered their private affairs. This, for example, induced one sophisticated nine-year-old girl to decide to enter the School willingly after first having been very much against the idea. Her mother had often invaded her psychological privacy by discussing the girl's emotional problems with her, by interpreting her drawings and dreams to her. But even after a preliminary talk with the psychiatrist, the girl began to believe that at the School we do not pry into the unconscious, much less into the private life of the child against his will.

The psychiatrist, in explaining the School, discussed only such everyday matters as allowances, and told her that at the School there was no one to inquire about why and how she spent it. The girl listened and then said, "You're supposed to be interested in my dreams, not in such things as allowances." When the psychiatrist assured her that allowances and what goes with them are at least as important as dreams—and that such was the attitude at the School—she agreed to at least a visit. On this visit she experienced no interference when she chose to cut short her contacts with adults and instead joined a group of children for some time. After playing with them for a short while and observing them at supper, she decided she knew quite a bit about the School, and before leaving she declared she was ready to come and live there.

New enrollments are rare at the School, mainly because it takes a long time—on an average of two or three years—to rehabilitate children who are so severely disturbed that they need institutional treatment because they cannot function with their families or in foster homes. We do not usually admit more than ten new children during the year and we try to space these enrollments so that no more than three or four children will be entering at any one time. On the other hand, we try to limit the admission of new children to three periods of the year, so that for most of the time the children are not disturbed by having to make new adjustments.

Enrollments usually take place at the beginning of summer (the end of the academic year), at the end of summer (when the academic year begins) and after Christmas. Although the School is in session continuously, these events, in the minds of the children mark off the main subdivisions of the year; they are prepared for changes to take place at those times and hence are more ready to accept them. After these signposts of the calendar are passed, they want to settle down to "normalcy," to a more or less undisturbed life, or at least to a life undisturbed by newcomers. Hence these times of the year, if at all, are the ones when children least resent changes in the membership of their group.

The groups, incidentally, are relatively small, although for various mechanical reasons beyond our control (among them the nature of the building we live in) not always as small as we would wish. The dormitory groups vary from four to eight children, although we have found that a dormitory group of six children would probably be better for the type of children and the age groups we serve. Classroom groups are somewhat larger so that we have five dormitory but only four classroom groups, the classes varying from seven to twelve children. In addition to these groupings which are more or less regular, many other groupings are either planned or come about spontaneously to fit the occasion; children from various dormitory or classroom groups may share a common workshop program, go on trips together, work a common garden plot, and so on.

In speaking of a garden plot I do not refer to any work that the children are required to do. If they want to, they can do gardening and plant what they like. But they don't have to. And even if they do seed a plot, there is no pressure on them to keep on with it because that would make the gardening a chore instead of something enjoyable. All housework, including cleaning, tidying up, etc., is done by maids. And while there is nothing wrong with having normally functioning children lend a hand in simple tasks around the house, the children at the School were enrolled there because they cannot function to begin with, and are there to try to learn how. During this process their relations to those who will have to convince them that this is a better world than they thought, should not have to be burdened by a struggle to get them to perform tasks someone else could as easily do for them, nor by their having to submit mutely to adults who are experienced as overpowering. On the other hand, we expect the child not to rely passively on adults for performing those maturational and integrative tasks—such as playing, or learning in class—which can be mastered only with the active participation of the child.

Thus we try to prevent the expenditure of emotional and physical energy that would go into picking up clothing or toys, or making up beds. This energy the child needs for much more important tasks. He needs it to overcome his lethargy and his negativism, or to renounce the habit of living entirely in the world of his wish-fulfilling phantasies. We prefer him to save all his emotional energy for the task of relating himself to other persons. Once a child is relatively advanced in solving his problems or in overcoming his difficulties, there may then come a time when it is constructive to prepare him for fulfilling those tasks which the outside world will expect him to meet when he returns to it. Then he may be asked to help with sorting out his laundry or making his bed, but only when the task is performed *with* and never *for* an adult. They must be tasks that are directly connected with his person and his individual well-being, and recognized as such by the child.

For example, the child who wishes to wear dirty clothing cannot be expected to understand that the sorting out of what should be sent to the laundry and what to the cleaner is a friendly activity. It is only after the child has a genuine desire to be wearing clean things that his helping to get them to the cleaner may become relatively pleasant to do. Then, and only then, will his performing such a task imply not an expenditure of vital energy but rather a gain. This may be because he is doing something constructive on a plane with the adult, or because of the pleasure the adult experiences when the child has at last shown some spontaneous ability to behave in a socialized way— a pleasure the child senses, and which usually increases his ego strength.

This kind of cooperation between child and adult in an important activity becomes possible only after the child has accepted his life at the School as meaningful, as "real." When a child first comes to the School he rarely accepts the School setting as "real" all at once. Even if he takes advantage of some of the more pleasurable features of his new life, he usually clings for some time to his past life setting (usually the family) as his everyday reality. He conceives of his life at the School as a passing thing, an excursion into a strange and different world where experiences are devoid of real meaning and one's actions do not commit one. So long as he harbours such feelings he does not view life at the School as anything worth coming to grips with.

The reasons for such an attitude are manifold. One of them is the fact that as long as the child expects to return very soon to a setting pretty much like his past one, it seems an unnecessary waste of emotional energy to adapt his actions, not to speak of his personality, to the School setting, only to have to adjust himself all over again in a week or a month. Another reason is that the child is afraid that if he behaves as freely as he is encouraged to do at the School, his behaviour will lead him into severe conflicts with his parents, whom he expects to rejoin very soon.

And finally it must be realized that the child has a heavy investment of vital energy in his old personality, including even his repressions: it was hard work to develop the deviate personality he felt he needed just to be able to get along with, or even to fight against, his parents or society. It was hard labour and agony, for example, to repress the desire to do things his parents disapproved of. It seems most unwise to the child to undo this labour as long as he thinks his parents will be forcing him to resurrect old repressions after a few weeks or months. Of course, children do not reason these things out in an orderly way, but their feelings for situations of vital concern to themselves are often more accurate than adult reasoning can retrace.

For these and similar reasons, the child often spends several months in which he just seems to be marking time. But the child is not idle. His time is actually spent in testing to see if he must really come to terms with the School, with the values and the way of life it stands for. During this time he may try at all costs to get around the need to have to change his ways. He may try to convince his parents that living at the School is not the right thing for him, or the School that he is so bad that he is "beyond repair." Old symptoms may become aggravated and new ones appear, particularly during home visits. All these efforts are made to avoid the bigger, more far-reaching efforts that are implied in responding to the School's challenge to change himself or his views about life.

It is very difficult to convince a child that the setting created by the School is as legitimate a form of reality as the setting of his previous life was. Children live only in the world they grow up in and have not yet learned that several different ways of life may be equally legitimate, not to speak of the difficulty of realizing that a new and strange way of life may be better than the one they have known. Although the most salient features of the School setting may be very attractive to the child, he can accept them as such only after he is no longer afraid we are being nice to him only later to take advantage of him; after he no longer fears that accepting an easier life will lead him into deeper conflicts with his parents, or require him to give up ways of life (delinquency, deafness, etc.) that he feels he cannot yet get along without.

For example, it takes many children quite a long time to find out that meals can be enjoyable. So long has the mealtime been a battleground for his conflicts with adults that for months whatever happens around meals is unpleasant for the child, so negatively sensitized has he grown to that situation. To these children meals have meant only humiliation or the experience of being overpowered by adults; having to sit still and be bored, or having to eat foods they disliked; or meals may have meant the great chance to get back at adults for other sufferings through an obstinate refusal to eat.

It is only after the child has accepted the everyday life at the School as being real, that the potential satisfactions we offer become things he can "take." Then for the first time the child can begin to accept the help we offer him in meeting the tasks of life. Only then will he use our help in solving the conflicts that exist within himself, or between him and reality. Only then will his experience at the School become useful in changing his outlook on life, and his opinions of himself.

Since, or perhaps because, the new child's relations to adults are badly damaged, most newcomers are much more interested in other children than in adults. While they may remain indifferent for some time to all adults, or at best take a ruthless advantage of them, they are immediately fascinated by group life, whether positively or negatively. For a time some behave as though they were entirely engulfed by it. Hence, a few remarks on the group may precede a discussion of the new child's first concrete experiences.

In the minds of the children their dormitory group is the most important of all; it is their "family" unit. In order to preserve it as much as possible as an organic unity, we try not to add more than one new child at a time, and not to add another before the previous newcomer has become a well integrated member of the group. This does not mean that the children of such a group function always, or even most of the time, as a unified group. On the contrary, the coherence of the group often reveals itself best in the child's ability to venture out from its security to new areas of living. What is important to each child is that he knows that his group is an always available haven of security for him. Through his positive relations to the other children and adults, or the willingness of adults to take ill humour without retaliation, the child can always replenish the emotional energy he expends on his ventures into the outside world.

A new child tends to roam from group to group because he has not yet found security in his personal relations, and hence one association is as good—or more accurately, as bad—as another. In addition, he is afraid to commit himself emotionally to any one set of persons. Then comes a time when the group support is very needed and very important, because the child is still so insecure with all outsiders that he sticks to the group all the time, or at least to those of its members who are not otherwise emotionally engaged. Later, when the child feels secure in his group, he will leave it for moments at a time, but only if other children of his group are in sight. And finally he will leave it more frequently, to form shortlived associations outside of it from which he returns periodically to the security of the group.

It is often through the members of a coherent group that the new child gets his first inkling of the climate of living that characterizes the School. This happens less because of his desire to understand, than because the others are ready to form relations with him, to take him into the group. The newcomer is usually indifferent and frequently inimical to the group. His past life has taught him to expect the worst of others, and so he does. But the group—without forcing itself on him—genuinely welcomes him, which is contrary to past experiences and often a real "shock," because it is so unexpected a challenge to re-examine his picture of the world and his relations to other children. The group, for its part, tries to help the new child to become one of them not because it is the nice thing to do or because adults suggest it, but out of an inner necessity: the presence of an outsider makes them uncomfortable so they wish to make him an insider.

This is true, of course, only if the group can exist undisturbed by new additions for a considerable length of time. Otherwise, the frequent changes do not allow for the development of a group climate which is strong enough to take in the newcomer.

If the various members of a group still feel unsure of one another, the newcomer is either hated because of the additional threat that his coming implies, or he is wooed as a potential ally and hence not received as a person, but used as a tool.

In a way, the reception of a newcomer into the group is a test of its coherence, a test of the security which the children of the group find in one another. To the casual observer, groups that have reached different stages in group integration may seem to function on the same level of coherence so long as they remain undisturbed. But as soon as a newcomer enters, they react differently. In the least coherent, and hence least secure group, the children will turn against the newcomer, either by behaving as if they are so much of an ingroup that there is no chance for an outsider to ever become one of them, by allowing various children to compete for his friendship, or by being openly hostile to him.

Children of a better integrated group may make a show of in group "belonging," of a coherence much greater than it actually is; they will go out of their way to make the newcomer join them in a hurry. They behave either as if they were accepting him as a practical test of their mutual coherence (the newcomer's eagerness to join is needed in maintaining the fiction that they are an integrated group), or as if to convince themselves through a show of coherence that the addition of a child is no threat to their mutual security.

A truly well integrated group will meet the newcomer with friendly indifference. The children who form such a group feel so secure that they can take the newcomer or leave him. If he wants to join, well and good; if not, that's all right with them, too. If a newcomer is introduced into such a group the children will explain to him what they are doing and invite him to join in, but otherwise they go on pretty much as they were. By and large they let the newcomer alone and show respect for his privacy, which is precisely what the children of a less integrated group are unable to do.

To the new child, too, the casual reception he gets from the coherent group is most reassuring—and so are the casual remarks of an "old-timer"—while the obvious overtures by members of a less coherent group will add to his insecurity. If *they* do not know where they stand with one another, how can he hope to find his place within their group? Moreover, he will recognize their interest in him for what it is: the desire to gain favour with him for their own benefit, or to overcome the anxiety his arrival has created.

Similarly, a welcoming party for the newcomer is successful in setting him at ease only if he is not made the center of the party but just a participant like everyone else. The purpose of such a party is to take the edge off everyone's uneasiness rather than to make the newcomer immediately and artificially a bona fide member of the group. The party in "honour" of a newcomer with him as the center of attention is sometimes advocated to help a new child feel "at home," but this we have found less desirable. The honour may flatter his narcissism, but narcissism will be least useful in gaining him membership in the group. Moreover, it arouses some justified fears about later being able to live up to the exceptional position such a party seems to raise him to. The awakening after the party will be all the ruder if his first experience in the group was that of being its most important member. Thus, a party with the newcomer as the central person is undesirable in terms of the way he experiences it.

From the point of view of the new child's acceptance by the rest of the children these parties are even less desirable. In reality, it is the old members of the group who are entitled to special attention because they are being asked to take in a newcomer and also to share the adult group leaders with him. The addition of a new child means actual hardship for them and they cannot be expected to be happy about his coming as a return for his being imposed on them.

Arranging a party with the new child as the center of attention is often an effort on the part of the arranging adult to deny the real distribution of hardship, if not to turn it into its opposite. Knowing that the difficult task of adjusting to a child is being imposed on the group, some adults behave as if that were an enjoyable event, thus denying the hardship they impose on the children. Statements such as "we're all so glad to have you join us" only convince members of the old group that their interests are being betrayed. The adult, instead of protecting the group's interest against the newcomer, seems then to identify with the interests of the newcomer instead of the ones he knows longer and better.

We find it preferable to admit openly that the addition of the newcomer is a painful imposition on the old group members, one that we regret and for which we apologize. We explain why such things are unavoidable because of the mechanics of the institution and we make it clear that the party is given much more for the old members than for the new one. If, besides the other fun of the party, each child (as well as the newcomer) receives a toy, their loss is in part compensated, or at least symbolically so, by the adult and the School.

A party arranged for all children of the group rather than just the newcomer is also more acceptable to a new child who has formed no relationships as yet, because he feels that it does not oblige him, as a party in his honour might do. This was obvious from the behaviour of Alice, aged eight, who suffered from deep-seated anxieties that had kept her withdrawn from all contact with reality. Her personal withdrawal she had covered up most of her life by "goody-goody" behaviour, interrupted by occasionally violent and dangerous attacks against her mother and a younger sister whom she hated even more.

At the party we gave on her arrival she ate very little as if she wanted to show us that she knew very well she didn't belong yet. Candy that was offered to her she put in her pocket, as if to tell us she was not ready to share bed and board with us, or that she knew perfectly well she was still without status in the group. She might also have been testing to see if such taking of food was allowed. (Other children at these parties test to see if they can overeat or waste food.)

After the party the rest of the children paid little attention to

Alice although she made her bid for it by talking about her family. Since the others hardly knew her, this subject was a topic of no interest to them. Finally, she announced to anyone who would listen that she was very fond of her little sister. But this kind of talk was too much for Priscilla, who had also hated a younger sister violently and had also tried to cover up her feelings at one time by overt expressions of love. Priscilla, from her own experiences, may also have sensed the insincerity in Alice's statement. Since she had learned by now to admit to her real emotions, she told Alice casually that she, for one, was *not* fond of her sister. Alice looked at the counselor, expecting disapproval of such an impolite denial of social conventions. But nothing further was said and Alice felt that in spite of her statement, her true emotions had been understood and shared by Priscilla and perhaps even by the counselor. She responded by putting her toys away in her toy chest, a first gesture of her feeling at home.[1]

As with many other children, Alice used her first day to explore the School in its relation to her dominant feelings of being unloved and uncared for. She wondered who would fix her things when they got broken, and whether her toys would be safe. Then she asked who would buy her shoes, and when Lucille told her that the counselor would, and that she herself had just gotten new shoes the day before, Alice remarked that her father had promised her a new pair but had never gotten around to getting them for her. That such criticism of her father was taken as a matter of course and that the counselor made no effort to reassure her or to make excuses for her father gave her the courage to state other complaints about her parents. For one thing, she had lost a tooth, she said, and put it under her pillow but had never gotten her dime from the Blue Fairy.

When she awoke the next morning, Alice began further testing to see if the counselor would protect other children—and by implication, herself—against malice and practical jokes. She eyed a sleepy-looking child in a bed near her own and suggested to

[1] Participant observer: Joan Little.

the counselor: "Tell her her mother's here, that'll make her get up." When the counselor replied she would do no such thing, she became bolder about criticizing her mother by making the apparently irrelevant comment that she was ashamed of her mother.[2]

Thus within the first twenty-four hours, Alice had brought some of her main problems out pretty directly—her fear that she would never be properly cared for, that her mother was inadequate to the degree that she had to be ashamed of her and that her father was unreliable in his promises. All these she could state more or less openly after the lie about her sister had fallen flat and after she saw that the expression of true feelings was supported at the School even when it violated politeness and conventions. In becoming frank about stating her feelings it was also a comfort to know that her counselor would prevent her from acting dangerously hostile toward other children and thus protect her from things she was afraid she might do if there was no one to control her hostility.

Alice's entry into the School was made easier by her placement in a rather well integrated group where all other children felt so secure with each other that they were free to support her in expressing her feelings. But the placement of Paul, aged ten, was due to an emergency (several suicidal and at least one homicidal attempt) and could not wait for an opening in a group that had already developed an adequate coherence. Things were off to a bad start as soon as the counselor had shown him around the house and introduced him to the other boys of his dormitory group. Bob (aged eight) felt he could not rely on the support of his group with the threat of a new child coming up, because he was not established in it very well himself. His own insecurity, plus the age difference, made him afraid of competition from a ten-year-old boy, so he tried from the beginning to put Paul "in his place."

In a superior tone he asked Paul if he had brought his ice skates along since the children planned to go skating after the

[2] Participant observer: Joan Little.

party. Paul was taken aback and felt badly about not having ice skates, or about not knowing how to skate, or both. "I forgot to bring mine," he said, and at the same time he took hold of the counselor's hand as though looking for support when he thus found his dignity attacked. She kept hold of his hand and asked him to sit down beside her, but he refused to sit with the others at the "party" table, and seated himself at a small one where she joined him from time to time. Apart from the others, he pretended to read comics, but actually he watched very carefully to see what went on. When the other boys offered him food, he declined, saying he wasn't very hungry. Toward the end of the party the children spontaneously formed a band and marched around the room singing. Paul hummed the tune but did not join them, though he waved his pop bottle in time to the music.[3]

Thus while the children in this group were not secure enough with one another to make Paul feel safe about joining them, his freedom to observe their behaviour gave him some inkling of the atmosphere of the School. Soon after the party he retired to his bed, but remained watchful. When he saw another boy begin to suck his thumb after getting into bed, Paul left his own bed under the pretext of fetching something, but actually in order to walk past the other child, trying very hard to be casual about it. When he was sure he had seen right, that nobody seemed to care if a big boy sucked his thumb, he returned to his bed and put his thumb in his mouth with relief.[4]

Thus, by observing other children who, if not further ahead in overcoming their difficulties are at least further ahead in not being afraid to enjoy themselves, the new child arrives at some feeling of what the School has to offer.

[3] Participant observer: Gayle Shulenberger.

[4] Incidentally, although Paul had begun on his very first night to return to primitive forms of satisfaction, he soon became frightened and felt we were dangerously indulgent. He complained for some time that we were spoiling him and asked the counselor not to permit him or the others what he felt to be undesirable behaviour, such as messing with food or wasting it, or getting presents too often.

The less secure the children of a group are, the less they are able to mitigate the anxieties of a new child and the more it becomes up to the adult to convey to the new child that he is now living in a setting where his needs will be satisfied wherever possible. This is more difficult because the emotionally disturbed child, as I have said, trusts adults even less than other children. He must be helped in beginning to recognize that his dread of the world of adults is not wholly justified, that not all adults misunderstand him, or wish him ill.

Sometimes the expression of the child's need and his testing of adults are so direct that even during the first day (or days) of his stay it is possible to provide him with experiences that will make his defenses against legitimate needs start to crumble. After that he can permit himself satisfaction of at least some of the desires which have so far remained frustrated. This satisfaction does not always lead directly to good personal relations in severely disturbed children, and nothing would be wronger than to expect that it could. On the contrary, just because a child may quickly feel secure about the satisfaction of some of his instinctual needs, he may dare to reveal the severity of his emotional disturbance more openly. But this means he will also be freer about showing his negativism, his distorted ideas about others and their actions, about the world and also himself. Newly gained feelings of strength and security are often spent in more vigorous acting out. In a way, though, this augurs well for their eventually being brought into the context of a personal relation: the child no longer acts out secretly and in isolation, but in the presence of a significant adult; or he directs against that person the negativism which is no longer bottled up inside.

Paul, before coming to the School, had made all his destructive attempts when no adult was present. But within a month after enrollment, he had brought his self-destructive tendencies into a social context, and then expressed them mainly in symbolic ways. He no longer tried to destroy himself or others, but what was worn next to his or their bodies. First, he tried to set his own pajamas on fire and when he was stopped from doing that, he made a heap of the other children's pajamas a few days later and tried to burn them. But both efforts were made only after he was sure that his counselor would immediately be available, and after she extinguished the small fires he experienced obvious relief.[5]

Sometimes the new child's behaviour is so threatening to even a coherent group that the children draw away from the newcomer and then the School has to be interpreted mainly by adults. Of course, it cannot be said too often that emotionally disturbed children do not trust any verbal statements. Adult actions they trust somewhat more, but most convincing is the feeling-tone conveyed by the act. Nevertheless, the behaviour of adults remains a poor substitute for the conviction that is carried by the statements and behaviour of other children. Still, we must often rely on ourselves when the new child's behaviour is such as to forcefully alienate the group.

Mary on her first day, is a case in point. This child was nine years old when she came to the School, and while her behaviour showed psychotic features, it was rather her asocial actions that had led to her placement. These included stealing, violent attacks against children and repellant cruelty to animals. As soon as Mary was introduced to her group, Grace, one of the others in the group, did her best to make Mary feel at home. She asked her a few questions and when these brought no response she seemed to sense that a new child could not be expected to reveal personal matters if she herself did not take the initiative. So she told Mary that her parents were dead.

This broke the ice for a moment and Mary replied that she herself had been living with an aunt. Then Grace volunteered that things weren't bad here, much better than in a foster home she had lived in where she had been kicked around. To this Mary replied with high glee and a nasty smile that she had once hit a girl over the head with a lead pipe so badly that many stitches had to be taken in the child's head (a true statement)

[5] Participant observer: Gayle Shulenberger.

and that the children here had better watch out and not cross her. This attitude perturbed the other children enough to have them draw away from her.[6]

Fortunately, the security the others had already gained at the institution and with one another sufficed to keep them from being frightened by Mary. Therefore, they did not need to react with a show of how dangerous they could be, as children in a less secure group might have done. But her behaviour was enough for them to wish to steer clear of her and they left her strictly alone which, of course, did not make Mary feel any more at home.

Since this avenue of coming to terms with the School was now closed, it was up to a counselor to try to show Mary in some practical way, and despite her great negativism toward adults, what the attitude of the School is toward children. As the counselor was taking her around the School, Mary showed some interest in the paints she discovered in the play room. At the same time she told the counselor how once, when the painters were redecorating her home, she had started to play with the paint but then got it all over herself and got a bad licking. The counselor made no attempt to assure her that such behaviour was accepted at the School (a statement Mary would either have considered untrue or an effort to play up to her because she was so dangerous); she merely told Mary that these paints she could use right away if she wanted to.[7]

Gingerly, Mary took up the paints, but soon she became more courageous, and asked what would happen if she got paint on herself. The counselor told her "nothing," that she would just wipe it off, and she showed her how easily you can do that with turpentine. At that, Mary dipped her fingers all the way into the paint jar and made paint blotches all over her arm. Then she held out the arm for the counselor to wipe. While this was being done, she asked, "What do you do to girls who stink like turpentine?" at which the counselor only laughed. Thus reassured

[6] Participant observer: Joan Little.
[7] Participant observer: Gayle Shulenberger.

she opened up with a long stream of questions—who took care of the children and who did what with them and when—ending up with some questions about playing with clay, though despite encouragement, she hadn't the courage to try it that first day.

Mary, on her original visit to the School, had been encouraged to ask questions but there was nothing she had wanted to ask. Only after a concrete experience had shown her that we understand children, did it make sense to her to listen to what we had to say. Previously she had shown no interest in learning about the School. Perhaps she preferred not to be talking to strangers about what she had on her mind; perhaps she had no interest in talking with us because she did not trust us to tell her the truth; or it may have been just her extreme general negativism to adults. Now, as she listened, what impressed her the most about life at the School was the assurance that she could rest or go to sleep whenever she wanted to. This statement she tested immediately by retiring to her bed. Once there she seemed relieved enough, but probably because she felt the need to retire from temptation after she had given in to it by soiling herself with paint and by overcoming her negativism about asking questions freely.

Since we respected her right to behave negatively and to avoid contact with us, the immediate sequence to this incident did not happen until approximately a month later. Although in chronology it does not belong to the first encounter, psychologically it belongs so closely to her first experience at the School that it may be mentioned here.

When Mary next consented to go with her counselor to the playroom, she painted the face of an unhappy little girl, and when her counselor asked who this was, she indicated clearly that it was a picture of herself. But then she added that the girl had no name, that she was just any girl, "a girl without any name." Her feeling seemed to be that she had no personal identity of her own.[8]

After thus revealing one of her more serious problems, she

[8] Participant observer: Gayle Shulenberger.

immediately withdrew again from all contact with her counselor and fell back into solitary eating. But since she did this in the counselor's presence, she was able to re-establish contact after eating awhile because the fact that her behaviour was not criticized brought back some confidence, if not in herself then at least in the School. Then she asked the counselor to read her a story she knew very well. It was the story of a caterpillar (in Mary's words, "an ugly worm") who after many adventures turned into a butterfly. Midway through the story her tension rose and she said, "Do you know what happens in the end?" "Yes," the counselor said, "but why don't you tell me?" So Mary told her excitedly how the ugly, unhappy worm turns into a beautiful, happy butterfly. It was the first time she had shown any positive emotion and it was as if she had hope now that some day she herself might be changed from a nameless, just-any-girl, into a happy, distinct individual.

To be able to believe that, at least for a moment, to believe that she could become a distinct person, that satisfaction and happiness might be available to her, was really the beginning of progress in treatment. This was really Mary's first day of being "in the School;" before that she was never more than physically present. Thus, in a way, it was her first day of "living" there, although she had been there some thirty days and nights.

While the true beginning of Mary's life at the School was removed by one month from the day of her arrival, it is possible, with other children to create this experience at the very beginning of their stay.

Frank (aged eleven), was an acting-out delinquent whose behaviour was traceable to early and continued deprivation due to placement in inadequate and ever-changing foster homes. When his mother finally married again and established a suitable home his attitudes had become so asocial that he was constantly at odds with society. One of his efforts to compensate for many past disappointments took the form of overeating, which resulted in obesity.

His parents' efforts to have him lose weight by dieting were interpreted by him as due to dislike on their part. During his first meal at the School he announced that it was important for him to reduce and he asked the counselor not to serve him too much and to remind him to watch his diet. He was told matter-of-factly that he could eat as much or as little as he pleased, that it was entirely up to him, and that we had no wish to influence him either way. As it turned out, he hardly touched his food. The counselor assured him that it was all right with her, except that he would probably get hungry later on if he ate nothing at all. This apparently convinced him that she meant it when she said he could eat as much as he liked, and he fell on his food wolfishly. He requested four helpings of the main fare and five of the dessert, and after he had eaten most of that, he asked "Is that all we have to eat?" He was given another helping, after which he was ready to admit he had had enough.[9]

On the same day Frank set about learning how far he could go in the use of "bad" language. Although his own talk was full of obscenity, he criticized other children, saying: "You swear an awful lot here." Then he turned to the counselor and asked, "How come you let them talk like that? Don't you stop them?" She told him she saw no reason for interfering, but then he wanted to know, "Is it because you can't stop them?" (Only weakness, he felt, could explain why it went by unpunished.) On this very first day Frank also wanted assurance about enuresis and asked what would happen if he ever wet his bed. When his counselor told him, "nothing," except that his sheets would be changed, he asked to be wakened in the middle of the night. This request she refused, although he pestered for a promise of some kind, and when he saw that she meant what she said, as in the case of his food, he was vastly relieved.[10]

Next, with surprise, he investigated the stuffed animals which he noticed on the beds of the other children. "That's kind of

[9] Participant observer: Patty Pickett.
[10] Participant observer: *Idem.*

funny, isn't it?" he said. "All of them having stuffed animals. That's like babies, isn't it?"

From the very beginning, Frank was exploring to find out whether satisfaction of his special needs (such as the need to overeat) was available to him, and whether these things took precedence in our minds over abstract norms (how much a boy of his age "should" eat); it was also important to him to find out if the free and honest expression of his feelings (through "bad" language) was possible, or whether he had to hide his true feelings behind pretense and "polite" language. Moreover, he found out that his infantile or neurotic tendencies (bedwetting) were taken for granted as legitimate needs, or legitimate in terms of his disturbance. The fact that he and the others could play with stuffed animals may have told him vaguely that children at the School can be childish or mature as they wish, or as their emotional need for it may be, and that they need not conform to standards of maturity out of line with their emotional development of the moment.

Unlike many of the children who come to the School, protection against parental interference was not a major worry with Frank and therefore he was not at all curious about it. As a runaway child he knew the answer to the problem of too much parental or adult interference. He had his symptomatic behaviour: he could truant. Children whose personality structure does not permit them to eliminate parental control by acting out or by running away but who, for example, must swallow their hostility, seek assurance first and foremost that we intend to protect them from their parents. Until they feel safe on that score they cannot permit themselves to do any exploring at all. Without that assurance it makes little difference whether or not we allow them to satisfy those asocial or infantile (but nevertheless real enough) needs, pleasures which their parents always frowned on or frankly prohibited.

Hank, a seven-year-old negativistic boy, had retaliated for years against what he experienced as parental rejection by aggression and violent temper tantrums. With these tools he had successfully intimidated his parents and other children—so muc. so that neither public nor private schools could keep him. From earliest infancy the parents had enforced, among other things, a rigid regime of cleanliness and "good" behaviour, and had exercised pressure for prematurely grown-up ways. So it is understandable that his first concern at the School was to investigate those aspects of living which had always placed him under greatest stress.

First he wanted to know how much safety there was at the School from parental control. From the moment he came, he expressed his resentment of his mother, but in doing so he showed how he rebelled against her control, and at the same time submitted to it. As with all other children when they come to the School, we asked him what he would like to be called. He said, "Hank, not Henry" and then added that he hated the name Henry because that was what his mother liked to call him.

When he was taken up to see his dormitory, he said he preferred to sleep in the upper bunk of a double decker bed, because his mother always thought he might fall out of an upper bunk and would want him to sleep in a lower one. When he saw the stuffed animals, he immediately defended himself from the temptation to childish enjoyment. "Oh, no," he said, "none of that stuff for me—I'm grown up; I don't like stuffed animals!"

His anxiety about cleanliness showed itself immediately. The bathrooms are adjacent to the dormitories, which most children accept without any ado. But Hank said he wished his bathroom were right in the same room with his bed, and for some time he pretended it was, so central an issue for him were the functions served by the bathroom.

As he unpacked his tooth brush that first day, he told the counselor, "You know, I love to brush my teeth." She laughed a little, and gave him to understand she was not very convinced. So he repeated his statement. Then, as it brought no response, he switched to some innocuous topic, but after a few minutes of small talk, he asked her, "What happens around here if you don't brush your teeth?" She told him we were not very concerned about it but that his teeth might get dirty, and he admitted, "That's right, they might. But I still forget to brush my teeth sometimes." She assured him that all boys sometimes forget to brush their teeth, and with that he was apparently satisfied.[11]

Yet in spite of this conversation, no real contact had been established. Hank remained very distant, as if the counselor and the other children did not really exist. The next evening, when he was in the tub, he began to tell her that he usually quarreled with his mother when she made him take his bath. As he told her these things, he went through a ritualistic soaping, rubbing, and rinsing of each separate part of his body, washing each one several times. "I have to do a very close inspection job," he said, "because I don't like to take chances." She assured him no one was going to inspect how well he cleaned himself, but it made no impression. "Oh, but I can't take it easy," he said, "my mother told me not to." The counselor continued to assure him without pressing the point, to which he replied, "Oh, but my mother might move in here with me, and then she'd see." The counselor promised him that was entirely impossible, but he was still unconvinced. "Well, Mother might come as a counselor," he said. "You never can tell." [12]

Since he had no faith in her statements as yet, he kept asking other children if it was true that parents never visited the School. It was only after they had all told him repeatedly that visits from parents are rare, that the children are told about them beforehand, and that parents never enter the part of the building the children live in that he allowed himself to become less compulsive about his washing. Then his anxieties about cleanliness and elimination and his numerous other compulsions slowly gave way to more natural behaviour and he became more relaxed.

Hank maintained his distance until the end of his second day at the School. That night, at bedtime, the counselor read him a

[11] Participant observer: Ronnie Dryovage.
[12] Participant observer: *Idem.*

story, then sang him a few songs and finally brought him his night snack. When he saw the food appear, he unbent at last. "Gee," he said, "three things we get when we go to bed—stories, songs and something to eat." This time there was real contact between counselor and child. He then asked her to buy him a stuffed animal and she promised he would have it the next day. That night, Hank fell asleep in a matter of minutes though his long history of insomnia and night terrors was to reappear again and again before he knew genuine night rest.[13]

While it is true that Hank's compulsions and the most asocial expressions of his fears and hostility disappeared very soon, basically his anxious and hostile personality structure could change only very slowly. In general, the assuring and protective environment of the School soon permits the child to give up his pathological defenses against early fixations. For this reason, it was possible for Hank to relinquish his bathing ritual when the necessary assurance was offered in the very situation in which it began. But undoing his strong anal fixations and starting him on the path to changing his personality did not happen as dramatically as his giving up of defensive behaviour. The reason may be that the compulsive defense of the bathing ritual was externally imposed by the parent rather than one that was developed spontaneously by the child.

Similarly, the parentally imposed pretensions that one is grown up at seven and no longer wishes to play with childish toys (or that one loves to brush one's teeth), are given up rather quickly, as were Frank's pretended wish to diet. But these do not really imply progress in personality integration. Instead they should be viewed as necessary steps in treatment which need to be taken before important changes in the child's personality can take place.

However, our purpose at this time is not so much to discuss treatment processes as such, but rather to show how all life activities can be put to beneficial use: what some of the specific

[13] Participant observer: Ronnie Dryovage.

possibilities for fostering personal integration are which may be found in the repetitious day-to-day tasks, and what chances they offer for helping the child to solve his emotional problems. To this end, sketches from typical days at the School will be presented in the following chapters.

3

events in sequence

WRITERS, and particularly masters of the psychological novel and drama, have usually brought their heroes to life by permitting us to see them in action; they allow us to understand the hero's development by showing us what various personal relationships have meant to him and the way he responded to their challenge. We learn about the critical moments in the life of the hero and how what took place then and there went to shape his personality. In a word, the artist selects out of the whole stream of living those human interactions which, like signposts, permit us to fill in the gaps between.

Yet when we approach the problem of personality development scientifically and try to gain an understanding of it from the psychoanalytic literature, we find that most reports expect us to understand even the most complex personality deviations through what the patient recollects or what the patient and the analyst together reconstruct. By and large we are expected to follow the process of personal development, not on the basis of experiences that shaped the individual, but rather through the adult patient's reflections about them or the child's re-enactment of them.[1]

[1] Outstanding exceptions are August Aichhorn's *Wayward Youth* (New York: G. P. Putnam's Sons, 1936), where observations on delinquent youngsters in action are presented, and more recently, Anna Freud and Dorothy Burlingham's *Infants Without Families* (New York: International Universities Press, 1944).

In order to understand what produced the deviate personality we have to rely on recollections that emerge within a very particular type of relationship—the one between patient and analyst. But this is a relationship quite removed from those everyday activities and experiences which originally produced the distorted personality. It is a relationship which is different from all others, often rigidly controlled and with a logic all its own. It usually excludes those settings, actions, experiences and interferences which deeply condition all other relationships. And even if, as in the analysis of small children, the analyst acts much more like a "real" person, the analytic situation is often deliberately defined as very special, while rules of behaviour that apply to all other life situations are deliberately set aside or modified.

True, in child analysis play material replaces the spoken word to some degree, and actions with dolls or toys come closer to the child's real activities than the free associations of adults do to the adult's life experiences. But the doll the child sets on the play toilet, even when he identifies the doll as himself, is still not the real child; the most carefully reproduced toilet is not a real toilet; nor does the handling of the contents of the toilet have the same consequences it would probably have in real life. They are symbols, and as such not much different from those other symbols, the spoken words.

But in our treatment efforts which try to embrace the child's total life, we have opportunities for insight into the workings of personality development that fall somewhere between what the artist and the analyst can offer us. Because we live with the children for twenty-four hours a day, we do not have to rely on symbolic substitutes for events that took place in the past to be able to understand what may have happened at that time. We can observe directly how those past experiences influence present behaviour. But much more important is the fact that we observe and even participate in all activities which currently form the child's life. We see (and are often part of) the experience that brings about significant reactions. And although, as in analysis, we still have to rely on the child's statements or our own efforts to piece things together before we can understand why an experience has deep effects, at least as far as the experience itself is concerned, we need not rely on the child's recollections; we not only observe the child in action, we interact with him. And just as the artist permits us to understand the hero by allowing us to be present at critical moments, so we at the School can observe the child directly as the things happen that may one day change his feelings, then his outlook on life and finally his personality. It is our hope that such direct observations may also help us to understand what kind of experiences are constructive and what kind are destructive to a person—and why.

Of course direct help of this kind which includes the whole range of a child's daily activities is no patent medicine we can lightly prescribe in all cases, and not only because it is costly and time-consuming. It is undoubtedly true that some disturbed children need the security of knowing they deal only with symbols. They are so fearful of real personal contact, of real situations, or of realizing the meaning or purpose of their behaviour in everyday reality, that they can reflect on them only when they are sure what they say is "just talk" between them and the analyst. In this way they avoid the anxiety which the actual experience arouses, an anxiety which would keep them from the understanding they need before they can modify their actions, their opinions, and finally their personality structure.

While this is true for some children we have found that for other children, this dealing with symbols in place of the experience itself is needlessly time-consuming. In still other cases it actually prevents the child from coming to grips with his problem. This is particularly true for children who already deal with life largely or entirely in terms of symbols, to the detriment of their relation to reality, children who use symbols mainly with a "private" meaning, apart from what they normally signify. These children are quite deeply fixed in their magical thinking, or have lost too much contact with reality in other ways. Using the term loosely, they might be called delusional or schizophrenic, although on the basis of their actions some of them are classified as delinquents.[2]

By and large, however, we feel we can help the child within real situations and without recourse to symbols. But this we can do only if the child is convinced he is now in a setting which is far more secure than the ones he knew, and if his everyday activities are protected from the consequences he was previously right in expecting and fearing.

Thus Aichhorn could not only afford to let his aggressive group destroy their living quarters, but could even turn the act to beneficial advantage. This was because no punitive action by society resulted from their asocial behaviour and because the situation and emotions that flowed from such actions were immediately dealt with within the context of the youngsters' real and immediate setting.[3]

To cite another example, the discussion of night fears at bedtime would serve little purpose, and assurances about security from dangers the child imagines to be lurking in the darkness would fall flat (or might even backfire) if the child did not also receive tangible evidence that if he feels anxious during the night, he can immediately find protection from an understanding and trusted adult.

[2] Escalona has discussed the differing treatment needs of psychotic children and has suggested that differing treatment methods should at least be experimented with. (Escalona, S., "Some Considerations Regarding Psychotherapy with Psychotic Children," *Bulletin of the Menninger Clinic*, XII [1948], 126-34.) But even Escalona seems to think more of treatment situations which are set apart from the main current of the child's life, which may explain some of her scepticism. Such children need —if at all possible—to live in an environment which is beneficial in its totality; twenty-four-hour-a-day treatment and not just for one hour a day. Dr. Fromm-Reichmann's and Dr. Rosen's experiences with adult psychotics seem also to support this notion. (Fromm-Reichmann, F., "Notes on the Development of Treatment of Schizophrenics by Psychoanalytic Psychotherapy," *Psychiatry*, XI [1948], 263-73; Rosen, J. N., "The Treatment of Schizophrenic Psychosis by Direct Analytic Therapy," *Psychiatric Quarterly*, XXI [1947], 3-37, 117-119.)

[3] Aichhorn, op. cit., 167-85.

Such assurances, when given before the child falls asleep, seem more effective, for example, than when given in a play session during the day. Exploring with the child at night into the shadows he has transformed into dangerous lions is also more effective than assurances that lions cannot possibly enter his bedroom, when these assurances are given in broad daylight in a room not his own and perhaps miles from his bedroom. In general we have found a specific affinity between certain treatment efforts and the settings in which they are made. The affinity between the specific setting prescríbed by Freud and the method and results of psychoanalysis is recognized, but careful studies about its nature, its advantages and drawbacks are still lacking. Reports on experiences with other types of therapy such as active therapy (Ferenczi), short psychotherapy (Chicago Psychoanalytic Institute), etc., do not clarify this issue as long as the specific relation between setting and procedures on the one hand, and their consequences on the other, are not discussed in much greater detail and on the basis of comparative studies. Nor do reports about positive results with one or the other of these settings or methods solve the issue. It goes without saying that these comments must also apply to our own treatment efforts at the School. It lies with future researchers to draw their evaluations from careful comparative studies which are thus far still lacking.

With these qualifications in mind, we might say that in our type of work, we believe we can help a child best if our efforts are not restricted to a special treatment room or the playfield, or to the child's bedtime, or meals. Each time and setting has its particular therapeutic possibilities of which we must take advantage. Each routine activity also offers specific chances to become the carrier of particular experiences, as I shall try to show in later chapters.

Here it should be stressed that a therapeutic handling of the child's total activities permits us to set them in balance to one another. For example, in order to prevent chaotic living it may become necessary to impose restrictions on some routine activities just to be able to grant utter freedom in those others where the child seems at the moment to need to be entirely, even unreasonably free.

Nevertheless, when in this or in following chapters particular times of the day, or particular activities are singled out for discussion, the reader must not imagine that what happens in the morning, for example, is unrelated to what happened at bedtime on the previous evening, or on the play field the preceding day. On the contrary, the specific reward of handling particular activities correctly is reaped mainly through their cumulative effect. Precisely because most of our efforts are not restricted to the treatment room, and because we do not rely mainly on the reliving (in phantasy or memory) of past emotions and events, we must put every one of the child's life experiences to helpful advantage, whenever and wherever they chance to occur.

In view of these facts, a discussion of the specific integrative propensities to be found in the various activities should be introduced by at least one example to show that what happens at any one particular moment or in any particular setting has its roots in many earlier events. This example may further show that when, in the chapters to come, specific situations are artificially detached on the printed page from the general context in which they took place, they actually form part of a closely knit sequence of events. It may also help to illustrate the various aspects of a single child's relation to one adult, and how varying settings give a varying flavour to the relationship and thus lend themselves to the working through of different problems.

This account is about a particular week in the life of Tom, aged twelve. Tom's parents were married when the father was already in advanced age. In age, Tom's mother was therefore closer to her son than to her husband. When he was old enough, Tom became her play companion for the times when they were alone, but when the father was present he had the conviction that they competed for his attention. And, as if this situation was not difficult enough, the mother often behaved in ways that were experienced by the boy as seductive, only (as he felt) to desert him for his rival when the father appeared. Mother and son were also competitive in intellectual matters as well as in games and sports where he felt that the mother competed with him as with an age-mate. But while she thus seemed to stimulate him prematurely, both in sexual and intellectual ways, she neglected to satisfy his infantile emotional needs.

Some of the disturbances that arose from this complex family structure found expression and became partly resolved in a series of events at the School stretching over a period of more than a week. It began with Tom's severe disappointment in his mother when a letter he believed she had promised him did not come. Again, as so often in his previous life, he felt she had first raised his hopes and then disappointed him. This resentment toward his mother he turned against the maternal figure of a counselor whom he accused of forever depriving him.

When he first came to the School, Tom's feelings of utter desertion and neglect had been combined with delusions of violent persecution. At that time, he expressed the conviction that all women he knew were constantly plotting to kill him. This changed, later on, to more specified charges of persecution and he then felt they wanted to rob him of his genitals. All this, of course, was accompanied by equally drastic or even more violent phantasies of how he was going to take his revenge by torturing and killing any number of men and women. But by the time of the following series of events, his accusing women of wanting to injure his body had changed, by and large, to less violent delusions of persecution. He no longer accused his counselor of wanting him to starve, but only of wanting him to go hungry, of wanting him to feel bad, or of never giving him what he wanted most.[4]

[4] Participant observer for the whole series of episodes, unless otherwise indicated: Patty Pickett.

As mentioned on p. 11 three counselors and one teacher are in charge of any one group. They take turns and are usually "on duty" a maximum of four and a half shifts a week to avoid overwork and the con-

Starting out with the realistic complaint that he felt bad about not having gotten mail that day, Tom soon exaggerated by saying he never got any mail at all. In this he was no longer accusing his mother, but the counselor, saying that he never got to do anything nice, that he was never taken to interesting places, or on trips, although he noticed that all the others had very good times with her.

From previous experience, the counselor knew that to point out how irrealistic Tom was in his accusations would only have aggravated the boy, because what he was really reacting to were not actual events but emotions left over from a real enough past. So in a casual way, she suggested that Tom and she might go out for a walk or on a shopping trip, since this was allowance day and he might like to spend his allowance. But Tom said he had no intention of spending his allowance, that he had other plans with it. "I'm going to save it," he said, "and buy food."

The counselor told him she couldn't see why he wanted to spend his allowance on food when there was always plenty of it in the kitchen, but she also assured him that if there was anything special he wanted that wasn't on hand, she would be glad to buy it for him. And she added what he already knew—that we felt that every child at the School should be able to have any-

---

comitant emotional strain. Each shift is approximately seven hours long. The week itself is divided into fifteen shifts, not counting the time after the children have fallen asleep and before they wake up. During the night we have found that one counselor "on duty" will suffice for all children, since it rarely happens that more than one child wakes up and needs comfort at the same time during the night.

Thus any one counselor is "on duty" only four or five times a week, and for less than half a day at a stretch. But most staff members find it convenient and desirable to take many of their meals at the same time the children do and in the common dining room, even if they are "off duty." In this and many other ways casual contacts take place which prevent emotional gaps from arising between periods "on duty."

In critical periods, such as the one about to be described, the counselor involved, out of his own volition, and feeling his importance for the child, makes himself available to the child for shorter or longer periods of time even when he is "off duty" to help the child not only to weather the crisis but to turn it to positive use.

thing he wanted to eat.[5] But Tom only said, "I don't like any of the food we have here or any you could buy me." The counselor repeated that she wished he would tell her what he liked so she could get it for him, but he cut her short, saying, "There's nothing you can give me that I like and that's all." Thus, he had not only transferred his resentment of his mother (who had deprived him emotionally) to the counselor (whom he accused of doing the same) but was also transferring the conviction that no pleasure could possibly originate with her, and if it did, he didn't want it. After this exchange, Tom retired into a corner to sulk, and turned his back on all efforts by his counselor or the children to be friendly.

Tom managed successfully to frustrate the counselor's repeated efforts to establish some positive contact. For example, a few hours later that same day they were together at the swimming pool and she offered to play ball with him, which was something he usually enjoyed. But now he was curt with her and told her, "No, I'm going to play with one of the boys." Yet her efforts to show him that she wanted to make things nicer for him were not wholly wasted. They enabled him to look for some kind of contact, but since he felt frustrated by a maternal figure he avoided all contact with her and turned to male age-mates instead. Still, his anger forced him to play with them aggressively by jumping into the pool almost on top of the other children in the water. Once in, he actually did jump on one of the other boys, trying to hit the lower part of the boy's body with the lower part of his own. When the counselor called out and told him to stop, he turned on her and splashed her aggressively in defiance, shouting, "So what! So what if I jump on him."

For the rest of the day, all efforts by his counselor to regain friendly contact with Tom ended in failure. But he opened up just enough to admit to her that—contrary to his usual be-

---

[5] Once each week the children themselves take turns at making up a whole day's menu. Otherwise, the regular menus are based in large measure on what the children themselves like, and their suggestions are usually carried out. In addition, they are free to have drinks, candies, sundaes, etc., pretty much as they like.

haviour (when he bent every effort to engage girls in provocative games)—he had no desire to play with girls now because, in his words, he just couldn't stand them.

This aggressively withdrawn behaviour toward a maternal figure in particular, and toward females in general, had its counterpart in his openly aggressive advances toward boys, only the boys kept their distance because his efforts seemed too hostile and aggressive to them. For example, on the second day, he reverted to his earlier violent phantasies and announced provocatively that he was going to draw horrible pictures and write horrible stories or poems. As he drew and wrote he made comments to the effect that he was going to "cut the man down; stab, stab, revenge, revenge!" At the same time, he provoked the burning curiosity of the other children through his remarks, only to coyly try to hide what he drew or wrote until he felt sure every child within earshot had reached the highest pitch of excitement. Then he made sure that they all saw his creations, of which the following verse and the drawing [plate 8, facing page 131] are examples:

> "Beside the trail there lies in wait
> A man engulfed in thoughts of hate
> His fury at the breaking point
> He'd shot everybody in the pleasure joint.
> And with his gun he went to bed
> Ready to fill everybody full of lead . . ."

For the rest of that day he continued to discharge hostility very massively.

At one point on the following day, when a male counselor was in charge of the group, Tom ignored him, but since he seemed to remind Tom less of the frustration his mother caused him, he made no efforts to provoke the other boys or act aggressively toward them; instead he simply isolated himself. The efforts of the male counselor to help Tom out of his feeling of isolation and rejection by trying to talk to him or play with him, were of no avail. When his male counselor finally succeeded in getting him to join in a game, he soon reverted to feelings of persecution. He quit after one or two minutes, declaring, "I'll never win a game. You never let me win." [6] Later efforts to draw him out again were given up because they only seemed to aggravate him.

For almost all of three days Tom remained in this frustrated and angry isolation which vented itself in repeated accusing outbursts, although only in the presence of the female counselor. It was as if only in the presence of a maternal figure could he work out those problems which began with his disappointment in his mother.

Late on the afternoon of the third day the persistence of the counselor was finally rewarded when he joined her in a game of ping-pong. (Of all games, Tom liked ping-pong best. He was a good player and often won, and for this reason the counselor tried and finally succeeded in establishing contact at the ping-pong table.) Throughout the game, Tom accused her monotonously of wanting to beat him, of wanting to win, and aggressively told her he would see to it that she didn't. Remarks such as: "You don't need to think you're going to win," "Don't think you're so smart," "Don't think you know how to play this game," "I've got you here, see," "See how stupid you are," accompanied each serve of the ball. "See! Here comes the ball, that shows I'm going to win the point! That shows I can do it!" His counselor managed to withstand this provocative testing without being unnerved, and kept assuring him that she knew he could play a good game of ping-pong, that she knew he had a good chance of winning. When he finally won (legitimately), he said, "See! You didn't think I could do it!"

The following, or fourth day, Tom behaved in a more positive way toward his counselor. Although she was off duty that day, she was in the house and Tom was free to re-establish relations with her if he chose, which he did, after much hesitation. He agreed to play her another game of ping-pong and went through with it without abusing her. But he continued to unload his aggressions against the boys.

[6] Participant observer: Clarence Lipschutz.

On the fifth day, when she was once more in charge of the group, he confessed to her his terrible fear that the other boys were ganging up on him. All day he stayed very close to her, telling her how the other boys were persecuting him, how they talked about his secrets and plotted against him. "They're always talking about me," he said. "They're all ganging up on me! They're all trying to make life miserable for me!—I don't think one boy in the whole dormitory likes me. I don't believe one boy in the whole School likes me! Why is it I don't get along with the boys? The only people who like me in this School are the counselors, and even some of them don't like me. Maybe you're the only one that likes me."

Nothing anyone tried to do to help Tom see things a little more realistically seemed to make any difference. Although he admitted that from those conversations of others that he could understand, it was not always clear they were talking about him, yet he said, "I don't know. Maybe they don't, but it always seems to me that they're talking about me. I always think they're calling me names, and I'm positive they do it lots of times." A few minutes later one of his best friends went by and said something harmless enough, at which Tom burst out, "I hate your nasty blue eyes and your pretty blonde hair! I hate them!"

The next morning and throughout that day he continued to stay pretty much away from the others but close to his female counselor. As soon as he awoke in the morning he complained loudly that his rectum itched, "God damn it!" he exclaimed over and over again, "it itches so bad I can't stand it!" and he scratched himself furiously. Suggestions of some applications he could put on it that might relieve the itch were rejected with obscene comments and this continued throughout the day. But at the same time he stopped being seductive or provocative with his counselor (as he had been before the episode began), and clung to her presence quite childishly as though for protection. During the preceding days, the more she had tried to please him the more angry he became. Now her efforts to please him seemed to comfort him.

The following morning, the beginning of the eighth day, he again woke up complaining a great deal about various aches and pains, but this time none of them specific. At one moment his foot hurt or his leg hurt, then it was his head, and finally he hurt all over. These complaints were very different in character from his usual provocative complaints; he expressed them very much as a small child might. To his counselor's friendly, comforting attitude he now responded at last, but in ways that a very small child might adopt. Later that day, and on the following days, he relaxed into a friendly and relatively stable relation to counselors and children. He spoke more freely and realistically about his past and present difficulties and showed other signs of unfreezing. But these consequences go beyond the purpose of my example.

During these eight days, it was as if Tom were reliving and working through with his counselor some of the feelings and difficulties that began with his relation to his mother. It was his mother, after all, who had touched off the series of events by not sending him the letter he felt she had promised him. This disappointment he experienced as a repetition of many previous instances in which she had first raised his hopes to an unmanageable height, and then disappointed him again and again, a disappointment he experienced as total rejection.

At first Tom had re-enacted feelings of deprivation which were so deep that no one, and nothing, seemed capable of satisfying him. Then in desperation he developed ideas of omnipotence: nobody but himself, he concluded, could provide him with happiness. In line with such feelings he retired into isolation. But isolation is difficult to keep up, particularly for a child whose problems originated in a very close relation to at least one of his parents, however deviate the relationship was. Isolation is even more difficult to maintain in a setting where children and adult try to draw the sulking child into friendly relations.

In this, as in so many other situations, the group exercised its therapeutic influence on the individual. If there had merely been the relation between Tom and his counselor, her efforts to make contact could have been rejected or denied much more easily, because such efforts in a one-to-one relationship can easily be interpreted as a demand, as an aggressive intrusion on one's privacy. But the presence of the group and its legitimate interests served to make them less concentrated, more diffuse, and hence less threatening. Moreover, Tom's efforts at interpreting the counselor's friendly efforts as persecution met with the tacit disapproval of the group, and hence could not stand up under the test of reality which the presence of the group forced before him.

As a child Tom had felt deserted and deprived by his mother. He had turned to his father not as a result of the oedipal development but in desperation, in a bid for some love and attention. But since his motives in doing so were much less the desire to love and be loved than the result of a long series of frustrations, he was aggressive in the way he strove for attention, and his oedipal conflict could not resolve itself through identification with the father, or through any positive relation to him that was permanent.

Thus influenced by events of his past life, Tom felt rejected by the counselor, turned away from her and all other females, and turned toward members of his own sex, but in a hostile way. When the friendliness of his female counselor began to hit home and he could no longer deny the existence of women (which he had tried), he made an effort to deal with her in terms of the deviate solution he had once found to his oedipal conflict. Since his mother seemed unwilling or unable to satisfy his emotional needs, he had turned to his father for those things. And when his father, too, failed to provide what he longed for, and remained more absorbed in the mother than in him, he had tried to take her place. In terms of his hostility he tried to do that not by making himself more attractive to the father, but by proving he was better than the mother: by beating her in areas where he was better than she, for example in games—in ping-pong. But the counselor in that situation, reacted positively to his victory, which was the opposite of his experience with his mother. Hence the counselor appeared in a more positive light. Moreover, after the massive discharge of aggression which extended over a period of days, he had drained himself of some of his most violent aggressive emotions, and his past pleasant experiences with the counselor slowly asserted their influence.

In addition to these factors, Tom also felt guilty about his aggressive, homosexual attacks against the other boys, and once his violence was spent he began to be afraid they might retaliate. What he himself had wanted to do to them, he now feared they might do to him. He felt homosexually persecuted, first by the boys, and then by the physical pain at a part of his body related to his homosexual tendencies. The dependent care he received from his female counselor, who at this point represented protection for him against homosexual dangers, permitted him slowly to recover. His ego grew strong enough to combat his delusional ideas of persecution and to turn his hostility inward rather than discharge it at random. This storage of tension revealed itself in vague physical complaints which slowly dissolved as he continued to receive tangible proof that his counselor wished to please him. This in turn helped him to slowly resume a satisfying relationship to her, at least for the time being.

In the following days, Tom became more and more able to accept gifts and services from his counselor. More and more he could recognize her as a person in her own rights instead of a symbol of what he remembered as his mother's worst features. After a great deal more testing of this counselor over a long period of time, and after he became able to put their relationship to good use, Tom was slowly able to realize the better aspects of his mother's relation to him and to establish a more workable relation to her and to his father. But these developments no longer belong to the example, and only came about slowly during the many months that followed.

This example also shows how an episode that started with a transference relation (the transferal of feelings belonging to the mother onto a female counselor) found its resolution when the transferred, neurotic relation again turned into an honest-to-goodness personal relation. This is in line with our efforts in trying to change transference (neurotic) relations into true ones. Similarly we try to change neurotic attitudes (such as defeatist feelings about one's ability to achieve) into experiences of success, and these in the very setting in which the individual initially approached life in a neurotic way.

But our main purpose in describing these happenings was to show how mistaken an impression we might give if the events of early morning—to which the next chapter is devoted—or of any other time of the day, were to be viewed in isolation. True, Tom finally found his way back to his counselor after awakening, on the morning of the last day in the story. But although what happened that morning had important meaning in terms of the development of Tom's ability to relate to others, it did so only because of what had happened before: on walks, at the swimming pool or at ping-pong. Each of these experiences was potentially beneficial but became truly valid only in their meaningful sequence.

The actual events in this case have been greatly over-simplified, doing no justice to the various strands that existed between the events I have related, and the many others I had to leave out.

The scene of personal contacts changed continuously, but each setting offered specific opportunities for Tom to act out and work through particular aspects of his complex difficulties. The scene changed from the dormitory, with the disappointment of not receiving mail when other children did, to a walk on the street, to the play room, then to the swimming pool and back to the dormitory with its impact on other children. Then it was shifted back to the play room and ping-pong, followed by walks, contact with other boys, and then the nurse's quarters and the offer of soothing ointment. Finally, a resolution was found in the dormitory, in the morning, at a time when emotional contact on an infantile level is found more acceptable by the child.

Each of these separate situations was experienced in line with the everyday activities going on at the time. The desire to win in competition could not have been better expressed than at the ping-pong table. The aggressive attacks against the other boys could nowhere have found a more socially acceptable outlet (or one less harmful to other children) than in the water, at the swimming pool, and the final relief was experienced in the morning after awakening, when childlike dependency is particularly suggestive.

Needless to say, these events were discussed by all those who had contact with Tom (counselors, teachers, nurse, etc.) at staff meetings and in more casual conversations. Thus, every staff member dealing with a child is aware at each stage of all major, and also of most minor developments, and can act accordingly.

4

from dreams to waking

WAKING up in the morning, getting out of bed and getting dressed, are often difficult tasks for our children. They have lost out too often to meet the new day with much confidence. They lack the emotional strength needed to overcome their lethargy and their desire to retain the security and comfort of a nice warm bed.

Although we do not know exactly what the children may have experienced during the night, we get the impression, from those who tell us about their dreams or what bothers them when they happen to wake up during the night, that the less prepared a child is to meet the ordinary tasks of living, the more likely he is to have bad dreams and night fears, both of which make it harder to face the new day.

When they first wake up many children are eager to tell us their dreams, but this presents several difficulties. For one thing, we are naturally interested in whatever has upset the child during the night. We want to help him with the fears which the dream, for example, may not only reveal but may actually have aggravated. We also want to help him to recognize and work through his unconscious desires, anxieties, and so forth. But while these and many other reasons speak in favour of our listening to the dreams of some children, there are equally valid reasons suggesting that other children should not be encouraged to prolong their irrational phantasies because it may only make it harder for them to approach the new day realistically.

In making such decisions the counselor cannot even rely on how the child begins to speak about his dream, because often, during the telling, the child remembers frightening parts of it that he forgot when he awoke, and which come to light only now as he concentrates on the dream. Such newly recalled or associated material may often heighten the child's anxieties and have such a devastating influence on the rest of the day that he is powerless to come to grips with reality.

In deciding whose dreams he ought to listen to, it is not enough that the counselor be familiar with the child and his problems, though that helps. The reason is that in dismissing the dream the child may also feel we are dismissing him, too, and this rejection he experiences within the context of the dream he wanted to talk about: to the injury (the anxiety created by the dream) is then added the insult of the counselor's not wanting to listen.

In any case it is not easy to decide whether a child is strong enough to handle the residues of his unconscious as they reveal themselves in his dreams (and should therefore be encouraged to talk about them); it is equally difficult to know that another child is too insecure to go ahead with the tasks of living after he has just faced in broad daylight what lay buried in his unconscious. Such decisions can never be made in a general way.

To make matters more complicated, even if the counselor knows that one child may be encouraged to tell his dreams safely while another should be prevented from doing so, the counselor must also be able to foresee the results of his decision on the other children present. What will it mean to the others, with their fear of unconscious desires, to see that the counselor does not listen to dreams, or what may it mean to them to listen to the unconscious as revealed in the dreams of another child?

Only intuition and empathy will help the counselor to encourage those children to review their dreams whose egos are strong enough to face and work through the dream material—

most often their anxieties—and to see to it that others do not. The counselor must be guided here by his often unconscious impressions of how strong the child is at the moment, or how shaken he seems to be as he thinks about his dream. These indications of the child's strength or weakness at the moment are much more important and much more reliable when it comes to making decisions about how to handle the child's expressions of his unconscious than any preconceived notions based on theory.

Quite often it is neither in going more deeply into the dream material nor in evading its coming to light that the situation finds its wisest solution. Tom, here, is a case in point.

For more than a year after his coming to the School, Tom had to tell his counselor every morning about the dreams he had had. This he did while he was still half asleep. But to discuss his dreams with him at this or at any other moment during the early period of his stay at the School would have been fatal; he would only have escaped further into a world of imaginary fears and lost whatever little hold on reality he had. Nevertheless, once he had poured out his dreams in a steady recital, and once he felt sure that his wild hostile and sexual phantasies aroused no special interest on the part of his counselor (as he had hoped and feared they might) it slowly became possible to present him with reality. Then his talk moved to anxious anticipation about what the day might bring, but though these fears were still delusional they were much closer to reality. Gradually the frenzied outpouring changed to quieter conversation and only then, but still very slowly, could Tom accept assurance in terms of concrete fears about the coming day. Next he became able to interrupt himself long enough to eat ravenously—he awoke starved each day—and finally he was more or less ready to get out of bed.

In quieting this child, the counselor had to be careful not to reassure him too early about his safety during the day. Not only could he not listen, but he would have taken her assurance as a sign of the anxiety he aroused in her and would only have discounted whatever she told him. Moreover, Tom would also have resented her interrupting his outpourings and that would have increased his feelings of persecution.

In this case, then, it was just friendly and passive listening that eventually reassured. It showed Tom that his counselor was interested in him, without giving the impression that she was captivated by his sexual or hostile provocation. Her relaxed quietness as she listened to him seemed to suggest that his anxieties as well as his efforts to seduce or be aggressive were not quite as devastating to others (or to himself) as he feared they might be.

After Tom had discharged some of his tension by talking, his ego slowly regained whatever little control it possessed over his unconscious and irrational thoughts, a control that was shattered by the memory of the dream experience. The counselor, like a good and strong ego, was neither threatened nor overpowered by Tom's unconscious; she simply faced it without either accepting, supporting, or repressing it.

After she had thus proved her good will and given the child time to get back some ego strength, she could further help his ego along by showing him that he had anxiously exaggerated his fears, not of his unconscious, but of the dangers the new day might bring. In line with her ego-supporting function she helped Tom to see the coming day (and himself in it) more realistically. Then he was slowly able to talk more reasonably about his fears, and the outpouring which had himself as its center—but which also had behind it the determination to shut out all interaction with another human being—could slowly give way to the conversation of two persons in good contact. Once this stage was reached the counselor could begin to feed Tom with cookies or candy. Such obvious proof that response to his most basic needs was assured gave him back some small trust in life and this in turn gave him the strength to give up the security of the bed.

If we had offered him food during the first outpouring of his partly unconscious thoughts, he would have viewed it as an effort to "stuff his mouth," to block the discharge of his emotions. He would have felt it either as an effort to choke him, or if not him, then his unconscious, and to force both of them back to repression. But food offered during a more or less sensible conversation became a symbol of returning to human contact with his counselor, and with it to the reality of the day. The double experience of being able to discharge safely a tension of unconscious origin (through talking) and of relieving the tension of hunger (through being fed) restored enough strength to Tom to enable him to get out of bed.[1]

More than two years later, when Tom was no longer flooded by wholly irrational fears, and when he already had a large measure of control over those of his tendencies which he had not previously understood, his telling of dreams on awakening could be handled quite differently. Then it was no longer necessary to disregard his dreams and it was not only possible but desirable to deal with them at the moment of wakening. Then the counselor supported Tom's ego on another level when she supported his efforts to relegate both the dream and its content to the area of the unreal, the phantastic, and to view his night fears in the clear daylight of a rational outlook.

During this period, Tom might begin by telling his counselor in the morning that he had had a very bad dream. In one of them, for example, he had been driving wildly, going back and forth all over the road, utterly lacking in control over the car. With little or no prodding he added that he didn't care about the dream as such. What perturbed him was that he was afraid that he would never be able to learn to drive well.

Without going into the unconscious fears the dream indicated, including his doubts about ever being able to master all the tasks that maturity might confront him with, the counselor assured Tom that in view of his age he was not only not expected to drive a car but was legally prohibited from doing so. She added that the reason was that no child of his age was able to drive safely, or correctly. She also reminded him how well he was able to do things that were in line with his age, and how all of them were things he'd been anxious to master. She elaborated

[1] Participant observer: Patty Pickett.

on how this was the best proof he could have that, as he grew up, he would also be able to do the things that would belong to each later stage of maturity. Moreover, she reminded him that nobody was compelled to drive a car, and that if he disliked the idea, there was no need for him ever to do it. This way of reminding Tom how adequate he was at his own age level helped him to overcome the more or less realistic anxiety the dream had created; the dream itself, since he was now a better integrated person, he had been able to discuss as phantasy even before the conversation began.[2]

This ability to view a dream as a dream and not as a true picture of reality, was largely the consequence of Tom's spending a much greater part of his day in meeting reality, while in the first phase of his stay at the School most of his day was spent in wild phantasies and in daydreams that were totally unreal and filled with anxiety.

During the beginning of his stay at the School a discussion of his dreams would have provided Tom with just one more experience of defeat. It would have shown him how little conscious control he had over his irrational tendencies, and a conversation about his dreams would have ended in his having to meet the day in the grip of such tendencies, knowing full well how helpless he was to control them. Much later, a discussion of his dreams provided Tom with the experience that with some help —the counselor's support—his rational self could evaluate the residues of his dreams, and could see them as phantasies having no direct bearing on his actual life. Then a morning discussion of his dreams only strengthened his ego in meeting the day where before it would surely have weakened it.

While Tom brought his dreams to the counselor's attention directly, either by talking about them, or by obviously showing their effects, other children use more roundabout ways in securing our help. Paul, after he had made considerable progress, began to fear, and with reason, that his stay at the School might

[2] Participant observer: Gayle Shulenberger.

be drawing to an end. He then became quite perturbed about his future. Although plans for his future placement were repeatedly discussed with him, as well as the arrangements we would make for his well being after leaving the School, the thought of what lay ahead still worried him and particularly at night. This he was unable to admit directly since he was familiar enough with our assurances and knew that we lived up to them. His ego saw no reasons for his fears and this kept him from stating them openly, which was also in line with his better control over unreasonable fears. But he was bothered enough to be unable to start out in the morning with any feeling of security.

Instead of stating his fears, he projected them onto his counselor. The first thing he told her when he awoke was that she looked like a lost child who had no one to take care of her. He told her that her hair was uncombed, and that he knew from observation that she owned only two decent outfits. It took quite a bit of friendly assurance and further conversation before Paul remarked that "even at that you have two more outfits than I have, because I don't even have a single good suit." So Paul was assured that the reason he had no good suits was that he didn't need them at the School, because all the boys there wore only non-matching pants and jackets of which he had several old ones and a few new ones, and that once he left the School he would be given whatever suits or other clothing he needed.

Later, when he was asked why he never talked about these things during the day when the counselor tried to discuss them with him, he replied: "During the day when I'm doing things I don't worry about it, so why should I talk about it? You're not around in the middle of the night when I wake up. Then I have nothing to do and I worry about what's going to happen to me." Thus, even Paul, whose night fears had become quite realistic, still needed support in the morning to be able to start out successfully, a success he still needed quite badly to strengthen his confidence in himself and his ability to deal with the world.[3]

Paul's anger at his counselor in the morning for not protect-

[3] Participant observer: Gayle Shulenberger.

ing him enough from his night fears found direct expression in his critical comments. But it is only after a child has become relatively integrated that his hostile behaviour on awakening— or at any other time—will have such a definite source and be so goal-directed that it is relatively easy to deal with.

For a long time the children are helplessly tossed about by their contradictory emotions, particularly at night and in their dreams; of course, this is also true during the day, but somewhat less so. When they first wake up they are still totally overpowered by their violent and contradictory feelings. George expressed this quite directly one morning, after a prolonged stay at the School had taught him to face up to his emotions but not really to integrate them yet.

As usual, when he condescended to talk at all in the morning, he spoke about his night fears and nightmares. Then he complained that the dormitory was too cold, and that he almost froze during the night. As the counselor made a move to get George extra blankets to make sure he wouldn't be cold again, other boys in the dormitory complained that it was too warm and stuffy. This complaint George also agreed to, saying, "I thought there was a dragon in here last night blowing burning air at me." The counselor pointed out the contradiction, asked him whether or not he wanted another blanket or two and asked which was true, that he'd been too hot or too cold during the night. George's answer was an apt picture of his true state of mind. He said, "I'm frozen with fear and steaming with rage." [4]

As George's fear slowly "unfroze" through the friendly efforts of the counselor, his "steaming rage" asserted itself against her more and more aggressively, since it was no longer held in check by his paralyzing fear. In this as in many other cases, some integration can be achieved at first only on the asocial level of hostility. At the very least, freeing the child from some of his fears will also free some of his energy for living; but before this energy becomes available for constructive tasks it will first serve his hostility for some time. Still, such a separation of emotions, though

[4] Participant observer: Gayle Shulenberger.

they block one another, is a necessary step in unfreezing the child. We have made similar observations on many other children who can rarely express their conflicting emotions, and almost never as clearly as George did.

Most children at the School will order the counselor about angrily for some time, and particularly in the morning before they get out of bed. For example, they may ask the counselor to bring certain articles of clothing to their beds, only to throw them on the floor with abuse because they were not exactly what they wanted, or because things were too slow in coming or weren't placed exactly where they wished to have them put down. Other children go so far as to have the counselor bring to their beds, one by one, each piece of clothing they possess, only to reject each one angrily, and at that not only once, but two or three times. Only after they have thus gotten rid of some hostility are they able to consider getting dressed. Then they can and will accept almost any of those pieces of clothing they have just finished rejecting so violently.

To discuss such behaviour with the children while they are still angry would serve little or no purpose. Their behaviour is not goal-directed as such, they neither dislike their clothing nor are they angry at the counselor as an individual. It is a kind of behaviour the child adopts because it offers a much needed discharge of hostile tension. The tension itself has originated in the child's unconscious which has been ruling unchecked over his mind during the night. On awakening, the rational controls have to reassert their power over the irrational tendencies. The ego has to come back into its own, or the child will be unable to make contact with reality, will be unable, for instance, to leave the bed. In order to regain control over unconscious tendencies it is as if the child's ego had to convince these irrational drives that if they will only submit to some measure of realistic control the ego will be much surer of finding satisfaction.

Thus the child's behaviour toward the counselor in the morning is a brief repetition of how ego control is first established in the infant. Initially the ego was developed to provide the child with the real satisfaction of instinctual desires, so much more preferable than the imagined satisfactions of his phantasy. The child's hostility toward the counselor then seems to represent the efforts of the reawakening ego to control the unconscious hostility. It is a test. It is as if the child needed to be aggressive toward the counselor in order to convince himself that the ego is trying to bring the hostile tendencies into a social context, not to suppress them entirely but rather to permit them to find effective outlet and satisfaction.

If the counselor, at this moment, should forbid such a discharge of hostility against himself, the child would have little chance of learning that his hostile desires can be discharged in ways that are relatively more ego-correct (through talking). They might explode, then, in much more dangerous acts of violence and physical aggression, or force the child back into self-centered isolation. If he cannot discharge hostility against a person the child will seek imaginary satisfaction in aggressive phantasies which separate him dangerously from reality, particularly from friendly relations to other people. In this connection it is also important that through such token discharges of aggression not only are some amounts of hostile tension released, but also the child sees for himself that such discharge is possible. This allows him to postpone further discharge for a little while, anyway, and both together permit even a relatively weak ego to bring the remaining hostility under some kind of control.

Thus in regard to hostility the same factors hold true as in the telling of dreams. The counselor must rely not only on his knowledge of the children but also on his spontaneous empathy in order to decide how to handle the child in the morning.

If the child's hostility is due to some discomfort that the counselor can relieve either through talking or realistic assurance (as, for example, in Paul's criticism of his counselor) the counselor should make an effort to work through the child's hostility and help him with the underlying problem that gave rise to it. But if the child's aggression toward the counselor is more the outward expression of an internal battle between the child's efforts at control and his asocial drives, then it is best if the counselor suffers the child's aggressions quietly and submits—as far as he can realistically do—to the child's hostile whims. Only then will it be possible for the child's asocial drives to transfer their energy to the ego because the child's conscious efforts seem to serve the discharge of hostility and not its control. Yet even by serving the child's hostility in this case, the ego is still exercising its main function, that of establishing contact with reality, of recognizing reality, and finally of modifying the child's behaviour in line with what is real.

These various steps in establishing ego control over asocial, instinctual tendencies are often recognized clearly in much of the child's behaviour in the morning. First he grumbles his commands to the counselor. The sounds are more like barking than words. The eyes are partly closed. The child is still engulfed in the world of his phantasies and there is very little contact with reality. As the counselor submits to the child's commands, slowly the second step in ego control is reached. The commands are now enunciated more loudly, but also more distinctly. The single-word commands change to sentences. The child's eyes open wider, and finally remain open, looking more and more at the outer world of reality, and less and less to the inner one of phantasy. But while this closer inspection of reality is first attempted to satisfy the child's hostile needs, the counselor's subservience cannot fail to provide the child with narcissistic satisfaction.

Then the third step in ego control is slowly achieved. The counselor, as a servant, satisfies the child's self love. But in order to assure the continuance of this service he must be recognized to some degree as a person. So the child begins to talk to him in a two-way communication. The child's ego need no longer rely entirely on his hostility as the source of energy for its strength. Satisfied narcissism provides another source of strength (while at the same time, as noted above, the pressure of hostility is lowered through discharge and hence the need for its discharge grows less).

Finally, the provider of narcissistic satisfaction (the counselor) becomes valuable, not necessarily as a person in his own right yet, but as a provider of pleasures. Thus in this three- (or more) step process the rudiments of a social contact have been established. These contacts, in turn, provide the most effective balance against the unconscious asocial tendencies which have ruled over the child with little restriction during the night. With the help of this contact, as well as the child's greater ability to view the day more realistically, it becomes easier to look forward to the next twenty-four hours with more optimism.

Aside from the asocial, hostile or anxious tendencies of the child which make it most difficult for him to get back to reality in the morning, there are still other difficulties he encounters at the beginning of the day. Unconscious phantasies or realistic fears are not the only things that characterize the child's night life. Just being in bed offers a great deal of pleasure, pure and simple, and what is often more important, it provides a seemingly total security from the external world. (As a matter of fact, in order to restore and protect the child's night rest we have to go to great lengths in assuring exactly that comfort and security to the child.)

In the morning, on getting up, the child must give up the pleasures of a comfortable, warm bed, as well as the joys of his wish-fulfilling phantasies. He is deprived of the protection and security he derives from the absence of an external world. Thus the counselor must not only help the child with the difficulties that stem from the unconscious but must also behave—and try to arrange the world the child meets on awakening—in such a way that it becomes obvious to the child that by changing from the world of his bed to a more active way of life he stands to gain greater pleasures, without running graver risks.

It is always the main task of a counselor to do both: to help the child's ego in its fight against inner asocial tendencies and to

arrange the child's world in such a way that he can meet the
tasks of living with confidence. All therapeutic functions of the
counselor are greatly in focus during the awakening period; it is
perhaps the time of day when the child needs his counselor most.
On awakening (and on falling asleep) the child is most concentrated on his unconscious and his counselor, because at these
times there are fewer distractions or demands from the outside
world—the activities of other children, the need to learn, or the
wish to play—and hence also less interference with the counselor's efforts.

In this morning setting, as on many other occasions, the staff
member must not only play a role which supports the child's
ego but must often function as if he were the child's ego, a role
which the child will then slowly take over. (He may even have
to support the child's superego, which is less desirable but nevertheless necessary for time periods in many cases.) The counselor
must take the child by the hand, as it were, and introduce him
to the new day by saying good morning, by patting his hand
or by holding it. Even the child who responds to the counselor's
good morning with the assertion that it's a hell of a morning
and why can't they leave him in peace, has taken a step toward
communication.

How closely linked are the receiving of satisfaction, the accepting of reality, and thus the strengthening of the ego, can be seen
in those children who, while still half asleep and all covered up
including their faces, will stretch out their hands from under
the cover for some food; this they will first munch under the
cover until they finally appear to ask for more. Thus, in order to
satisfy a physical need or an instinctual desire, they meet reality at
least tentatively, and begin to act purposefully and in a socially
acceptable way, i.e., act ego-correctly.

But to help them in making such contact with reality, the
reality must not be too unpleasant, and at least one of its pleasanter representatives must be present. Therefore, first and foremost, the counselor must be there when the children awake, and
he must try not to waken them before they are ready.

Mechanical necessity forces us to waken all children within a reasonably short span of time—though if we didn't, they would wake one another up in far less desirable ways. Hence the falling asleep time must be so handled that when the children awake they have by and large satisfied their need and desire for sleep at the moment; if they wish they can sleep later on during the day. This is usually easy to recognize by their response as one enters the room: if at least some of them then do not move, make a noise, try to open one eye, they are not really through with their sleep. If they are, then the quiet entering of the room or the opening of the curtains is usually enough to waken one child or another. With even one awake, a little quiet conversation does the rest. Some children like to be awakened with a song, others by hearing the counselor humming when they are just about ready to wake up.

Other counselors sit down at the table and quietly set up toys or some games for the children. In this way they show the child without words that good things more tangible than those of the dream world are to be had in the world of waking. Thus, the counselor, besides supporting the ego, must literally combat the id in its own field, without promising pleasures we cannot later provide in reality.

It would be poor policy, for example, to describe events of the coming day in too cheerful colours to a child who is depressed. In his case it might be better to show understanding and empathy for his fears so that he does not feel so alone about facing the seemingly impossible task of living through the day without disaster. Here again, it is most important that each child be treated as a distinct individual and in line with his ability to take care of himself at the moment. For example, children who are well ahead in the solution of their problems can now reestablish some contact with the outer world on their own.

These children should be given a chance to take their own good time about doing so. One must avoid pushing them about getting out of bed or getting dressed before they are willing to conform to such social demands—or if willing, are also strong enough to do so. Therefore some children, after they are partly awakened, are left strictly in peace. One of them, for instance, likes to lie in bed quietly for some time; one day perhaps for ten minutes, another day for forty-five. In his own good time, he will then join in the conversation, or address himself directly to the counselor. The counselor's response must convince him that the new day extends him a welcome reception, at least from his counselor.

Another child becomes more and more ready to meet the day as he receives detailed reassurance about what it will bring. He has developed on his own the sequence in which he wants to receive information, beginning with the most general and proceeding to matters of more and more personal concern to himself. While he is still half asleep, he wants to be told what the weather is like; then how far the others are ahead in dressing; then what he is going to wear, what kind of activities have been planned, or any he might engage in; and finally, whether the counselor will spend time with him individually. As he gets these assurances about the personal details of his day he can afford to grow more and more awake.

In general, in these morning contacts, even more than in others, we must not assume that the child's ego can join forces with us in dealing with irrational tendencies, or that the ego is strong enough to handle the task at hand in a realistic manner. If we seem too anxious in helping the child, we may give him the impression that we, too, assume that without our help he cannot do things successfully. In general, much of this support has to be given in non-verbal form. As a matter of fact, there is hardly another time of the day when the children are less ready for verbal intercourse than in these morning hours.

Although we fully realize the great importance of non-verbal communication, yet because of the historic development of psychoanalysis, our thinking and planning still proceeds far too much on the verbal level and relies too heavily on the tool of verbalization. We do not even have an adequate terminology at our disposal for reporting non-verbal interaction except in terms that are mainly behaviouristic and of little help if a dynamic understanding is required. Neither is our skill in the observation of non-verbal influences, the meaning of contacts, etc., as great as our grasp of verbalization. We hope that further work with children—and particularly in settings such as ours where observations can be made at all times of the day and of all activities—will permit us to become more aware of the meaning and importance of non-verbal contacts and eventually help us to understand how they actually proceed. As our knowledge of them increases, we will be able to set them to use more and more skillfully.

Often, the traumatic experiences which first caused deviation in the personal development of our children took place so early in their lives that the children were not yet able to verbalize about them. Often, too, they took place at a stage in development where the ego was as poorly put together as it is in older children at the moment of wakening. This again makes the morning hours valuable for establishing contact in the most direct way, and in an emotional setting where such contact and help will count most.

Staff members who are with the children during these first hours of the day try to handle each child in a different way. Richard, for example, was one of the children who was just awakened and then let go for a while; he was given a chance to collect himself. But his counselor had to help him by reminding him at intervals—perhaps as many as three or four times—that she was still there and was interested in him and his getting up. She did this either by talking to him, coming to his bed, touching him, or by calling his name. She waited for him to call her for help in getting dressed and when he did that, she knew he was ready to meet the day, ready to accept not only her but her help.[5]

Wakening Walter, aged ten, was more difficult. Walter seemed to withdraw during the night even more deeply than the others. When he fell asleep at night only his body was covered, but

[5] Participant observer: Patty Pickett.

every morning he was all covered up, even his head. His counselor would pat lightly on his blanket and talk softly to him until somewhere from beneath the covers a hand would appear. If the counselor took it and held it quietly for a few minutes, Walter would finally poke his head out. But even after such contact he was still too removed from reality to meet it, and pretended he had gone back to sleep. Repeatedly she would come back to his bed and talk to him for a minute; each time he would again pretend to have fallen asleep, but each time he was in better contact than before. The conversation would increase from a soft "hello," to comments about how he felt and what he might like to wear. Then he would slowly let her help him get dressed, though he was still not quite in this world. She had to help him in orienting himself by letting him find out certain things for himself. He was usually pleased when he had figured out for himself which day of the week it was, and what activities would be going on that day. By then he was ready to get up and start to play, but this process took on an average of forty-five minutes.[6]

Things were again different with one of our twelve-year-old boys. This child, when he opened his eyes, had to be surrounded first by his favourite toys and then, one at a time, the counselor had to bring to his bed various pieces of clothing. He would lie there quietly as he watched the increase in those objects which represented the reality he would have to be dealing with. First it had to be the pleasurable reality of toys, and only with them on hand could he accept the more difficult reality of getting dressed.

We had tried having these things around his bed when he was asleep so that he found them on awakening; but that would not do. If he saw them all around him in the morning, he would withdraw again. Just as he could not meet reality all at once, so his possessions had to reappear one at a time. It was only after he had inspected one object at a time and again become familiar with it that the next one could be added.[7]

For some of the children, waking up has to proceed in several

[6] Participant observer: Josette Wingo.
[7] Participant observer: Patty Pickett.

distinct steps, each one serving a particular purpose in preparing the children for the day.

Some children have a routine they must go through every morning to convince themselves that they have some measure of independence from the adult and can succeed with their peers. Paul, for some time, was very touchy and disagreeable, if not downright nasty in the morning. Soon after awakening he had to pick an argument with someone, any argument would do. When he felt he had made his point and in this way established his independence from the other children and the adult, he would declare in a satisfied voice that he had to go back to bed because he hadn't finished sleeping yet. He would then return to his bed for some five or ten minutes, pretending to be asleep. Sometimes he would actually sleep for those few minutes, often sucking his thumb vigorously at the same time. Then he would get out of bed and pick another argument, but less aggressively so. If this went well, and particularly if he felt he had really put his point across, he was ready to get dressed without further ado. For Paul, at this time, it made little difference how he managed to convince himself that it was safe to get up, since in contrast to previous experience, his opinions and independence were respected at the School.[8]

Jerry (aged ten) showed a negativism in the morning that was neither the chaotic expression of random hostility nor any effort to establish his independence in a general way. His need for ordering the counselor around was directly connected with what had always been a major area of conflict between himself and his mother. At home he had always been the victim in these conflicts and had finally been forced to store in physical symptoms the tension and hostility created by a lifetime of rigid maternal control.

Jerry had suffered from various incapacitating allergies. At the School these allergies disappeared very soon as he began to discharge his long pent-up anger and frustration outwardly against the person of the counselor. In the morning particularly, he insisted that the counselor lay out his clothes, but each piece she

[8] Participant observer: Eugene Miller, M.D.

brought him he rejected angrily. After she had gone through every one of his shirts (some six or seven, or more) and he was convinced she had brought out all he owned, he would condescend to accept one of the ones he had just finished rejecting. The same process repeated itself for his socks, pants, shoes, and so on. Just as he had once had to submit to his mother's nagging in the morning about not dressing carefully enough, he would now nag the counselor. Since his mother had always forced him to wear what she chose, and had always made him get his clothing himself, he now had to prove to himself that he could wear what he wanted to and could even have his counselor bring his clothes to him.[9]

This was no discharge of hostility proper, nor any effort of Jerry's ego to gain control by serving asocial, unconscious tendencies. Jerry's behaviour served the relatively simple purpose of convincing him that things were entirely different at the School from the way they had always been at home, and that since he could now decide on those matters which pertained to himself, he could afford to meet the day with some measure of security.

While children like Jerry have to start the day out by asserting an independence they never knew in their previous lives, other children have to start out by proving they can permit themselves infantile pleasures, and that such pleasures are available to them without loss in status, and without having to give up more grown-up advantages because they also enjoy childish ones.

One ten-year-old boy, for example, was called a baby by another child (a newcomer) because he let himself be dressed by his counselor. The newcomer was not ready yet to permit himself such pleasures or such laziness, because he was afraid they would cost him the respect of the others. At the same time he was jealous of a child who could permit himself such an easy way out of a difficult task. The counselor took a firm stand against anyone's calling the boy a baby and explained he had every right not to dress himself if he didn't want to, nor did that make him a baby. She referred to his achievements in school and on the playfield to show one could hardly think of him as a baby, re-

[9] Participant observer: Patty Pickett.

gardless of whether he enjoyed being dressed in the morning or not. This not only helped the boy she was dressing, but gave the jealous child something to wonder about. It made him see that one day even he might be able to let down his defenses and enjoy the same pleasures without giving up more grown-up enjoyment.[10]

At these and other times, we generally try to create situations which lead the child toward maturity through his own wish for it, and not through adult pressure for higher achievement. If adults press for more grown-up behaviour, the child is never sure that their motive is not mainly to get out of an unpleasant task. He fears that they push him ahead not for his own good but for theirs, and higher achievements at that price will add little to real independence or maturity. On the other hand we have never yet had a child at the School who did not prefer dressing himself pretty much on his own once he had enough energy available for that and other tasks of living. These children get up and get dressed without much ado, although even then they like to preserve some token help, as if to symbolize that their present independence—as opposed to precocious maturity—implies no giving up of any truly desired pleasure. But the pleasure they now want is neither subservience nor any real help in having things done for them; they want only the counselor's readiness to help because of the mutual attachment between them.

Most new children resent being awakened directly, at first. This they can usually accept only after their egos are much stronger, after they are much further ahead in emotional stability. It is as if human contacts were unpleasant to the more disturbed children immediately after awakening. They seem to have to carry some of the dream world into reality and they need to avoid any rapid transition. Richard behaved as if he had to assure himself that the world of pleasurable phantasies, of protective animals, for example, did not disappear entirely on awakening. He had to talk with his teddy before he could talk with people. The coun-

[10] Participant observer: Josette Wingo.

selor had to select just the right moment to begin a conversation with him, because if he got too involved or too excited in his play with the animal, he was again out of reach.[11]

As mentioned above, these are things one can describe and even talk about. But there are other experiences, and other types of contacts, that are much more important in making the new day acceptable to the children.

While Walter needed physical contact, other children have been conditioned against it. Mostly they are children whose parents touched them rudely, either to wake them in the morning, or at other times of the day by way of getting them to do what was wanted. For similar reasons children who were rudely or forcefully dressed by their parents do not experience as pleasant, at first, any help that is given around dressing. Children who in these or in other ways have had disagreeable experiences with physical contact, and who cannot be reached through talk, must be convinced by some other means of the friendly intentions of the counselor. Here, in awakening the children, it is best just to put some cookies, or a piece of candy on their beds, or even in their mouths before one starts talking with them.

Other children who distrust all adults, and believe only what they see, or what the other children say or do, are most helped in the morning if the counselor leaves them strictly alone. They begin to feel safe and become awake simply by watching the counselor's actions, how he talks with or helps another child; or they take courage by observing what the children do themselves. Some children can afford to wake up and come back into contact with the world only if they see that some of their friends are already playing with toys or sitting around the table playing games together.

Many a child needs the invitation to play from another child before he is able to leave his bed. Then he feels sure he is accepted. Some of our children, particularly those who have been at the School for some time and have made real progress, behave as if they know exactly what the fearful child needs in the morn-

[11] Participant observer: Patty Pickett.

ing. And they act accordingly, usually with much greater success than an adult might have had with the same tactic. They take some of their toys over to the timid child's bed and start to play with him, sitting on, or right next to his bed. They put the dolls or toycars or airplanes right on the sleepy child's bedcover and slowly involve him in their game.

The child who dreads meeting the day cannot help but become interested in the play that another child spreads right on his blanket. Soon he has said something, one word has led to another and he has joined in the game. The instigator, as if he knew how to proceed, then extends the limits of the game beyond the bed, takes it onto the floor just in front of the bed, then further out into the room, and soon the child who was hesitant to get up finds himself sitting on the floor, or at the table, wrapped up in the game, not quite knowing how he got so awake and out of bed. But the ban has been broken: he has stepped out toward reality and nothing bad has happened.

How the children do these things will naturally depend on their interests, their age, intelligence and maturity, and that of the child they are trying to involve in their game. Mitchell, aged eleven, would bring his chess board to the bed of another boy, quietly and deliberately setting the board and the men up on the blanket. First, he would move both the black and the white figures, as though only playing by himself. Soon the sleepy child becomes interested and tells Mitchell how to move his figures, and finally he moves his figures himself, becoming wider and wider awake.[12]

Children less mature in terms of their favourite games will use simpler means, although in doing so they will often proceed in much more sophisticated, or one is tempted to say, more therapeutic ways. After two years at the School, Lucille still needed some help in preparing to face the new day. But this help she now preferred to provide herself.

Her bed-doll which she appropriately called "Sleepy" she enlisted in her aid. First she would talk to "Sleepy," and then with

[12] Participant observer: Patty Pickett.

"Sleepy" (or through her) she would talk to another child. Not yet talking as Lucille, but as "Sleepy," she would, for example, involve Alice in a conversation. Not really Alice, though, but Alice's bed-doll "Sparkle Plenty." Lucille, talking for "Sleepy," and Alice talking first from under her covers and then with eyes wide open sitting up, for "Sparkle Plenty," would carry on conversations that began as if they were still part of dreams. But the need to communicate with one another slowly forced the two more and more toward reality. Eventually Lucille would leave her bed and visit Alice with "Sleepy" or rather as "Sleepy." The conversation would become less and less an expression of the children's unconscious and more and more part of an organized game. This play would then lead them to their buggies or their doll houses, and they would soon find themselves wide awake in what is the everyday reality of young children.[13]

Another year, and Lucille was well able to meet the new day with relative pleasure and quite a bit of vitality. Then it was Emily who was most fearful of waking up and who played "possum," hiding under her covers and pretending to sleep, impervious to all efforts of the counselor to help her in meeting the day. But Emily was no match for Lucille.

Lucille would plant herself firmly before Emily's bed, or sit on it, which Emily never resented as long as it was one of the children. Then Lucille would annnounce loudly any move she "saw" Emily make under the covers, and this became a game for the child in the bed. Lucille would say: "She blinked her eye, she can't be asleep," or "she smiled, she's waking up," or whatever else came to her head. As soon as she could catch Emily's eye, she would laugh and wave to her, saying "Come on, come on, wake up"; and Emily would be "caught awake" whether she liked it or not.[14]

Some children can only begin to function in the morning after they feel secure about their bodies and their bodily func-

[13] Participant observer: Joan Little.
[14] Participant observer: *Idem.*

tions. And the more disturbed a child is, the more likely he seems to be to need security in this respect.

It is thought that one basis for the development of the ego is that the child is forced to recognize the body as something separate from the rest of the world, and at the same time as something that is subject to voluntary, conscious control. The first achievement of the rudimentary ego is the ability to regulate the voluntary movements at will. The first experience at self-control is the changing of random activity into purposeful action. This experience serves as the model for all conscious control over action later on. Thus it becomes understandable why some children cannot start the day without checking up on their bodily functions.

A child who is insecure only about how he will stack up in general during the day is less disturbed than a child who is also worried about his body. It would seem that losing relative control over reality is a less far-reaching step in personal disintegration than losing control over one's body, which is more fundamental and therefore much more frightening. In brief, a child who has at least been able to establish control over his bodily functions is better off than a child who is not even adequate in that area.

On the other hand, if an individual is severely overpowered, or if his ego becomes seriously weakened for other reasons, the ego may even relinquish its control over bodily functions. Then somatic disturbances will serve the function of discharging tensions which the more adequate individual will discharge in purposeful activities. The child who is forced to eat against his will, will first fight back. He will react to what seems like aggression with counter-aggressions of his own. He will push away the spoon that is forced into his mouth and if this does not protect him from the food he dislikes, and it is still forced on him, he will spit out what he does not want to eat. But if even such purposeful actions meet with defeat and the child is prevented from acting on the basis of his own volition he may give up all efforts to have a say in what happens to him. Then uncontrolled and uncontrollable fighting back may take the place of controlled and controllable efforts to defend himself.

Where the actions of the ego—the deliberate effort to avoid unpleasant food—has ended in total defeat, the body may take over and uncontrollable vomiting may then take the place of deliberate actions (pushing away the spoon, spitting, etc.).

It should be stressed that in such a situation the child not only sees that a show of independence to avoid an unpleasant experience will not lead to success, although this in itself is most damaging to his self-confidence; he also feels that he is being punished for his efforts to do something on his own about an unpleasant situation.

Such punishment as a result of his efforts to control his fate, when added to the experience of being overpowered, leads many children to give up all active and conscious ways of dealing with an unpleasant reality. The body is overpowered since the ego (the child's conscious mind and will) can no longer protect it from harm by deliberate action. The body may then react in its own way, either actively by vomiting the food, or by giving in passively to the overpowering treatment, by becoming lethargic and unable to eat (by anorexia). In a word, the body, which is now unprotected by the child's purposeful actions, becomes sick. The road to recovery is the reverse of the one that has led to the sickness. A weak and inadequate ego which failed to protect the body from the impact of an enemy world (in our example the forced feeding) led to a sick body (vomiting, nausea; in other cases, anorexia, allergies, and so forth). It is some time before children who have suffered such defeat in the past can feel adequate in the morning without first making sure that their bodies and their bodily functions are in fair working order.

In psychoanalytic theory the body image is the basis for the formation of the ego. If this is so, one can easily understand why a poorly functioning body may lead to a weak ego. But the reverse is equally true and a weak ego may lead to a poor show of bodily coordination. In our children the fear that their bodies are in poor working condition persists long after the disturbance, the uncontrolled vomiting, for example, has disappeared.

By the same token, the fear that they (their egos) may be unable to control the movements of their bodies usually persists much longer than their actual failure to do so. Children whose movements were once beyond their control (spastic-like arm and hand movements, or uncontrollable kicking) still fear in the morning that they may have lost control over arm and leg movements long after they have gained real control. Hence we can understand why and how the return of ego control in the morning depends largely on the children's conviction that their bodies are functioning adequately, that they can move them as they wish, that their egos are actually "in control," at least of their own movements.

This ability to control, to manage one's limbs, is the image that seems to promise the child he will also be able to manage other tasks which life or the day may present. Support for the idea that the control of one's body is the basis for better ego strength may be found in the correlation we can regularly observe between the disappearance of uncontrolled movements (tics and twitching muscles, but also uncontrolled hitting out, kicking, and so on) and more adequate intellectual and emotional functioning.

Progress in treatment toward more conscious and more reasonable control over actions and emotions is sometimes heralded and sometimes followed by the disappearance of uncontrolled movements and better coordination, but never have we observed significant progress in mind alone or in body alone.

Some children have to try out their ability to move before they dare to leave the security of the bed. Others have to inspect their bodies, or need to have them inspected to feel sure things are in good order before they can start out the day.

John had been totally overpowered by adults almost from birth on. A disease of the mouth had prevented him from developing any spontaneous activity around eating and he was forcefully fed from the beginning of his life. Eating became so unpleasant to him, that he continued to reject food even after the mouth disease cleared up. In order to feed him, first a nurse and then his parents had for years restricted all his movements so that he wouldn't kick away the food, or move away from it. This restriction of movements, plus the inadequacy of a poorly nourished body and a mind continuously set against an overpowering environment, were enough to prevent John from ever developing real control over his movements. When he was eleven, and after several years of treatment at the School had cleared up his eating difficulties, catching a ball, for example, was still virtually impossible for him because he lacked the necessary coordination.

In the morning, before leaving his bed, John needed to explore his ability to move his limbs at will. He would begin with gross and uncoordinated movements of arms and legs, shaking them sideways and up and down. From such gross movements he would proceed to finer movements of fingers and toes. Then after convincing himself of his control over voluntary muscles, he would try some coordinated movements, and after seeing he could master them he was ready to make the coordinated movements needed for getting out of bed and getting dressed. Any distraction during this testing of his ability to move would have been deeply resented by John and had to be avoided. If he was ever interrupted, he would immediately withdraw to his bed, and it would be some time before he started the whole procedure anew.[15]

In inspecting their bodies first thing in the morning, the part of the body the children are concerned with varies greatly. Some are most concerned with their skin and look for scratches or pimples. But we have often noticed that particularly in the morning children are preoccupied with their feet and toes. It may be that this concern with their feet is because the feet make the first coordinated movements in and after getting out of bed. It may be that the feet are particularly important as organs of locomotion and—something very important for the fearful and the

[15] Participant observer: Josette Wingo.

runaway children—as organs of flight. Or it may be that the feet and the toes are selected because of certain symbolic meanings attached to them. We have never succeeded in finding a generally valid explanation of this morning preoccupation with feet but whatever the reason, quite a few children need to see that their lower extremities are all right before they feel safe about starting the day.

In view of one of the commonest and severest anxieties of children it is understandable that they are concerned in the morning, as at many other times of the day, with the adequacy of their genitals. But in many cases it is difficult to know whether they handle their genitals in the morning to be sure they are still there and in good order, or because of a still absent control over masturbatory tendencies, or whether they do it in an effort to convince themselves that pleasures are still available even if the world seems forbidding, and so on.

Still, the actions and reactions of some children seem to indicate clearly that behaviour which may look like masturbation pure and simple is actually intended to assure the child about the adequacy of his genitals. Bill, for example, felt little inhibition about masturbating rather openly at any time of the day. So it is hard to understand why he should have needed for some time to test the strength of his penis in the morning by hanging objects on it. Apparently he needed the assurance that it was still "holding up" in the morning before he could start other tasks of the day.

Other children may attach different meanings to the way they handle their genitals. Harry, for example, would manage to get hold of a mousetrap and affix it to his penis in the morning. This behaviour was meaningful to him on many different levels. For one thing, he gained some pleasurable physical sensation. He also punished himself for some of his behaviour during the night (or on preceding days, or in the past). But what was perhaps most important to him was that in spite of the heavy punishment nothing bad happened, either to him or his body. Even the mousetrap could not sever one part of his body from the rest of it. This was the reassurance he needed to dare to begin the day.

Harry was by no means the only child who needed assurance in the morning that no dangerous punishment would interfere with his well-being during the day. Not many children go as far as Harry did, but much of the children's pestering of counselors in the morning has also the meaning: "I want to see if I have to be afraid about being punished for what I may do today." If a child's misbehaviour in the morning does not lead to unpleasantness, a very important assurance about the day has been gained: the world of adults then appears much less threatening than the child may have feared.

The most innocuous way in which a child seeks assurance that his body is in good shape for the day is through one form or another of exhibitionism. Children parade around in the nude, in front of counselors or other children. While in some cases this is more an effort to seduce than anything else, the majority of our children seem much more concerned in finding assurance that their bodies are pleasing, or adequate, or at least not repugnant. That this is the reason for most exhibitionism can be seen from the child's reaction to casual remarks by the counselor to the effect that his body is all right, an assurance the child will soon follow by dressing himself.

Before a child has gained sufficient courage to expose himself, or to openly and directly test the organs of his body (and even afterwards), his concern about his body may take subtler forms. Then the very insecure children (but also the relatively secure ones who still fear that their bodies are not quite up to par) reveal their fears in the morning by complaints about major or minor aches and pains, both on the surface and inside of their bodies. These children have to show parts of their bodies to the counselor and need repeated assurance that they are all right—always provided that they are. Many of our children have received such assurances before, but the physical or psychological reality of their lives meant they were in pain nevertheless. Therefore they do not easily trust assurances, particularly when given by a maternal figure (the female counselor) because it was usually their mothers who gave them vain comfort that did not tally with fact.

The result is that these children need assurance from some person who seems to them more trustworthy in this respect, an expert, a nurse, or sometimes the physician.[16] The nurse must take care of visible and invisible scratches and pimples, while at the same time being careful that complaints do not take the place of personal relations. She must also take care that her services do not replace the more adequate and healthy satisfactions, because otherwise the children might cling to their somatic symptoms. One of the ways she can do this is to give her attention to all children, regardless of whether or not they complain. The need for band aids or salves, for imaginary or barely visible ailments, decreases considerably if the children begin to notice that they receive no more warmth from the nurse for their ailments than they would get if they dropped in on her for a friendly chat without complaints. The nurse visits all children while they are still getting up so that they can tell her directly about their fears.[17]

Even expert assurance about imaginary, but nevertheless keenly felt pains is not always enough for some children, particularly

[16] The University's Department of Pediatrics takes care of the medical needs of the children. Since our children are very fearful and subject to imaginary ailments, they make difficult patients who try the physician's patience. The splendid help we receive in our work from the whole Department of Pediatrics, and particularly from its chairman, Dr. F. Howell Wright, is here gratefully acknowledged.

[17] Nearly all of our children enjoy regular health very soon after enrollment—even those who for years have been subject to frequent ailments. After they have been at the School for approximately a year they are rarely sick, with the exception of the usual contagious diseases of childhood. Hence the nurse is not usually very busy in her capacity as nurse and can spend most of her time as a companion to well children. She takes them shopping, plays with them, and generally participates in their everyday lives. This has the great advantage that the children know they can have her time, sick or not, and soon most children who want her company prefer to get it on a shopping trip to a store, or by going out for a soda with her, instead of through imaginary ailments.

during the morning hours when the pain often stands for a fear of the day and what may happen in the course of it.

One method we have often found useful is to have the nurse ask the child to get up for his breakfast and play until school time if he wants to, or return to his bed after breakfast if he prefers that. If the pain persists, or he still doesn't feel well by school time, he can then send for the nurse or come to see her, and she will do more to help him. It is not the purpose of this procedure to have the child forget about his pains while he has his breakfast, or plays out-of-doors. But very often what actually happens is that the greater contact with children and counselors on a more realistic basis, the acceptance the child experiences by them, and his testing of his adequacy gives him enough of a feeling of security to be able to disregard small discomforts, or to be able to divert the libidinal energy he has centered in his body, once this energy can be set to good use in pleasant relations with others.

Equally, or even more important, is the fact that these bodily complaints without physical basis usually reveal the child's fear about his physical inferiority. Therefore his ability to function well in play is the most convincing assurance he can get that, in spite of his fears, his body is well up to the demands he may make on it during the day. This assurance then gives him more confidence about facing the less pleasurable activities of the day, such as learning in class. The direct experience of getting along in his personal contacts is more effective than any verbal assurance we could possibly give him. As a matter of fact, since the sick child is treated right away, very few of the children return to the nurse after an active game, because imaginary pains disappear once the body has been tested in reality and found well.

As indicated earlier in the chapter, getting up is as much a group phenomenon as it is a matter of our dealing with the children as individuals. Some children respond mainly to the challenge of the group activities, some need a great deal of attention, others need only a minimum of physical or verbal contact, or cannot stand it at all in the morning. Some want their counselors to be wide awake in the morning, and like them to sing marching songs. Other children would resent such a forceful approach and like to be hummed to, and so on. Some children have an easier time of waking up and making contact when the counselor himself is rather quiet and seems a little sleepy.

Obviously, one cannot sing and be still at the same time, but when a counselor feels rather quiet himself, he can spend more time with the child who reacts to him better in that mood, and can concentrate on those children who need him chipper in the morning on those days when he feels that way himself. Here, too, our system of having two or more counselors attached to each group has its advantages. They have different personalities, and differing rhythms, and naturally the one who feels wide awake and energetic in the morning prefers to take care of awakening the children, while the counselor who tends to be sleepy in the morning usually prefers to work the later shift.

5

the in-between times

ONCE the children are up and dressed they must leave the dormitory for the dining room, eat breakfast and then go to class. Each of these activities is separated from the ones before and after by an "in-between" period. The child lingers on with the old activity and the principle of inertia asserts itself. He wants to keep doing what he's been doing. He does not want to give up one activity for another which will mean new decisions and new difficulties.

Often we say to ourselves that the child is so engrossed in his play, for example, that he hates to leave it for the dinner table. This may very well be the case, but quite often he clings to the current activity not so much because he likes it so well but because he dreads tackling the newer activity, or because he is so drained of emotional energy that there just isn't enough left for him to manage the transitional adjustments.

The day is full of such in-between areas and much time and effort is spent in giving up the old activity and getting ready for the new one with reluctance to do the first, and anxiety about what the second may involve. There is an in-between time between waking up and getting dressed, between dressing and playing, between playing and going to breakfast, and so on throughout the day.

Moreover, time is not the only dimension which the child in

the latency period inhabits in an in-between sense. The affinity of children in this age group for the in-between areas also finds its expression geographically, and this is not strange, after all. The emotional needs of an individual, or an age group, when left to its devices, creates for itself a *lebensraum*, a space for living in accordance with the particular character of these psychological needs.

The space within which the activities of the infant or adult will proceed is the house, the apartment, the front porch or the totality of the community. The life space of the child in the latency period is mostly out-of-doors: the backyard, a tree house, the block, the vacant lot, the alley. It is the no-man's-land, the in-between areas, places where neither the infant nor the adult is too firmly entrenched. This becomes even more obvious in winter time. When children of this age group are given the freedom to choose their play spaces they prefer the hallways, the stairways, the in-between areas of the house, to the well-defined rooms, be it the child's room or the living room. But every parent also knows that these ill-defined spaces where the child likes to linger are also the ones where his play is more likely to become disorganized, to lead to confusion and to unmanageable excitement.

In order to test his developing ability to look after himself— in other words, to test his ego strength—the child in the latency period seeks the in-between spaces because of their freedom of choice and the challenge they offer him to test his own strength. But for the same reason he also fears them. The child who at one moment—particularly during the day and when other children are around—has preferred the alley or the stairway for his play, will at another moment be terrified about having to cross them, particularly when alone, or in the dark. His own room offers less challenge to his ego, but there ego strength is also less likely to go down in defeat.

At the School we have tried to create a setting which, in a way, provides the necessary in-between spaces for living that children of this age group seem to need. In doing so we were as usual following the leads of the children's spontaneous choices rather than any deliberate plans about modifying the buildings assigned for our work.

A few years ago, for example, we thought it would be nice for the children to have one large, really comfortable living room in addition to their dormitories, play rooms, shops, and so forth. So we built such a room and equipped it as well as we could. But as soon as the children took it over it turned into something very different. It became an in-between room. Something between a living room, a play room, a room for indoor sports, for music and for what not. Only then did the children like to use it. And when, to the comfortable chairs, the book shelves and the piano and record player were added a pool table, a bowling alley and a huge array of blocks and games, it had really become theirs for their use. It was as if it were contrary to the children's desires to admit any clear-cut division of functions between rooms or to take up activities in line with what a room is designed for. They really start to consider a room "theirs" and to enjoy it, to live in it, when it is no longer a "living room" or a "play room" but has become an in-between room allowing the widest variety of activities.

Similarly our shops were really fun for the children only when they lost their character as paint shops or wood-work shops and became in-between rooms in addition to the function assigned them by adults. Besides being a shop, such a room also became a living room as we added some comfortable chairs and a corner where a child could sit down and read. It also became a play and listening room by adding games and the radio. Then what had been "a wood-work shop" became "our shop" and was used accordingly.

By the same process, the type of dormitories we started out with were soon changed. Though we started out by trying to arrange them so as to allow each child as much privacy as possible, we soon learned better. The children felt uncomfortable in such relative isolation from one another and very soon we arrived at a dormitory arrangement which did not quite provide the privacy of "one's own room" but was still without the public character of a meeting room for a group. Each dormitory soon represented something of an in-between room, neither private nor group room, which permitted the children to shift with the greatest of ease from privacy to play, from rest to activity, and from one activity to another Even when lying quietly on their beds they are never quite "out of it," which they would be too afraid to be. Nor can any activity ever prevent them from returning immediately to the relative isolation of their bed if they so desire.

Our corridors and stairways are often preferred places and are particularly sought after as places for "private" talk among the children. But at the School they are not set aside from the rest of the rooms. Their importance is recognized, and also that they form a legitimate living space. They are at least as well lighted as the dormitories, and are so lighted day and night that the eeriness is avoided which many stairwells and corridors have for children.

Our play field, too, has taken on the character of something in between a vacant lot, a back yard and a well equipped playground. It has spaces for free roaming which are nevertheless connected to the swings, to the teeter-totters and the sand box.

Thus in view of what has been said about challenges to ego strength, about temptations to test oneself, and about the child's fear that he may not stand up in a test, it might be added here that while our physical setting may provide less challenge to testing oneself, it also offers less danger for the ego to be found wanting or to be proven inadequate. The physical setting of the School is organized just enough so that the child can still do some organizing of the space he finds himself in. Yet it is flexible enough not to confine the child's living, and not to discourage those sudden changes in activities and moods that are so characteristic for this age group.

While it was thus possible to provide our children with a physical layout that includes adequate in-between spaces, and to provide them in such a way that they are stimulating without offering too much unnecessary excitement, the handling of the in-between time periods is more difficult. To them, to the "unplanned" and unscheduled activities and the problems they raise, the rest of this chapter is devoted.

The particular difficulties of the in-between periods in human development are well recognized by now. It is understood equally clearly that these are not just awkward time spans, but are at least as full of important experiences and developments as any other developmental stage; their relative absence of stability no longer detracts from the fact that they have a meaning all their own, and a most important one, at that. It is now a truism, for example, that adolescence is such an important in-between stage in development. It is a period whose meaning would be misunderstood if one were to view it mainly as a time when the youngster is no longer a child and not yet an adult.

But while adolescence is a true in-between period it is not one of empty waiting. All too often it is a period during which almost too much is happening, more so than in the more stable developmental stages. It is equally well known that such in-between times—times of growing, times of stress—are equally difficult for the adolescent and for those around him. They confront adolescent and adult with the most intricate problems of continuous mutual adjustments. But at least adolescence is a period which is often full of open conflict, and hence full of activity. The tension is discharged in action and the adolescent is only for intervals a true "in-betweener." Most of the time he is either acting and feeling like a child, or prematurely acting and feeling like an adult, but he is rarely pulled both ways at the same time.

In this sense, the latency period, much more than adolescence, is an in-between period. It is not just the passive waiting for the next step in personality development, which accounts for it. It is more the child's inability to be an irresponsible infant again, someone entirely dependent, and his inability to really know how to take care of himself. It is a period when infantile pleasures are still very much desired but no longer truly enjoyable, while more mature pleasures are still things more feared than desired. As intensely as infantile pleasures are sought, they are no sooner had than they seem stale. It is also a period when more adult activities, if at all sought, create deep anxiety and lead to deep disappointment because the child is not ready for them yet.

During the ages between seven and twelve, the body is still growing, but less so than in infancy or adolescence. Mental processes also seem to be relatively at rest, as if the child were collecting his strength for the strenuously rapid development that will characterize the adolescence just ahead. The latency period should be a time of intensive mental activity, but a mental activity of a particular, receptive nature. The child in the latency period has to acquire in a passive way the tools which as an adolescent he must then actively set to use to develop into the person he wants to be. And as if to make the tension of this in-between period even greater, this receptive passivity is expected of the child at a time when sitting still for any length of time is practically impossible for him.

The latency period, like all in-between periods, is likely to be experienced as empty but nevertheless exhausting, and above all as boring. This feeling of unpleasantness or boredom is the overt expression of unconscious anxiety, or at least of strong tensions without any definite or conscious content. For this reason even normal children often experience the latency period as unpleasant and harassing, as are other normally occurring in-between periods, even in adult life. The waiting, for example, before a job-interview, the time spent in the doctor's outer office before a diagnosis is reached, or the "boredom" of the soldier between battles, these are typical in-between times for adults. The last may also serve as an example of why children at such in-between times look around frantically for an activity, even an asocial one, to forget with, to cover up their anxiety like the soldier before the battle. Like many soldiers, too, children try to overcome their fear of the future test by trying to prove themselves during the in-between times through their daring exploits. They hope for even a token success which will pacify their fears about their abilities, or else prove they are indestructible. Actually they only add new fear and tension to the ones the exploit was supposed to relieve.

Normally an adult should be more or less free of persistent anxiety, and if he has to put up with some of the in-between periods of life that he cannot avoid, he is likely to be able to do something about them. One of the most constructive ways of reducing the anxiety of the in-between period, which in its mildest form is felt merely as boredom, is to take action calculated to put an end to the tension of the waiting period. Only if the adult is unable to do something constructive about the problems confronting him will he try to deny his anxiety, to combat his boredom, or at least to prevent himself from feeling it by adopting some form of often frantic busyness. Although such efforts may be camouflaged as "leisure-time" activities, they are not really enjoyed. Hours spent in this way are actually not play times but time-killers, efforts to deny or forget tension. Unfortunately, in order to distract from the underlying anxiety, such activities must be able to absorb the individual. And in order to do that they have to be exciting. But then—like the daring exploits— they may add new tension to the old one they were supposed to relieve, such as in card playing, or gambling, for example.

By and large, however, the adult living a relatively normal life in our society experiences these in-between periods without too much tension. He has learned to make his peace with the fact that they come up from time to time. He has learned to master them—be they daily, recurrent occasions, or rare, as when looking for a job. Mostly he can do so because he is frequently in a position to know what the next steps are likely to be, what things he must do right away or very soon to end the period of tension constructively. The more self-reliant he is, the better he and his life have been integrated, the more successful will he be in making changes from one activity to another without in-between times, and hence with a minimum of strain. The more insecure a person is, the less he is able to make frequent and spontaneous changes from one life activity to another, and the more filled with tension his in-between times will be likely to be.[1]

But while an adult who is not too emotionally unbalanced can foresee to some degree what the activity he is about to engage in may be like, what the next reasonable steps ought to be, first to relieve his tension and then to bring about the permanent disappearance of its particular cause, the child is in no such position.

Children can neither foresee what the future has in store for them, nor would they be able to do much about it if they could. Moreover, in addition to the many in-between times they are exposed to, they live in what is one big in-between age. Children in the latency period, because they are so little able to take care of their problems, normally look to others for content, for filling out their "emptiness." That is why they make the best students, anxious to learn, to be taught, to take in. By the same token, however, they are the most insecure, even more so than the infant, who is far more dependent. When the infant has received full satisfaction of his needs, he is free of all fear; he has gotten everything he wants, he does not care about the future. The child in the latency period never really feels secure about the future. We must constantly assure him about what it may bring, for without it he feels lost. And while these feelings are still manageable for the normal child in the latency period, they are highly exaggerated in emotionally disturbed children.

The often observed decline in "artistic" creativeness when the child grows into the latency period is another sign of this development. The infant, relatively secure in the love of his parents will let his imagination roam freely. But in the latency period the child is afraid. He has fears about his future, about his ability to achieve, about his status with other children and with adults. So he tries to conform, and his imaginary outpourings become

[1] The compulsive arrangement of the sequence of life activities represents a neurotic effort to avoid the tension created by "empty" time spent in waiting for the next event to take place.

more realistic, less phantastic, but by the same token more stereotyped.

Theoretically, things could be made easier for children and adults if one activity led logically to the next, if what followed were a continuation or a consequence of the preceding event, or if every activity led obviously and directly to the satisfaction of a recognized need, as in the food gathering activities of a primitive society. Then in-between times could be avoided. But ours is not a society which permits us to arrange the child's life so that he can proceed smoothly and naturally from one activity to the next with hardly a transitional period.

The day in our society is not organized in line with a life rhythm that is based on the needs of the child or his spontaneous interests. If they were quite free to arrange their lives, few children, if any, would choose to sit in class from nine to three, to play from three to six, then troop in to dinner, and so on. Even at the School we are not free to arrange our schedule in such a way as to follow the child's life rhythm, since every child's rhythm is different. Moreover, we would ill prepare children for a return to normal life—to public school, for example—if we taught classes one day from seven to nine in the morning and the next day from six to seven in the evening, or not at all. Not to speak of how our teachers would arrange their lives if the teaching time were to change unpredictably from day to day. On the other hand, we do not wish, and cannot, without defeating our purpose, force the children to live by a rigid schedule prearranged in all details. In practice, we strive for a workable balance which we hope is a happy one, by providing relative areas of freedom (much of the day outside of class and several long recesses during the hours set aside for school) and relative areas of preplanned activities (the time of classes, the three main meals, hours in the swimming pool, etc.).

In line with our desire to follow the children's needs and inclinations as much as possible, and not to force them more than is absolutely necessary, we allow them much greater areas of freedom than a comparable group of normal children might enjoy. But this in turn involves bridging an even greater number of in-between areas, in which the child may exercise his freedom of choice. If we insisted, for example, on the children playing one game for one hour and then another one for the next, there would be no more than one in-between period in two hours. But since they are free to break up their games as they wish, there may be five or ten in-between periods during that interval.

To choose the next activity may be quite a time-consuming activity in itself when dealing with six emotionally disturbed children. And some activities, such as baseball, may require many more participants than six, who will all have to decide whether they want to begin this game and not some other one, and where they want to play.

What we must do in this case is not only avoid letting the child realize he is afraid of the new activity, but try to prevent such an anxiety from creeping up on him. We must manage to ward off his doubts of success, his anxious imagining of the event in its worst possible aspects.

Once the last game has ended and the next is not yet under way, the "unplanned" interval occurs, a typical in-between period. This is the moment when the seriously disturbed child is apt to be flooded with boredom if not anxiety. He shouts desperately: "What do we do now, what comes next? Let's get going. Come on," and in doing so succeeds only in creating confusion and in prolonging the unmanageable period for himself. The feeling of purposelessness, of emptiness, the fear of not being chosen by the captain, of not winning the next game, all this and much more the child feels in the in-between period. These feelings more than any other experience, destroy his feeling of worth, of self-respect. As a matter of fact the frantic activities of many neurotic children, the continuous moving around of the runaway child, are often nothing but efforts to avoid this very emptiness, and with it the anxiety which might then come to consciousness if some other activity did not arise to prevent it. What happens to the children in these times is similar to what many adult neurotics recognize as their Sunday or holiday blues.

Many such adults function well during the week-days when the necessities of life take most choice-making out of their hands. But as soon as they have empty time on their hands—meaning that they have to make autonomous decisions on how to spend it—they must either set out on some frantic entertainment, or feel depressed. This depression is in part due to their inability to select an activity which would tend towards the solution of the unresolved problem (in this case of how to spend time in a way they really enjoy) or toward the lessening of fear. The inability to do so impresses them again with their lack of independence (or ego strength) a realization which in more serious cases leads to a feeling of worthlessness and deep depression, while in milder cases it remains on the level of boredom and emptiness.

Children are subject to the same feelings, but since they are closer—developmentally, and in time—to the infantile tendency of discharging tension through random movement, they try to discharge the tension and cover up their fear and emptiness through frantic activities or demands for them; all of this they actually fear since they fear all new and unknown events, and are convinced they will never succeed. Occasionally, therefore, during in-between times, the most constructive approach by the adult is to declare outside-of-choice those activities which the child seems to fear, although they may be the ones he most loudly demands.

In the situations we have just been discussing, the in-between time is a logical consequence of the child's having to make autonomous decisions. Other in-between times come about for mechanical reasons, but not entirely so. For example, it would be possible, theoretically, to herd all the children from the breakfast table to the classrooms, thus doing away with some unscheduled time. But that would mean having breakfast so strictly regulated in time that all children would have to be through eating at the same time, and that would be most undesirable. It would also imply that going to class could never be a freely chosen activity, not even in regard to the time of arriving there, the way the child enters the classroom, and so on.

Obviously, if our wish is to strengthen the ego, we must give the child ample chance to exercise it, so that in time he may acquire the ability to make reasonable choices. Only then can the repeated experience of having managed to arrange his own life give him the security to meet future events with self-confidence. If we move the child about like a pawn, he will never become a person. Thus while the in-between times often tax the child's ego strength severely, they are times which can be used very constructively in developing his ego strength.

Compared with the adult or the child, the infant has no conception of time, or of the future; everything is present to him. A promised event is expected to take place immediately and if it does not, the infant is deeply disappointed and convinced it will never take place. If it is not something vitally needed, he will cry for some time and will then make his peace with the fact that the event will just never take place.

The child in the latency period reacts quite differently. His sense of time is quite well developed; he knows that future events will eventually take place, but he can hardly bear the strain of waiting for them. His ego is well enough developed to realize the difference between present and future, and that planning in the present is necessary for assuring pleasant events in the future. But it is not well developed enough for him to integrate the tension of waiting. This he will show by his pestering which he will keep up for long periods of time unless stopped in some way.

Even the limited success of the normal child in integrating the tension of waiting is beyond the ability of the emotionally disturbed child. Similarly, the task of integrating the various arenas of living which the normal child can achieve (though often with great difficulties), is more than the seriously disturbed child can master. The lives and personalities of most of our children are already so seriously fragmentized by the time they have come to the School, that we must bring coherence into personal chaos, a coherence which may serve them in later personality integration as they integrate the various aspects of their life at the School.

Therefore, the help the child needs in overcoming his fear of the next activity is not limited to bridging the in-between moments. It should also establish the unity of life which he does not now recognize as existing between the various activities. A life that is divided into separate parts cannot easily make sense, hence it cannot be mastered. And life makes no sense to the children who need institutional treatment. The in-between times must stop being empty spaces that separate disconnected actions. They must become sensible links in a sequence of events. They must convince the child of the unity of his life through the only example that is pervasive enough to force him to establish, in its image, the unity of his own personality.

This coherence is facilitated, of course, by the fact that counselors (who exercise some of the parental functions), teachers, nurse, and so on, all form a unity of living which includes the children as members of equal importance. Connections between class and play are much more easily established—and it is also easier for the child to realize that what he learns in one area will help in the next—when he goes to class with the same children he plays with, and if the same adults plan for both.

While we thus simplify the in-between experiences in terms of the personal contacts involved, we also try to reduce them in number, and in extension of time. An example is the handling of anticipatory fear in the case of excursions, etc.

It should be clear by now that our children are characterized by deep feelings of inadequacy, and by the consequent exaggerated fears that they build up around future events. This prevents us from informing them ahead of time of any activity not regularly scheduled. Only if they know exactly what to expect on the basis of repeated experiences of their own are they able to look forward to a new one without anxiety. Our statements alone, they do not trust.

Even things that are fun for normal children to do, or things they look forward to with pleasure, are events these disturbed children feel sure will end only in defeat and displeasure, if not open disaster. Many reasons account for this attitude, although they differ with the individual case. Suffice it to repeat that the children's relations to their parents must have been severely disturbed to have made institutional treatment necessary. Since the relations were so disturbed, one may well imagine that activities which are fun for other children were either not available to them, or were more likely experienced as unpleasant—whether because the parents made promises they failed to keep, or if they kept them, things nevertheless turned out badly.

The most frequent anticipatory fear of our children, which is quite often in line with their past experiences, is that promises will not be kept. This means that each promised trip, for example, revives memories of other promises not kept (which itself is unpleasant), and in addition makes them doubt our present promises. In either case the tension is almost unbearable, so that as a general rule, we make no promises we cannot keep within twenty-four hours. It usually takes up to two years of regularly kept promises before a child becomes inwardly convinced that our promises will be kept, that planned activities will actually take place. And what is said here of not keeping promises goes as well for the pleasures of any other anticipated activity.

It also takes approximately two years before a child stops expecting all future activities to end in displeasure or defeat. On the basis of past experience they are convinced that a trip to the beach will be unpleasant, that they will have to return before they have had time to enjoy themselves, that they will be forced to stay longer than they want to, that others will criticize them or show them off, and so forth.

To argue such points with them is useless, and would only lead to mutual aggravation: the future is always uncertain, and it is the future we speak to them about. Their past experiences are certain, and those they know for sure turned out bad. Only after the child has had enough pleasant experiences on trips, and these have finally outbalanced the memories of unpleasant ones, will he develop the attitude that there is at least a fair chance that he may enjoy the coming activity, because only then will he find in his more recent past enough evidence to back up our present promises.

With every pleasant experience which is not counterbalanced by an unpleasant one the child becomes more and more willing to believe us when we describe a future activity as fun. And with each plan that turns out well, the anticipatory tension will also diminish, though some remnant will remain, since waiting even for pleasant experiences creates tension. Moreover, and quite realistically, we must admit that the child has it in his power to frustrate our best intention. We have to admit that no one can prevent him from having a bad time if he is set to create one for himself. But here, too, the group often helps: when a child sees everyone else having a good time he may slowly get the idea that it is his own doing which prevents him from enjoying himself.

In this context one may realize the difficulties under which the staff of an institution of this kind labours: we have to provide pleasurable experiences for children who are convinced a priori that they won't be pleasurable. Clearly this attitude defeats many of our efforts, since a negative attitude on the part of some, let alone the majority of the participants, can change many experiences from positive to negative ones. And finally, when our efforts have succeeded and the child, on the basis of his past experiences, can look forward to future ones with justified confidence, we have discharged our duty and the child leaves the School, to be replaced by another one who is utterly convinced that whatever we arrange for him will be unpleasant.

An analogous instance from physiology seems permissible at this point in stressing once more the importance of in-between times. Modern physiologists have come to believe that the correct working of the connective tissues is much more important for a healthy body than was previously thought, perhaps even more so than the working of muscles and bones. The study of the latter was formerly so emphasized because they seemed the more important physiological structures since they did the "actual work" and also since the changes occurring in them seemed more readily observable. Similarly we, too, have found that in-between periods arising between areas of definite activities are most trying for our children, although they are much less discussed than the more obvious planned activities. These are moments when the children need a great deal of help, and ones we must plan for very carefully.

One way of providing some relief in these periods of waiting is to show them that some satisfaction is assured because something pleasant has already begun. For example, it is much easier for children to reach a decision about whether to go on a treasure hunt or not, if the counselor who suggests it at the same time shows the prizes and makes sure that they all understand that each child (and the counselor, too) will get a prize no matter who ends up first. When planning a game of baseball, no release for the need to play, and no discharge of tension through motility is yet possible—they have to wait until the game is under way. But while the arrangements for the play are being made it is possible, for example, to feed the children something they like so that satisfaction of one desire softens the tension created by the need to make decisions.

Additional giving of food, always only as a tangible indication of our good intentions and never in the place of, or as a substitute for, personal relations, will also help the child to accept a decision which may go against him, a decision he might not be able to accept if a full mouth did not give him a clear proof of our good will and thus take the worst edge off his anger. Many times additional feeding of candy has saved the situation for counselor, child and group. A decision on an activity may have been reached by majority vote, and the decision may have gone against a child's will. (Of course, he is not forced to take part in the activity; he can stay home, or do something else by himself —or join another group of children. But this is not what he

PLATE 5. This boy is unhappy about life, and with good reason. As always, he covers up his feelings by being angry at the world. He has been playing with the boys, but something has suddenly reminded him of his past, and he feels lost and rejected again. He withdraws from the group, and the world as well. He expects the counselor will try to be nice to him, but it doesn't help much. At home everybody stopped everything when he had a tantrum. The world turned round him. Now he sees that others are not influenced by his anger, and since they just go on playing his anger is not effective as a weapon any more. Yet when another boy spontaneously joins the counselor in telling him they all like him the world begins to look better again.

PLATE 6. Children who can really follow their inclinations in the way they want to do things can also play without interfering with one another even within a small area. And this is just as true for the dormitory (*above*) ...

[PLATE 7, FIGS. 1 and 2.] . . . as for the schoolroom (*top*) or the craft shop (*bottom*). In any case, doing things is one of the best ways to counteract the feeling of worthlessness from which most of these children suffer.

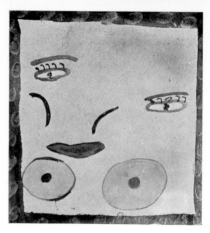

[PLATE 8, FIGS. 1 to 4.] *Top left:* One of the "horrible pictures" Tom drew, in which "a man engulfed in thoughts of hate . . . shot everybody in the pleasure joint." *Top right:* It is as if, in her painting, Mary was trying to express all that made up her emotional world. Without a father, and totally neglected by her melancholic mother, she remained, emotionally, in the world of the baby, eyes looking fascinatedly at the mother, herself all mouth, and breasts the most important thing in the world. It is how she, as a baby, experienced her mother. And as if to emphasize the primitive sensations, she put fingermarks all around the border, just as her first sense of touch developed when she put her fingers up to her mother's breasts and face. *Bottom left:* Grace's attachments were only to animals. She preferred to be in her grave rather than remain with human beings who had never made life anything but miserable for her. She paints herself leaving the world of the sun (*upper right in the picture*); her beloved ghost horse kisses her hand goodbye while she walks to her grave. Border and predominant colour in the picture: black. *Bottom right:* Fear of mutilation is one of the most pressing anxieties of most of our children, and in retaliation they wish to inflict on others what they think others are intending to do to them. This drawing is by Hank: original in blood-red crayon.

wanted; he wanted his group to have done what he wanted them to do.)

The counselor, knowing the decision has not pleased him will try to comfort him, while he may frantically protest. But it is difficult to protest in anger and accept food at the same time. While the child munches the candy the counselor has a chance to make the decision acceptable to him, be it by pointing out how much he cares about his taking part, or by mentioning the part he will play in the game if he decides to join in after all. In this way the counselor can forestall the child's further angry outburst, or his saying he refuses to participate—a statement, once made, which is hard for a child to go back on because he thinks he lowers his status, or because the annoyance of the others about his opposition, once voiced, may make it more difficult to rejoin them.

Yet while all this is generally true, an indiscriminate reliance on food for reducing anticipatory tension would be no more than a mechanical device. And the use of devices is always undesirable when compared with spontaneous personal relations geared to the specific problem at hand; food or other tangible offerings can be useful only as a token or carrier of human feelings—otherwise it remains dead.

Of course, the choosing of activities itself is not without dangers because if the child should decide on his own steam to take up an activity and the activity should then end in defeat or disappointment it would only convince him again that he cannot look after himself and all efforts at autonomy would be given up in despair. Therefore, at such in-between moments the child must be presented with reasonable choices, each of which is acceptable to him, and each of which could provide him with a positive experience rather than one that would weaken the ego.

For example, adults who wish to make sure that the child will choose the activity they want him to, may offer two choices to the child one of which is pleasant and the other unpleasant. But this is not really presenting the child with a choice and is interpreted by him only as a ridiculing of his desire for autonomy. Genuine choices can be made only between activities which are more or less equally attractive. Thus in-between times can be used most constructively for developing a child's ego strength by giving him the experience of having made a decision whose correctness is borne out by fact. The result then becomes valuable proof of his ability to make decisions in general, to get along, to look out for himself in the world.

Although this seems obvious at sight, most present day thinking on group life does not take it sufficiently into account. Many group workers are anxious to have an activity begin and for good reasons, as was pointed out earlier in speaking of the planning and waiting and the tension they entail. Moreover, there are many handbooks on the various activities and in fact a whole literature on the subject; compared with which the literature is scarce on how one can utilize those in-between times in terms of choice-making as a means of developing self-confidence and ego strength.

While transitional periods that come between free-time activities can be used to permit absolutely non-directed choices, the times between free and directed activities (such as going to class), present problems that are somewhat different. Nevertheless, even there we try to give the child as much freedom as possible in arranging the details of transition, as I wish to discuss in the following pages.

6

the challenge of learning

MOST children enter the School with an active aversion to learning, to going to school or to any pressure to do so. Even children who did well academically before they came to us are afraid or have mixed feelings about school, only in their case it is not so much a matter of learning difficulties as the fact that they never got along well with other children. (If a child learns well and can also get along reasonably well with other children he does not need institutional treatment.) Therefore what happens before school begins is often decisive, and constitutes one of the critical in-between periods of the day.

Classes are held in two connecting buildings which can be reached through a short passageway; together with the dormitory building, they enclose the School play yard. So in physical distance going to class involves no more than a few steps. But our children measure distances mainly in terms of emotions, and to a child suffering from a fear of the classroom, the distance of a few yards seems unconquerable. While the closeness between classroom and bedroom, and the fact that they do not need to cross public grounds to reach their classes, is a convenience for our children, this closeness in itself is not enough to bridge the emotional gap which separates the truant from the classroom, although eventually it will help to mediate between him and the class.

George, to cite a more or less typical example, had been a runaway child almost as soon as he was able. At the age of three he was already roaming the streets, getting food for himself by entering houses through windows or backstairs and then taking provisions from the ice boxes. Later, in his sixth year, he made an attempt at drowning another child to get possession of the other child's fishing tackle. This and other violent attacks on children, plus strong delusions of persecution, kept him perpetually on the move.

When he entered the School in his eighth year, going to class was of course out of the question; just being in a room with other children threw him in a panic because he was terrified that his "enemies" might catch him if he were cooped up with no outlet. It took more than a year before he was going to class fairly regularly, but for several years the time just before class continued to be very difficult for him. He needed the help of his counselors every minute between breakfast and class time to keep from running away. And even with his counselor he had to run or to walk before class every day as if to counteract his runaway tendencies by indulging them in small doses.

Other children work out tensions that arise before class for other reasons by playing active games, or by having a violent go at the swings. For still others, motion alone is not enough. Mary, for example, would run over to the schoolroom as soon as she was dressed, sometimes even before she had had breakfast, to make sure that her teacher was there. She would stand and watch the teacher as she laid out the work for the day, sometimes helping her, but more often just exchanging a few friendly remarks with her.[1]

Mary's past history had been characterized by the sudden disappearance of the most significant figures in her life, including her mother. It was in the schoolroom, and from her nursery school teacher, that she had learned of her mother's sudden death. The teacher, to whom she was also very attached, "disappeared" at the same time because Mary was moved to another district following the death of her mother. Thus seeing for her-

[1] Participant observers: Kathryn Howard and Joan Little.

self that the teacher was still there and had no news of disasters for her, was something she had to experience every morning to be able to look ahead to class without tension. Generally she was sullen and irritable before the visit, but once that anxiety was over she ate her breakfast in peace and played freely for the period before class.

Sometimes running away before class or being hesitant about entering it can be traced to the child's fear of losing his freedom, his independence. Then, regular attendance in class can be assured only after the child has established his independence from the teacher, or has overcome his fear that once in the classroom his freedom to leave may be restricted. Leo, for example, had to convince himself of this by the very way he entered the classroom.

At the beginning, every time he came into the room, he would announce loudly: "I'm going out again. I'm not coming in this time." But the teacher went on with her work, distributing papers, helping children, etc., and did not look up. When Leo finally came in, all he did was run around provocatively, and when this produced no reaction he went to the rear door, then back to the side door, pretending at each one to be leaving the room. Finally he did leave, but only to poke his head in every few minutes, shouting, "I'm going out. I'm not coming in." While behaving in this way he also smiled and seemed happy. Finally he came quite close to his teacher and shouted at her, "Do you hear me, I'm going out. I'm not going to work."

The teacher after having said once or twice at the beginning that that was up to him paid no more attention and went on with her work. At last Leo left the room saying, "You have to catch me," and stayed out for several minutes. When nothing happened he finally came in, took his seat, and with no further acting out took up his assignment (a bit of simple work) which was all prepared for him. Nothing further was said, nor was it needed.[2]

After several days of this ritual Leo felt sure of his freedom to leave the classroom whenever he wished, and this security per-

[2] Participant observer: Anna Lukes.

mitted him to enter it regularly, on time, and without fear.

Runaway children, even long after they have more or less over-come the impulse to truant, are still more than ambivalent about learning. For months they need help every morning in fighting their runaway tendencies and in managing to withstand the tension they experience before class time. Some children need to be told of a pleasurable experience that awaits them after class, if they can only manage to survive until then without breakdown. Others are helped by a quite realistic discussion of why they should learn and what they stand to gain by it—not in the far distant future, but in the relatively immediate present—including presents given in or right after the class.

In some children the anxiety about learning is only part of a broader fear of exploring the world or of learning about it. They are afraid that by learning, by exploring, they may stumble onto some devastating discovery. Such fears usually find their expression in learning inhibitions. Actually the child is not afraid of learning per se, but of finding out about secrets within the family that he thinks he is not supposed to know. Occasionally his fears may be justified. But much more often it is some chance remark or observation he has misunderstood and which led him, at a very early age, to think that somewhere some horrible secret was hidden, a secret so terrible that he must avoid learning it at all costs. His ideas about such horrors are wilder than whatever it is parents may be trying to keep from their child, such as dissension between parents, siblings who have died, addiction or insanity in the family, or other types of family disorder. It is not only the proverbial skeleton in the closet that these children are afraid of stumbling upon through learning, but more their horrible exaggerations of it.

Another frequent source of learning inhibition is the fear of learning about sex, a knowledge which the child fears may lead him into trouble, as his parents may either have warned him, or more likely may have intimated by their disapproval of his exploring or manipulating of his genitals.

To be physically removed from whatever persons the child is

afraid to learn about, takes some sting out of the fear of exploring. And the same is true about fears of acquiring sex knowledge. Since the parents who told him one should never try to find out about sex (as by inspecting or by touching the sex organs of another child) are far away, the impact of their supposed taboo on learning is less powerful.

If parents live in another city, for example, it becomes obvious that they cannot know in detail of explorations going on hundreds of miles away. It is equally clear that any school studies conducted so far away will not easily lead to a discovery of any family secrets the child is afraid to unearth. Still, physical distance from the sources of anxiety is not enough in itself to restore the child's ability to explore after such serious blockage. In these cases many experiences must be arranged to show the child that exploring is by no means as dangerous as he imagines before he will dare to explore by himself. Here, as always, it is the personal relation more than the technical procedures that make for the success or the failure of our efforts. Only because the teacher has been tested repeatedly and has been found to be trustworthy will exploring with her seem less fearful—because her presence lends the necessary security. Only after exploration with her has proven safe over and over again, and has also been repeated in various contexts will the child eventually be able to explore on his own. First, however, it must occur always in closest proximity to persons or places that he knows he can trust.

In particular, the symbolic function of reading seems most likely to suffer from fears of exploration. In many cases, we have found the exploring of nature a most successful approach in overcoming the general fear of learning, and of reading in particular.

The psychological reason seems to be that every child grew familiar with certain aspects of nature long before he ever knew about complicated family relations or family secrets and became afraid of understanding what they were like; long, too, before he knew of reading as a means of acquiring knowledge. Moreover, nature does not demand comprehension of what seems to the beginning reader to be the magic connotations of symbols, such as words. The child thinks that if he studies nature, he will understand only nature. Whereas if he learns to read, he fears he will learn to understand everything, including that which he thinks he is not supposed to understand. On the other hand, knowledge of a part of nature, of his own body, was the first knowledge he acquired; finding out about his body was the first exploring he attempted. And precisely because this exploring of nature, often of his or another child's genitals, was where exploration was restricted if not openly forbidden, it seems clear that the exploration of nature is a logical place to take it up again.

In helping such children to study nature, we have found the use of the microscope and the magnifying lens very valuable. It seems that they convince the child, in a way he can accept, that he is able to see things that have up to now been invisible or baffling to him. Of course, this is not to imply that all one need do in such cases is thrust a magnifying glass into the child's hand and tell him he can "now go and explore;" it is again only his relation to an adult that will give him the real courage to learn.

Sometimes particular family constellations lead to particular reasons for learning inhibitions. Felix' problem could be traced to the death of his father when Felix was still very young. His father had been an engineer whose job it was to test the speed and endurance of cars, and he was killed during one of these tests. Felix' mother married again, this time a prominent lawyer. Despite the stepfather's best efforts, Felix developed the notion that to be loyal to his first father, he must never acquire an education that was as good as his stepfather's. To make things more complicated, this was combined with a hero worship built around the daring of his father. Felix decided to become a daredevil, too. By not studying, he flaunted his disapproval of knowledge, the highest value of his stepfather. By not succeeding in school, he also punished his mother for having married again instead of devoting herself entirely to him, or to the memory of his father.

The Challenge of Learning ‹ 139

In terms of his father's daring, he climbed over high fences, performed numerous stunts, and wound up as the leader of a gang, thus again defying the values of his stepfather-as-lawyer. In this way he tried to show that it is not those who study and live carefully (like the stepfather), but those who dare (like his father and himself) who are true leaders of men.

Felix' rehabilitation, too, had to start without any direct attack on his academic difficulties. Instead of moping in class or obstructing the learning of others, as he was wont to do, he was encouraged to construct wooden racer cars in the workshop and equip them with simple electrical machinery. Racing them downhill satisfied his desire for daring and gave him status with the group. Later, through subtle guidance, the need to understand the construction of machinery became an incentive to study reading. Here, also, his interest in speed was utilized. He learned to read by means of flash cards which were exposed to his vision for short periods of time.[3]

Final success was reached when Felix overcame his resentment of his stepfather by achieving symbolically in the latter's own field, in law and in intellectual ability. One day one of the children was wrongly accused of something and Felix, his attorney as it were, defended him against the most intellectual children of his group and won his point. Thus he made token peace with the memory of his father and also with his stepfather, and could proceed from then on without a chip on his shoulder.

Aside from the fear of exploring, many children are afraid of the classroom either because they fear competition after so many defeats, or because to them winning a competition means destroying a dangerous rival, perhaps a younger or older sibling. This last arouses such guilt feelings that they cannot afford either to compete in the first place or to win in a competition. Therefore we try to eliminate all competitiveness and encourage the child not to measure his own achievement against the achievement of others, but only against his own past achievements. Since our classrooms are ungraded and ages are mixed, it is

[3] Participant observer: Anna Lukes

relatively easy to show the child that judging himself against others is not a fair comparison and that success in such competition would really mean little when compared with his own performance of today as against that of several months ago.

Once the child is in class the most important therapeutic contribution the teachers can make is in giving the children a real chance to succeed in their work. To begin with, the classes are small, which is very important. Teachers can prepare individual assignments for each child, give him help when he needs it, and criticize or praise, when and where it is most constructive. The child is free of the pressure of homework or of any assignments he must do when the teacher is not present to relieve his anxiety, or when he feels he cannot understand or succeed.

Nevertheless, while the child is still far behind in his school work, the classroom situation, even with the greatest of effort, can at best be made bearable for him. Only after he has repeatedly experienced that he can make progress in learning, that classroom activities are enjoyable, that his fear of learning, of acquiring knowledge, is unjustified, can the classroom seem pleasant to him. This is true even for children who are encouraged to do nothing but play in class until they can slowly adjust to it. They may play then for some time and enjoy it, but may suddenly look up and see other children at work and realize unpleasantly that they are far behind others in adequacy. This tends to force them to abandon a setting where they feel so inadequate, for one where they even feel superior to their age-mates—a setting, moreover, through which they can discharge hostility against a world they are at war with; in a word it will force them again into truancy and delinquency.

All we can hope for in these cases is that the conflict between the desire to enjoy pleasant associations with the teacher (or the security of playing with nice toys where that is encouraged) and the contradictory impulse to run away from the classroom situation will become so strong that the child will feel some need to resolve it. Then our task becomes one of helping him to solve it in the direction of going to class both to learn and to play, rather than going there only to play. Hence for any truant or child who is suffering from fears about school there is an intermediate time when he is trying to adjust to the classroom but is not yet adjusted to it. This is a very critical period for him, when he needs special help in convincing himself that he need not run away or be afraid. Such children then present even more serious problems than the child who is still a truant in the full sense of the word.

But even while a child is still unable to attend class—and incidentally, the truant is rarely a child who does not want to go to school; he is usually a child who for psychological reasons cannot afford to—such a child is more likely during his truancy than at other times to reveal some of the reasons which prevent him from learning. In this sense, truancy from school really pertains to a discussion of classroom problems, particularly when speaking of a treatment institution. An example may illustrate how truancies permit us, and what is even more important, permit the child, to gain direct insight into some of the reasons why he prefers not to learn.

George, even when his parents used to bring him to school forcefully, had never been able to remain in the classroom for more than a few minutes at a time. As mentioned earlier in the chapter, he had been truanting virtually from the time he could walk securely. His severe delusions of persecution not only made him extremely aggressive toward others, but what is even more pertinent for this example, also made him afraid of any other person's company. This deprived us for some time of one of the best methods for domesticating truants; it made accompanying George on his truancies particularly trying and difficult, if not frankly dangerous. Still, being able to be with him when he was off on a tear somewhere was our only chance of forming any relation to him and later on it offered an opportunity to influence him in changing his way of life.

After many frustrating efforts, his then favourite counselor succeeded in gaining some measure of his trust, and he eventually allowed her to accompany him for stretches of time on his runaway bouts. This he did not because he liked her—he was incapable as yet of forming any positive relations or of harbouring any positive emotions—but because she had proven her usefulness to him by protecting him when he got into trouble over his stealing or his attacks against others, and also by providing him with food and with toys. When she slowly began to use their relation to exercise a socializing influence, a situation occurred in which he stated for the first time some of his reasons for being afraid of learning and the catastrophic consequences he was afraid that might have for him.

George, as was usual when he was running away, wanted to fish. One day, as he set down his fishing equipment at a particular spot on the lake, the counselor pointed out that he would do better to go someplace else because this was a place where no fishing was allowed. (She felt that while he still could not tolerate being forbidden to do something he was set on, he might be able to stand a change of location and get some idea of how one can make small adjustments to stay out of trouble with society, particularly if it implies no great hardship.) George asked her how come, and how did she know there was no fishing allowed there. She pointed to a sign and told him it said, "Fishing Prohibited," to which he replied, "I can't read so that doesn't apply to me."

This led to their first discussion of the fact that not knowing the laws because one cannot read is no excuse, and does not offer protection from punishment. It also led to the idea that if one knows how to read, one can select one of the many places where fishing is allowed instead of having to run the risk of doing something against the law—an experience with which George was unpleasantly familiar. For the first time then, it occurred to him that learning to read might have some advantages, and that not being able to read did not offer the protection he once thought it did. In addition, this conversation permitted us to use these and similar arguments with George later on.[4]

The connection between George's first wondering about the

[4] Participant observer: Ann Morrisett

possible advantages of learning, and his later success in the schoolroom became apparent only many months afterward in the
schoolroom.[5]

A year later when George was attending class more or less regularly, he was still fighting learning. He no longer felt persecuted
by imaginary enemies, but he was not yet over his paranoia. Previously, he had personalized and projected his hatred of people
and then felt injured and persecuted by them in return. Now,
in a way, it was his lessons he personalized; he hated them, projected his hatred onto them, and in turn felt they persecuted
him. At this time the fundamentals of reading were, as he put
it, his "worst enemy." It was another year before he mastered
reading, no longer hated it and hence no longer felt persecuted
by it. Then arithmetic took its place as his worst enemy, but by
that time his personal integration was much better and he was
able to do something constructive himself about his feelings of
persecution. But more about this development later.

At the outset his teacher had established a friendly relation
with George outside of class before he ever dared to enter it,
and when he was ready to do so he was expected only to play
there. In this way, we hoped that he would lose some of his fear
of the place of learning after he had first lost his fear of the
teacher. The relation to his teacher grew slowly more meaningful to him, but he still preferred to remain ignorant and wished
the teacher would quit trying to make studying seem pleasant to
him. At such times George would say to her: "Stop saying please
to me. If you say please all the time it's hard not to work." He
wanted to avoid the pressure of her friendly persuasion because
he realized it would not only force him into intellectual growth
but also into more polite behaviour.[6]

Some time later George's complaints showed more clearly the

[5] This, incidentally, may serve as an example of why it is difficult to
stick to the chapter headings, why a chapter on classroom teaching may
have to reach out to include runaway trips to the lake, and why a later
chapter on the children at bedtime will include in its narrative what took
place during the day on the playground.

[6] Participant observer: Ruthevelyn Pim.

conflict between ego and id as the ego became more and more assertive, but not strong enough yet to overcome the pressure for immediate satisfaction of all of his spur-of-the-moment desires. When praised for the progress he had made—and small enough progress it was at that time—George blurted out: "And what do I get for all this hard work . . . nothing! Just progress. No money, no nothing, just progress." Needless to say, his complaints were anticipated before he ever voiced them and the smallest step forward was heavily rewarded by toys, and in other ways. This was the time when George was no longer openly fighting by running away or by defying his teacher, but when his ambivalence about learning expressed itself mainly in sullen resistance.

After another few months George had actually mastered reading. Since he had not managed after all to remain ignorant, since the battle against growing up was lost, he was ready to admit why he had waged it. Then he told his teacher why he had hoped he might never learn to read, and one day shortly afterward when he was again unwilling to go on with his reading and was questioned about it, he explained why he was afraid to grow up and why he wanted to remain "dumb." He said that as a little boy he had "killed somebody. I pushed him under the rocks below the water." (Actually, as mentioned above, he had pushed a child into the river to steal the child's fishing tackle. This may explain why it was on a fishing expedition that he spoke for the first time of the advantages of not being able to read.) He was afraid, he continued, that if he grew up he might do the same thing again and be sent to the chair. If he knew how to read and write, everybody would say that he knew what he'd been doing, while if he remained a dumbbell, no one could hold him responsible.

Since George had now mentioned the most dramatic event of his past, it was possible to assure him that he would never be punished for what he had done as a small child, while at the same time impressing on him that his ignorance would never serve as an excuse when he grew up. On the contrary, it was explained to him, his not doing well in school would speak against him, because it would seem as if he had never made an effort to get along in society. While these and similar discussions later on did not make learning as such very acceptable to him— that could come only with actual achievement—it slowly broke down his notion that ignorance was a valuable protection.

Only in slow steps did George's need to run away change to more socially acceptable ways of discharging his tension before class, but eventually even his running around the block was replaced by some walking around in the play yard. As with most runaway children, there were times even after George had become fairly adjusted when his old urge to run away asserted itself, particularly in times of stress or when spring came again, or he felt generally distressed. Then his favourite counselor not only had to spend all the time between breakfast and class time with him but many other hours of the day, supporting his weak ego against the pressures of his asocial desires. She had to assure him of his progress and to enumerate his achievements before he could overcome his depression about still being so far behind, or get over his "what's the use" attitude.[7]

George knew he needed help in resisting his truant tendencies, and he either expected or wanted support, depending on his mood of the morning. "Here comes my hound dog," he would say, or turning to the other children with a mixture of pride (in her interest in him) and desperation (because she would end up by convincing him that it was better to go to class), he might say: "Here comes my hound dog; she's hounding me to school." But it was *his* "hound dog," and his special relation to her, that made learning at last possible for him.

When it was less a feeling of inferiority and more a desire to gain immediate pleasures, other methods were more successful. Then the running around the block had to be replaced by a more appropriate device, by a visit to the drugstore for a soda or to buy a small toy. To the toy George would cling all during class as a tangible symbol that studying did not mean having to

[7] Participant observers: chiefly Gayle Shulenberger but later, too, Patty Pickett and others.

give up his pleasures but meant getting additional new ones, as his counselor pointed out.

As George made further progress in adjustment, symbolic behaviour replaced his acting-out behaviour more and more and finally symbolic assurance was replaced by real personal relations: the security George derived from hanging on to a toy was slowly replaced by the security he found in his relation to his teacher. For some time then he had to rush from his breakfast to the classroom to avoid all the tension of delay not only by convincing himself that the classroom and the teacher were by no means as horrible as his anxiety coloured them, but also by having the teacher entirely to himself for some fifteen to twenty minutes, during which he could gain from her verbal assurance that his day's work would not be too difficult. Even more important was the emotional assurance that he was important to her, an assurance he derived from the fact that she was interested enough in him to spend her free time with him and come to class earlier for his sake. For some time he could maintain himself in class only when he was well settled with her and his work, before any other children had entered the room. Then his real relation to a teacher replaced the toys as a source of security.[8]

George had great manual dexterity and good technical understanding but he was still far behind in his reading and understanding because of his long-standing avoidance of the learning situation. School was bearable to him only because the freedom of the classroom permitted him to compensate immediately through his talents for any loss of status he was afraid he might suffer through his backwardness in reading. One day, for example, the children were reading in science about contraction and expansion through heat and their reading was applied, by way of example, to the cables holding up the George Washington bridge. George was entirely lost because the lesson was beyond his current reading ability and he became very restless, ready to give up and run away. At the height of this crisis he jumped up,

[8] Participant observers: Kathryn Howard, Anna Lukes and Ruthevelyn Pim.

went to the wooden blocks and constructed a replica of the bridge which won him great praise from the other children and brilliantly saved the day.[9]

Another method that proved of great value to George was permitting him to study what he wanted and when he wanted it. After George had accepted reading and was angrily fearful, in turn, of arithmetic ("had a battle with arithmetic" as he put it) this subject was dropped from his program for some time. When it was reintroduced, it still aroused the same anger, but this time he gave it expression in such violent form that he found relief enough to go on with his work. Specifically, when the teacher told him it was time he had another try at arithmetic he made a whip out of his belt and went around the room hitting out at the desks and the chairs and shouting, "I'm not going to do it. I'm just not going to do it." This also he could do because he had now gained enough security to attack his enemies (arithmetic) while before he had had such a low opinion of his abilities that he could only run away from a challenge. The teacher, watching his violent outburst, felt she had perhaps introduced arithmetic too soon and told him if he felt so strongly about it, she wouldn't insist on his doing it. But by that time, George's violence was spent. He just sat down and said, "Give me the work," and he did it without further reluctance and without any special difficulty.[10]

Some time after this discharge of aggression, and after George had made general progress in accepting symbolic material for what it was and not as real objects (or imaginary enemies) he also became able to deal with his anxiety and aggressions symbolically.

Although George now studied arithmetic sometimes, his general distaste for it continued for some time and no pressure was applied. One day his teacher promised she would go fishing with him and that if they caught any fish, they would fry them and eat them together. With this assurance of her good will, he

[9] Participant observer: Kathryn Howard.
[10] Participant observer: *Idem.*

found the courage to attack the dreaded arithmetic problems. He sat at his desk playing around with some scraps of paper, at first seemingly without aim. Then he began to make flags out of them. He arranged a pulley system with three flags, and when his teacher asked him why three, and what it all meant, he told her, "Well, it's a system; I'll explain it to you. See the white flag? That's for everything good. Everything I don't hate. Everything except arithmetic." Then he put the white flag down and picked up the bright red flag. Hiding his face behind it, he said, "This flag is for arithmetic. The reason it's a red flag is because every time I see arithmetic I get mad. I just get mad." Then he showed her the third flag, a white one marked with skull and crossbones. He concluded almost disdainfully, "And this is a flag I use when the other kids bother me." [11]

So after George had learned to accept and use symbolic material as such (letters, numbers, etc.) he spontaneously developed a symbolic system through which he could express his anger in a social and highly acceptable way, a way that permitted him to continue with his work undisturbed by the tension of the various threatening situations. All tension was now symbolically discharged through the flags. He actually used this flag system for some time, signalling to his teacher when he felt the other children were bothering him or when he was ready to study arithmetic, which he signified by raising the red flag.

In making the class setting reassuring for children who are afraid that learning means giving up primitive pleasures, we do not go so far as to let them bring the baby bottle to class to suck milk out of it. The reason is that we try to retain within the world of the School at least one setting which the child recognizes as requiring more mature and more integrated behaviour. This is the classroom. Nevertheless, some children are quite ingenious in providing themselves with the reassurance they derive from the ability to regress to earlier forms of pleasure, and they

[11] Participant observer: Kathryn Howard.

manage to do so in mature ways, as the classroom situation requires.

George, for example, reached his first outstanding achievement in reading (eight pages without interruption) immediately after such a tour de force. In science one day, he managed to construct a situation which in achievement represented maturity and in content signified that through greater maturity he would be able to provide himself with even more of the satisfactions he needed.

Following the suggestion of his teacher during a science lesson, he rigged up an elaborate siphoning system. He took several bottles and connected them with rubber tubing so that by blowing or sucking at one end he was able to force liquid through the various bottles and tubes. At lunch time he had to interrupt this activity, but during the meal some of the things he was saying to his teacher shed light on what he was trying to do. (At the noon meal, on school days, the children eat with the teachers; the other main meals they eat with their counselors.) Apropos nothing at all, he remarked, "Once my grandfather bought a cow so I'd always have milk. He used part of the garage for a stable." As he said this he punched a hole in a milk carton, stuck a straw in the hole and began to suck the milk through the straw.

That afternoon, when George returned to class after recess, he played with his tubing again, forcing the various liquids through the various bottles.[12]

In this way George proved to himself that through classroom learning he could better understand the way liquids behave, and may even have felt he had learned something about the milking process. This achievement and the praise he received for it made him very happy and boosted his courage so much that he attacked the dreaded reading with confidence and sat down to a highly constructive session with his book.

Some of the many and various steps in George's adjustment to the learning situation have been described in detail, because

[12] Participant observer: Kathryn Howard.

they are rather typical in their sequence: from the generalized fear of learning, through the relation to trusted persons, to the tentative attacks on isolated learning activities and then the final adjustment to the classroom. George's progress also shows why our approach must be flexible, and how much so. On any one day in class there are some children who are still fighting learning, others who are starting their initial adjustment to the classroom, while still others have overcome their fear of it.

As in all other learning situations the teacher's knowing what the child ought to learn is of little use unless the child himself is convinced he ought to learn for his own good. And while these two often coincide in the teaching of normal children, the other two steps have to precede them in cases of emotional learning blocks: first, the child's realizing what prevented him from learning, and second that his old ways (not learning) were ineffective even when viewed from what he feels are his own interests.

In George's case, he began to realize the origin of blocking when he said he thought that not knowing things would prevent his being held to account for his actions. This realization was gained in a number of often widely separated steps, only two of which have been mentioned. The earliest and least far-reaching was the protection he attached to his inability to read when he fished at the wrong place. Just because of its seemingly relative unimportance it was the easiest and hence the first area in which to begin to think about his learning block, thinking which slowly led to an understanding of its most important causes. This was his realization that he always thought being unable to read made him non-accountable even for a major crime.

True, we had a fairly good idea, before he told us, of why George was afraid to learn to read, afraid to grow up. George, too, was probably dimly aware before he put it into words of why he thought he was better protected from the law if he remained ignorant. But before these conversations we had no way of using our knowledge, just as the teacher's knowledge of why and what the student ought to learn is of little use unless she has the will of the student on her side in the learning process; and this she can get only after he, too, is convinced he should learn, and can trust that her guidance will benefit him.

For other reasons, too, it would be unwise of us to make use of our knowledge of why children behave as they do before they themselves have spoken to us about it. Most emotionally disturbed, and also many normal young children, believe that adults have powers of divination. That is why they often fear adults and make special efforts to hide their thoughts and emotions from them. But we are vitally interested in having the children neither fear us, nor hide their thoughts or emotions from us. Moreover, children who are unable to deal with the world realistically often escape into magic beliefs. The less adequate they are, the more they will do so. If we give them the impression that we have magical powers by seeming to be able to divine their unspoken thoughts, they become even more eager to develop that power. Moreover, if we can magically discover children's thoughts, whyever should they learn to read and write? Once they have mastered our magic they will know everything anyway.

All our efforts, and particularly with children who hate learning, must be directed toward giving them the impression that it is only learning that enables one to acquire knowledge. In this way we may slowly convince them of the value of learning and that there is no other way to acquire knowledge. And eventually, this may become yet another incentive to make them want to learn.

Moreover, and however much reason we may have for believing that we know what the child thinks or what motivates his behaviour, we can never be certain that our notions are correct. Nor can we ever be sure that he has reasoned out his motives for himself. If he were not yet quite clear about them and we were to verbalize them for him, he might not be able to accept our arguments. And even if he should accept them, he could never be sure afterward that these were his real motives, and that we did not impute them to him. Nor could he ever be convinced that he himself was, or would have been able to, discover the origins of his actions.

We are most anxious to strengthen the child's ego, to enhance his self-respect, his feeling of adequacy, to convince him that he is able to understand, to change and control his own action. Nothing is more conducive to developing these attitudes than the conviction that one can figure out by oneself just what motivates one, and nothing is more deflating than to have to think that others can understand the mainspring of one's innermost behaviour either better or sooner than oneself. Therefore, we do not use our hunches, or information received from parents, for example, unless the child has first informed us of it, or we not only think, but really know that he knows what goes on. But once he has told us about it, we feel free to make use of it at appropriate moments, even if the child has forgotten it, because such information has become part of our relation, is now common and no longer a private possession.

Initially we said that our efforts might be described as favouring the development of ego strength directly rather than through an uncovering of the unconscious. George's experiences may illustrate how we tried to support the ego throughout in its battle with asocial tendencies, and how we did not support the superego in its repressive function. We did not tell George that he must not be fishing at a place where it was forbidden; we did not paint to him the grim consequences of transgressing the law. We rather offered him (his ego) a choice, showing the advantages of social behaviour, and even more so of ego growth, of learning. But neither did we tell him why he was so afraid of learning. That he had to find out for himself, and to tell us in his own good time, of his own free will. Once he had told us, and it had thus become part of his conscious insight (and also of personal relationships), we were free to make use of it, sparingly and carefully.

Often a child becomes fearful when, in an effort to help him understand his behaviour, we remind him of some event of his past which he has told us about. The child may then frantically ask: how did you know? and feel much relieved when we can recall to him the time and place that he told us about it. In this way the child often becomes ready to take advantage of recall for understanding himself, while he rejected the possibility as long as he was not sure it was he who had told us about it.

As discussed in Chapter Five, periods of empty waiting are difficult, and anticipatory anxiety must be avoided as much as possible. Therefore, when the child enters the classroom he finds his work all laid out for him by his teacher. He knows exactly how much he is expected to do and whenever possible the teacher gives him help as soon as he asks for it so that no frustration over a difficult problem at hand will accumulate. If the teacher is working with one child, and another child asks for her help, she assures him she will be with him in a few minutes and is able to keep such a promise because the classes are small and the assignments relatively brief.

Again, even more important than the best planned procedures are the personal relations. Although the work is prepared for the child by the teacher, the attitude must be one of both teacher and child attacking the problem together. It is not a task set for the child by the teacher, but a task set by the teacher for the two of them to master together. To some children any adult-set task is unacceptable because what adults used to ask or expect of them in the past was usually bad for their physical or emotional well being.

While it may be possible in a progressive school for normal children to let the children set specific tasks for themselves, such a policy is impossible in a school for seriously disturbed children, or at least for those children who are not well ahead in their readjustment. Anyone even roughly familiar with paranoid, delusional, or autistically withdrawn children can well imagine that expecting them to set tasks for themselves would result in near bedlam, destructive for themselves and even more so for those who are further advanced and whose still feeble efforts at self-regulation would be crushed by the chaotic self-assertion of the more disturbed children.

Therefore, since the child must eventually be coping with adult-set tasks, ways must be found to convince him that accepting those tasks does not imply any giving up of rights to independence. The more we can show the child that we do not intend to interfere with his freedom to assert himself, the more likely he will be to eventually accept our assurance that the purpose of arranging the academic work for him is not to force him into some kind of strait jacket without respect for his natural desires (as he believes), but to present learning to him in ways that are exactly in line with his natural abilities and knowledge of the moment.

For example, a child can learn to read or write, if he chooses, in preference to studying arithmetic, as George did; he can read one book in preference to another, and so on. But such limited freedom is not enough to assure a child that his independence will be safeguarded if he is still in open conflict with all adults or with learning. These children need more fundamental demonstrations that their independence is not threatened by submitting, for the sake of learning, to some minimum of classroom routine.

In general, we have found that the more leeway we give the child in asserting himself in those areas where for particular reasons of his life history he needs it the most, the more cooperation he will eventually give us in most others. In one case the area in which he must show independence may be walking or moving around; in yet another it may be talking, or the freedom of verbal aggressions, and so on.

All truly progressive schools permit the child a great deal of freedom in expressing himself and in discharging tension or, one should say more correctly, these schools can prevent the accumulation of tension by not forcing the child to sit still. But few can permit freedom to the degree that that is possible in a treatment institution such as ours. This is because there are no needless restrictions of movement even outside of class, and the child is not tempted to take advantage of the freedom of the classroom to make up for restrictions in the home.

Moreover, the children in other schools may have unfavourable reactions to some types of disturbed behaviour or to provocative talk. Children at the School are so used to expressing their feelings freely that they do not react to such behaviour or disapprove of it in others. When, for example, the teacher was reading to the children from a book in which the sentence occurred: "Mothers love to care for their children," Bill volunteered, "My mother doesn't." [13] To this matter-of-fact statement the rest of the children did not react, because they were accustomed to hearing others as well as themselves expressing negative feelings about relatives as readily as positive emotions. In this way Bill's anger was immediately disposed of and did not interfere with his continuing to enjoy the story and then returning to his work.

In any treatment institution a very special emphasis is put on the full understanding of a child's needs and difficulties. The teacher who is part of such an institution is more aware than most teachers of what makes a child tick. Since her actions are not based on her opinion alone, but are backed up by observations made by all others who work with the child, her added security is a help when she works with a difficult child. She feels reassured, for example, if the psychiatrist tells her at staff meeting or in private conversations that a child's negativism is not due to any error she has made but that the child is equally negativistic to the psychiatrist. She can then watch and permit the child to discharge his negativism without growing insecure because she is not alone in thinking this is the constructive way to handle the child.

Another example may further illustrate: two of the children who are very gifted in painting suddenly stopped painting, and when their drawings became very stereotyped their teacher was worried. Going over this development at staff meeting revealed the fact that to some degree the children's previous concentra-

[13] Participant observer: Kathryn Howard.

tion on painting was an effort to escape into day-dreaming and a phantasy world, while their current disinterest was a healthy effort to cope with the world realistically. Then the teacher understood that what she had feared was a sign of regression actually signified good progress.[14]

In other instances the teacher's understanding of a child's emotional problems helps her to recognize emotional involvements and arrange things so that they do not interfere with the child's comfort in the classroom. For obvious reasons writers of primers and other schoolbooks introduce topics which are normally expected to interest the child and contain words that are part of the child's common vocabulary. Usually the material deals with stories that are supposed to arouse pleasant feelings in the child. Mother, father, brother, sister, baby, eating, and play situations therefore appear very often. But for many of our children these words evoke negative feelings or have strong ambivalent connotations, as Bill showed by his reactions.

But even on the much simpler level of word recognition, the child's past may interfere with his ability to perform in the present. Alice's intense jealousy of her younger sister (the "baby" as she called her disdainfully) and her mixed feelings about her father have been mentioned before. When her assignment required that she underline all words having the "y" sound in them, she underlined all words correctly with the exception of two: "daddy" and "baby." The teacher, aware that both words related to Alice's central difficulties, told her she had done fine, without going into details. Thus, without much ado, she showed Alice that she respected her emotional involvement and that it did not need to interfere with her academic success.[15]

Walter, like many severely disturbed children, learned to deal with his problems by isolating all meaningful events of his life from one another, and the events from their consequences. In order to maintain such an attitude he had to avoid all understanding, and with it all learning. He succeeded so well in play-

[14] Participant observer: Anna Lukes.
[15] Participant observer: Ida Bass.

ing the "goof" that he spent several years in an institution for feeble-minded children.

When Walter finally began to make progress in learning, he still tried for a long time to keep separate what he experienced and learned from that which was emotionally important to him. For this and many other reasons all words establishing connections were very difficult for him. Most difficult of all were those words establishing causal connections. But he had to learn them, of course, or he would never be able to give up his mechanism of isolating things from one another. Without an understanding of these words we could never even have shown him how he separated events and emotions that rightfully belong together.

To teach him the word "because" presented major difficulties. It required the patience and persistence that his teacher could offer him only because she understood what it would mean for him to master the word and the concept "because." After many, many failures Walter finally agreed to write the word on the blackboard. Slowly and painstakingly he drew, rather than wrote the word, and he drew eyes into the first letter "b," and then a hand at the top of the letter, a hand waving and reaching out; only then could he write out the rest of the word.

Walter was the child who kept his head, and particularly his eyes, covered up in the morning in order to avoid meeting the world, to avoid seeing it. Finally he would stretch out a hand from under the covers to establish a first contact. In class he showed graphically how for him to understand the meaning of the conjunction "because" meant to reach out into the world, to see it, and eventually to understand it. Without the teacher's understanding of Walter's problems she might not have been able to give him, at this moment, the understanding encouragement he needed. But she did understand why this word was so hard for him and she met him much more than halfway. It was her help that allowed Walter to go on with his feeble efforts to understand the "because" of his actions, and of life as it went on around him.[16]

[16] Participant observer: Kathryn Howard.

These two examples may also illustrate why it is important to hold some children to their tasks, while it is equally important for others that we do the opposite. Holding Alice to her task would have served no good purpose, since not being able to deal with the words "daddy" and "baby" did not block her total progress; in due time, her other progress would permit her to deal not only with the two words and the concepts they stood for, but also with the emotional problems they signified. Walter's situation was entirely different. Without a mastery of the concept "because" he could neither make progress with learning, nor with his emotional problems. Moreover, at that time it would have been impossible for Walter to understand the meaning and implications of the concept "because" anywhere but in the schoolroom. Only there, in the most objective setting, could he approach this difficult concept because the classroom stood in his mind for some distance from his immediate emotional problems.

The best way to avoid mistakes in deciding whether to insist that a child work on some learning task or other, or whether to disregard the matter entirely, is to follow the leads given by the child. Therefore, whenever possible, the children are encouraged to set their own tasks for themselves and then to live up to them. For example, they are asked how many sentences they wish to write, how many words they wish to study, and so on. Whenever their self-set assignments are within reason, no more is expected of them than meeting their own goals. Thus, if they feel well disposed toward learning on one day, they will set larger assignments for themselves than on other days.

Some children have been so pressed into conformity that the only way they could ever assert their independence was through negativism. Not learning in school was a type of assertion that became so important to them that it could be given up only after they had gained considerable self-respect through actual achievement. But before that was actually attained, they had to be free to express their old negativism, their old forms of independence in order to convince themselves that learning did not mean "to give in" (as they once thought it did), to give up independence. Such children need to be free to express their negativism and only after they have stated it most energetically are they able to settle down to constructive work.

Bill, among other ways, had been able to defy his mother by not learning to read. When encouraged to do so by his teacher, he replied, "Not goin' to, not goin' to." But the teacher held the book out to him and told him he was well able to read. So Louis read, "*Not* Rusty *not* ran *not* back *not* to *not* father *not* and *not* mother. *Not* his *not* name *not* is *not* Patches! *Not* he *not* looked *not* at *not* the *not* telephone *not* when *not* he *not* heard *not* Mr. *not* Wood *not* talk," and so forth.

After the teacher had shown she was unperturbed by his negativism, and after the need for assertion through negativism was spent, Bill became positively motivated once more and his application was good even though his resistance broke through again and again. But it was only by first making reading an experience in self-assertion through negativism that it eventually became a positive experience of self-assertion.[17]

In this as in other cases, teachers can follow their convictions about what is best for the child because their status within the School does not rest on the child's academic progress. They know that they gain more recognition when they can create a relaxed atmosphere in a class of tense and anxious children than when they can point to academic progress, which in many cases might have been gained at the expense of the child's security. The teachers do not need to please parents, nor be afraid of their criticism, and this gives them the freedom to experiment or to wait, when a child is not ready to learn yet.

One way to leave the teacher free of interference from parents is to keep her contact with them at a minimum. Naturally, parents are interested in getting to know their child's teachers,

[17] Participant observer: Kathryn Howard.

counselors, nurse, and whoever else has direct contact with the child and about whom the child may talk at length when he goes home on visits.

For just as understandable reasons, those who work with the child and often suffer under the impact of behaviour which parental attitudes may have created, are curious to get to know the parents. Thus the mutual desire to know one another is certainly present and legitimate. Experience, however, has taught us that such contacts do more harm than good. The teacher feels put on the spot when a parent asks her, for example, why his child has made no progress in learning for a whole year. The teacher may be utterly convinced that this was best for the child, and the only way to eventually overcome his fear and hatred of learning. Still, her very profession makes it difficult to state such a position without becoming defensive about it. It is much easier for the School's social worker or director to explain to a parent why a child cannot or should not be making progress in learning at the moment.

The relations between staff members and parents are mentioned in the context of a discussion of classroom learning because complaints about the lack of academic success are among the more frequent criticisms made by parents during the beginning of the child's stay at the School. Failures in learning are one of the touchier areas of parent-School contacts because in common thinking, continuous progress in learning is generally accepted as the basis for evaluating a teacher. Therefore the need for different standards in evaluating the teacher at a treatment institution seemed in need of some elaboration.

By the same token what has been said about the teacher holds equally true for the counselors. For example, next to complaints about lack of academic progress come the criticisms about lack of cleanliness, both as regards the child's body and his vocabulary. A counselor may be utterly convinced that it is necessary for a child's emotional development to let him get as dirty as he pleases during play, and in this conviction she may also be backed up by advice from psychiatrist and director. Still, the counselor, too, is very much a part of our society, subject to the prevalent standards and notions of behaviour. According to those standards, taking good care of a child entails the tacit obligation to see that he is neat and clean.

The parent's complaint to the counselor that he finds his child dirty behind the ears will tend to evoke an emotional response in the counselor who is directly responsible for the child's appearance and behaviour. So while he may be perfectly convinced that to let the child be dirty is what is best for the child at the moment, a parent's criticism will nevertheless revive unconscious (or not so unconscious) memories of his own training in cleanliness. He may then assert too defensively that letting the child be dirty was the right thing to do; or he may reveal in his reaction an unconscious feeling of guilt about not having taken better care of the child, about not seeing to it that he was cleaner.

We have found it best to have such criticisms or questions be answered by a person not directly or personally engaged in handling the matter under criticism. This is partly for the simple reason that whoever, in the last analysis, is responsible for such policies should also bear the responsibility of answering for them; but also because it is always simpler to refute—without emotional involvement—the accusations or criticisms directed against others, than it is to correct misapprehensions that arise over one's own actions.

Another reason that contacts between parents and those who do the direct work with the child should be avoided is that both have an understandable desire to "compare notes." The parent quotes a child as having told one story or another about teacher or counselor. The story may be a fascinating distortion, understandable only in terms of the child's delusional frame of reference or his hostile desire to hurt the parent's, teacher's or counselor's feelings, or it may be due to any number of needs which reveal themselves in this symptom.

The relatively less involved social worker or director is in a much better position to recognize such behaviour on the part of the child (and sometimes of the parent) as a symptom, and to deal with it accordingly. But this necessary mental distance cannot always be expected from a deeply involved person. The violently accused counselor, or the teacher whose actions are distorted by the child out of some inner need, may find himself confronting the child, or correcting the child's statements to the parents, even against his better insight into what would be best for the child's progress.

The physical remoteness of parents also has advantages for child as well as for teacher. Very soon after enrollment it becomes obvious to the child that neither misbehaviour nor failures in school can be used by him to frustrate his parents or get even with them. For example, the only way in which Max could get even with his very strict mother who totally controlled him, was to bring home bad report cards which upset her severely. During his first days at the school he insisted first that his parents and then that his counselors (whom he placed in parental positions), should be informed of his misbehaviour and lack of success in class. Only after he had realized that neither misbehaviour nor refusing to learn could be used to intimidate or annoy any adults, either at home or at the School, was he ready to settle down in class, both in regard to his behaviour and to studying.

I return now, from this digression into parent-staff relations to the freedom of the teacher to arrange the classroom in any way that will help the child most. With a child who fears printed matter, or is afraid to face several problems on a page, the teacher will use a sheet of paper and write out one problem at a time, or one sentence at a time and let him work with it until he is through. She will give him another problem to work on only if he wants one, and again in a personalized form, written out on a sheet of paper.

Children who are afraid to be watched while they study can learn only in relative seclusion, as if they were studying by themselves. Some children can study only when they feel protected on all sides; several children first began to read sitting curled up like babies in the kneehole under the teacher's desk. One boy who for years had been unable to recognize even the letters of the alphabet stayed there for months during class time. He would take a few flash cards to his hideout and whenever he was ready he would ask the teacher to replenish his supply. Finally, after he had mastered second grade reading—and with it his fear of reading—he emerged from his place of security. Only then was he prepared to be working in the presence of others. Like him, all children can decide whether and when they are ready for group activities in general, or for any particular subject.[18]

Since our classes are arranged neither by grade nor by age, children who have just successfully outgrown one emotional or learning difficulty are sometimes the best persons to help others with theirs. In this way they can test their own newly acquired gains and also fight the temptation to submit to their former behaviour in the way it is easiest to do that—namely, by fighting it in others instead of themselves.

To be able to group children on the basis of such considerations is often of great value. For example, Harry's teacher found it impossible at first to keep him in the classroom (Harry was then a seven-year-old delinquent). But when Joe, aged twelve, offered to help, she had a valuable ally. Joe had barely outgrown his own delinquency and valued his newly acquired status as a citizen of the classroom. Because of his recent past he had more of the necessary empathy with Harry than the teacher; but because of his still shaky controls, Harry's truancy was unbearable to him. At any rate he volunteered his help, and it was agreed that his desk and his chair should be placed beside Harry's.

Whenever Harry got restless, Joe sensed it much sooner than the teacher could have done. He would put his arm around the younger child consolingly and Harry was reassured by it, though he would never have permitted the teacher to touch him. Harry trusted Joe as a former delinquent, but was still suspicious of his teacher. If she came near him he became jittery, while Joe had

[18] Participant observer: Ruthevelyn Pim.

an easy time quieting him down. Joe himself enjoyed this very much, which was helpful both to him and to Harry. He particularly enjoyed the status he derived from the fact that he could control Harry where the teacher was helpless. In this way, there was no need for restraint, and later this permitted her to develop a good relationship to Harry much sooner than she could have done if she had needed to restrain him before.[19]

Not having to group children according to grade or age has other advantages, too. While rote learning and the repetitious activities it involves provide security for some children, it is beyond the endurance of others. But a child who has barely mastered a multiplication table and needs additional exercise in it may get it by playing store or through other games of that kind.

Sometimes even these games lose their interest, and then the techniques developed out of necessity in the one-room country school can be set to good advantage. But when a child is asked to teach his new knowledge to another child who has not yet reached that height of achievement, he not only does not mind but enjoys repeating over and over again the tables he would otherwise detest having to repeat. Similarly, a child might be most unwilling to reread a book he has barely mastered, and whose rereading might be profitable for him. But when we ask him to read it to another child he is more than ready to do so, and what seemed like a tedious exercise becomes a fascinating experience. There is nothing wrong with taking advantage of the pride a child feels in his new-won achievement to make it secure through repetition, always provided the teacher takes care that the teaching does not degenerate into a flaunting of superiority.

Overlearning to secure gains made is at all times sound educational policy. But insecure children need even more to feel absolutely secure about what they have learned, because any realization that they have forgotten what they thought they once knew is a terrible blow to the newborn conviction of their ability to achieve. We start the newcomer well enough below his own level of achievement to make sure he will succeed from the very

[19] Participant observer: Anna Lukes.

beginning. Similarly, we later protect him from disappointment by moving him most carefully ahead in his learning. Naturally, here, too, a middle course must be steered between protecting him against any possible failure and at the same time avoiding tedious repetition. Teaching others, a wide variety of reading material on the same level, playing games based on recently learned material, reading in connection with projects—all these are a help.

Playing together in the schoolroom, as well as teaching others in class, enlarges personal relations and bridges the gap between teacher and child. In a situation in which every child is a potential teacher, and most children have actually taught others, the fear of the teacher, of teaching and learning, diminishes.

Another advantage of mixing children of various ages and grade levels is that even younger, or less adequate children can take part in quite ambitious projects. The older child does the more difficult reading and planning, and the younger child can realize the greater stimulation that a more elaborate, mature project offers, not to speak of his pride at having taken part in so worthwhile a venture.

While this is true for younger children, it is even more true for older children who are far behind in academic achievement due to emotional difficulties. They feel bad about it, but they can compensate to some degree if they can nevertheless make a valuable contribution at their own age level to a project which is on their age level as a whole, but is beyond their academic level.

A twelve-year-old child who can barely manage second grade reading will gain confidence if he can draw paintings or graphs that are needed for a project on a fifth or sixth grade level of achievement. This tangible demonstration that in some things he does as well if not better than those who have reached the sixth grade academic level will encourage him. But it will do so only if in reading he is not expected to do as well as they, but can do his reading lesson on his own second grade level. Thus being part of a group working on the sixth grade level, and making contributions to it on that grade level in art, in construction with clay or wood, or by rigging up the stage and arranging the lighting for a play, is of great help to many intelligent but academically retarded children.

Sometimes it is good for a child to be moved from one group to another. In overcoming his initial learning inhibition, he may have experienced such severe difficulties in one group, or with one teacher, that although he may now be ready to learn, he still cannot do so in the old setting. Such children sometimes indicate a spontaneous desire to be placed in another classroom group. At the School, this is easily arranged regardless of the time of year, since all classes are ungraded and all teaching is planned individually. After such a move, the child may then suddenly make rapid progress in class.

Another and important aspect of classroom teaching in our setting is the contribution it can make to the understanding and solution of emotional problems not directly connected with learning. Well-organized classroom teaching presents concrete and definite tasks to the child. This, together with the more routinized nature of classroom activities, often permit him to state his most pressing problems to a teacher while her attention is focused on academic matters, rather than to persons whose wish to help him are more obvious to him. Moreover, children feel that since classroom activities must go on, the teacher will not follow up their statements any further than they wish her to, and the group will pay scant attention. Then they can express their problems in a relatively more objective way and without any far reaching involvement at the moment. On the other hand, the greater objectivity in evaluation of the well defined tasks is often most reassuring.

For example, both in psychotherapeutic sessions as well as with his counselors, Donald had repeatedly expressed great anxiety about whether he was making progress, and whether he would ever succeed in life. He was never able to work through these anxieties with them, nor could he accept as valid the encouraging statements of counselor or psychiatrist. The reason for his doubts became clear after he had been at the School for six months. At that time he told the psychiatrist: "When my teacher tells me I'm improving I believe her, because she knows. She can see how my work gets better. You other people can't." His teacher was therefore the first person to whom Donald was able to express his central anxiety about successful competition, because she was supposedly more objective in evaluating achievement, and was also (supposedly) not dealing with emotional problems. He also told her what he had not yet admitted to anyone else, that for a long time he had not wanted to make progress in class because he was afraid of outdoing his father.[20]

Concluding this chapter on classroom activities, I might add that those children who can take it go to class five days a week. The hours are from 9:00 to 12:00 (with a thirty to forty-five minute recess midway between), and then again from 1:30 to 3:00 (with another recess of from twenty to thirty minutes). Thus they spend an average of not more than three and one-half hours in the classroom during the normal school day. And again, if they wish, they can spend their recess time in the classroom, playing games, or whatever else they wish to do.

Even of the relatively short time officially devoted to studying, a considerable amount of time is spent in painting or drawing, in taking care of the animals in the schoolrooms (fish, turtles, hamsters, etc.) and other extracurricular activities, including playing games when an assignment is finished. Moreover, as said before, there are no study periods outside of class time, no assignments, nor any other written or academic work to be done after school. Even if a child wants to write letters home—which is infrequent—he can do so in class in place of a regular exercise in writing or composition.[21]

[20] Participant observer: Anna Lukes.
[21] The child's right not to write letters, if he does not wish to, is strictly observed. Parents are requested not to ask them, in their letters, to do so. Some parents take recourse to asking their children to acknowledge in writing the receipt of packages of candy or toys, in order to induce them to write. (The sending of packages as well as the writing of letters by parents is encouraged in order to prevent the child's thinking he has been

Nevertheless, once the learning inhibition is overcome, our problem is not that the children do not make enough progress because of the short time devoted to organized teaching and learning—on the contrary, we have to be careful then that they do not make too rapid academic progress and considerably exceed their academic age level. This might create problems for them on returning to public school, where they would either be thrown in with children who are several years their senior, or where they would have to sit in on the teaching of lessons they have long ago mastered. In either event classroom learning might again become dangerously unpleasant and boring. Because of the individual attention we give to each child, and because the task of learning is geared to the child's inclinations and is potentially enjoyable, most children, once their learning inhibitions are entirely removed, can easily make two or more years' academic progress in a single year's time.

Such excellent progress, plus the enjoyment of learning and the intellectual daring in attacking new problems on a realistic basis, then compensate the teacher for the trials and tribulations she has gone through with the child during the earlier periods when he was not yet adjusted to the classroom or to learning. It gives her the courage and emotional strength to carry on with a newcomer who is still in his negative period. Without these tangible demonstrations of the value of her methods it is doubt-

---

forgotten. Moreover, and in terms of his later adjustment, we wish him slowly to develop the conviction that his criticism of his parents was not entirely justified, and packages from home often help him to see his parents in a pleasanter light and in general add to his security.) In such cases the child is given the package and the parent is informed of why his letter was withheld. The parent's fear is understandable—that he may be forgotten if no contact in writing is maintained, since visits are rare—though it is unreasonable. No child ever forgets his parent after he has reached the age of reason. Actually the child whose relation to his parents was most disturbed will suddenly, after a year or two of not writing, begin to write regularly to his parents, but only after his difficulties with them have been worked through sufficiently, either for the old attachment to reassert itself, or for the child to express his desire to have decent relations with his parents. But this happens only after he is no longer so angry at them for what has happened to him in the past.

ful that she could go on year after year with her strenuous tasks.

In no case can the treatment of a child be considered completed until he is able not only to succeed in the classroom—careful tutoring could achieve that—but really wants to learn on his own and is able to enjoy classroom experiences. In addition, he must have become able to recognize which subject matter or learning experiences are most in line with his talents and interests; that is, he must have learned to achieve in accord with his developmental level and natural endowment—not as any other child may achieve, but as a particular individual who enjoys and takes advantage of his unique assets rather than one who is striving for a deadly uniformity. Both intellectually and academically, the child must have learned not only to accept himself as he is, but to strive to make the best use of his individual assets, within the limits of what society and he himself may expect of him, but emotionally independent of what an artificial norm may require.

7

food: the great socializer

THERE is hardly a time of day when some children
or other are not eating. In addition to our three main
meals, there are two regularly served snacks—one at about three
o'clock, the other before bedtime—but there is no schedule or
reckoning for the cookies and candies, etc., that the children
consume. We have found that candy eaten shortly before main
meals only rarely spoils the children's appetite, and that even
when it does, the children's health does not suffer. We do not
care when or what they eat, whether they eat mainly at meals,
or in between; our chief concern is that eating itself become a
pleasure to them.

We make it clear to every child that he is entitled to bread-
and-butter and milk whenever he wants it, and however much
of it he wants. We have found this the best and the easiest way
to relieve one of his most deep-rooted fears: that he may
have to go hungry. It is remarkable how even children who have
always had ample food will unconsciously equate a parent's disapproval with the unspoken threat of being deprived of food. By
the same token an abundance of food is experienced as an abundance not only of good things in general but of an over-all security.

We try to give the children the conviction that food is always
amply available, and the best way to do that is to be ready to

produce it at any time of the day or the night. It is in this sense that all times are mealtimes, though this does not lessen, but rather increases the importance of the main meals. With the children eating off and on during the day, they never get so hungry that they cannot afford to be social at table; thus there is no need to concentrate on the fare to the exclusion of the personal interchange that goes on at table.

The degree to which very deprived children will experience food as a symbol of all pleasures, instead of just nourishment proper, is typified by some of the statements George made during the earlier days of his rehabilitation. "You know," he said, "I'm one of those people who has to eat. Sometimes when I've just eaten a lot, I go out of the dining room and I get hungry again and I want some more food. And then, a little later, I'll ask for more even before it's time to eat again. I just like to eat and eat and I just have to have food around." [1]

This fear of going hungry can be the result of any deprivation the infant has experienced, so close, in infancy, is the connection between feeding and all other experiences. Julian's history shows very clearly the connection between early deprivation and delinquency, as one way a child can find of assuring himself that he can provide for his own needs independent of others. But the deprivation a child experiences, which may then lead to delinquency, need by no means be the result of his not getting enough food, or enough foods that he liked, as a young child.

Julian spent the first three years of his life in an orphan asylum where he was very well cared for, physically speaking. But the good care, including the well-prepared food, was not enough to counteract his feelings of severe deprivation which were due to the impersonal way in which his most essential needs were met. At the end of his third year he was adopted into a very wealthy family where he was overwhelmed not only with food, but with toys and all manner of material goods. When Julian was finally able to speak about the origins of his delinquency, he told his counselor that he launched into stealing by taking milk bottles

[1] Participant observer: Patty Pickett.

from milk wagons; that he used to take whole cases of bottles of fresh milk, drink as much as he could and hide what was left so he could always be sure of having milk when he needed it.

Julian went on to tell her that the milkman had accused him of the thefts but could never prove his case. This gave him the courage, he said, to steal other things, including money and jewelry, which he also buried in hiding places so as to have them when he needed them. But he insisted that if it hadn't been for the overpowering urge to steal milk, he might never have dared to steal other things—although this last statement we cannot be sure it is safe to accept at face value.[2]

Food is what first attaches many truants to the School; the security of a regular food supply is the great domesticator. Some children who became runaways as soon as they outgrew their infancy were first able to accept the School on such a basis. Of course these children cannot be expected to observe mealtimes. They come and go as they please. It is either hunger or cold that drives them to seek refuge, but more often it is hunger, because shelter they are shrewd about finding in basements, garages, or alleys.

While they were living with their parents, it was the food that drove them back regularly at night. But when they returned home hungry and exhausted, their parents received them with verbal abuse, if not punishment, so they suffered for the food before it was given to them, and this made even food, psychologically speaking, unacceptable. With so many strings attached to whatever they got, the children themselves became defensively unattached. In the end, even hunger could not move them to accept food as long as they had to feel it was being given to them by adults whom they hated and feared.

At the School, if we offered them food, they could eat it only if they could also maintain to themselves that accepting it did not oblige them, that we did not willingly feed them. They had to threaten us ominously with what would happen if we didn't hand over the food. The readiness with which the counselor got

[2] Participant observer: Patty Pickett.

food for them as soon as they appeared was interpreted not as an act of good will but as proof of our fear. As soon as the food was in sight they would grab for it. They snatched it from the table, or tore it out of the hand, again to maintain to themselves that it was only their boldness or our fear which kept them from going hungry. In this way they could eat without feeling obliged to conform in return.

Sandwiches, candy, milk, and so on, are placed on the beds of such children, where they will find it when they come back at night. At first they eat it without thought, but after a while they begin to expect it, and then slowly they begin to realize that it is not given to them because they have managed to intimidate us, nor have they wangled it out of us or robbed us.

Only much later, after a child has grown convinced of the advantages of having a bed and of getting food without strings attached, his liking of food and bed, which are also in the same house, gives him a first feeling of having a home. Then he may be ready to form some beginnings of a personal relationship, and in a step after this one food can again be used to help him master the next steps in domestication. When he then comes home tired and hungry and finds a person ready to feed him, someone he has learned to consider a friend, he may slowly open up to that person about what drove him to run away. When this relationship grows strong enough we can use it to further domesticate the child by setting some limitations on his truancies (such as returning before midnight). If the child then comes home considerably later than the time mutually agreed upon, he may be given not a wide variety or his favourite foods, but only what is considered the unconditional right of every child at the School: bread-and-butter and milk. If he asks for chocolate or cake, we explain that such things he may have only if he comes home on time, as agreed.

But imposing such restrictions or encouraging the child to set them for himself can be tried only by the person to whom the child has formed a relatively strong relation, though not necessarily a stable one; stable relations are still far beyond the child's emotional maturity at this time. If another person to whom he is not yet attached were to try to restrict him, he would lose his trust in the School and the gains made in domesticating him might be lost. He would either react with explosive behaviour, or would run away again without returning, because he would no longer feel sure of a friendly reception. From his "friend" even a casual reception he now experiences as pleasant and assuring; from all others it has to be most indulgent if it is not to drive him away again. Only if he is received by a person he is attached to will a child in this phase of development feel guilty about returning later than he himself has agreed to. But this guilt feeling is the only factor which will later on make him want to stay put.

At a much later stage in domestication, the taste the child has acquired for good food will further help him to give up his running away. The typical runaway child is far too anxious, too tense, too harassed to enjoy food; he needs it, he devours it anxiously, but he does not enjoy it. Nevertheless, during the solitary meals at night when he eats and talks with a favoured adult, the child will slowly learn to enjoy a meal, and the social contact around it. When adequately handled, this social contact plus the guilt feeling about running away will eventually domesticate the runaway child in all important respects.

After that, runaway children present almost no problem in the eating situation. Thus, while food is the best means of domesticating them, once they have learned to come regularly to meals and are able to sit through them in peace, they are hearty eaters who enjoy their food without too many difficulties.

Frank, who had been a runaway child, stated once how the abundance of satisfaction at the School, and particularly of food, made asocial behaviour unnecessary. Speaking of a staff meeting he had observed going on in the morning, he remarked to the nurse that he supposed we were "talking about the kids and their problems." Then he added, "You know, I had a problem. I used to steal and run away before I came to the School, but I don't now." When asked if he knew why he had changed, he replied, "Sure, at School you get everything you want. I don't have to steal." [3] (Offhand, this seems such a glib statement that I might add that up to that date, no one at the School had ever discussed with him the reasons for his truancies or why he had given them up.)

Early deprivation seems to lead to greediness in many respects, although greediness about food seems to be one of the most important and frequent characteristics of children who have not yet overcome the results of deprivation in infancy. Keith was another child who was adopted at the age of three by a very wealthy family. Things got off to a bad start, partly because he, like Julian, felt that he had been adopted less in his own right than as a companion for the parents' only daughter after they learned they could have no more children of their own. For both of these children, the deprivation they experienced before adoption was combined with the feeling that they could never achieve what their new sisters enjoyed: being the adoptive parents' own child. This added new fuel to the old feeling of never getting enough, and aggravated the greed it gave rise to.

Keith's feeling that nothing could ever satisfy him expressed itself most characteristically when his counselor took him shopping. One day they were downtown at Marshall Field's and after they had eaten and bought several toys for Keith it was obvious there was still something he wanted. When his counselor asked him what she could get that would please him, he said, "Buy me Marshall Field's [store] and I'll be satisfied." On other occasions, too, when he was given whatever he asked for and more, it was never enough. When his counselor asked what he expected her to do to make things more pleasant for him, Keith answered: "Just buy me every toy there is, and maybe then I'll be satisfied." Repeated statements of the same kind revealed that whenever he saw something he did not already have, it created unmanageable greed in him. One day on another shopping trip, when he had bought a number of things and could think of nothing else in particular he wanted he was still down at the

[3] Participant observer: Ruth Frank.

mouth. When his counselor asked what was wrong and what he wanted, he said, "Buy me all of 55th Street [the neighbourhood shopping district], maybe then I'll be satisfied." It was the same in the dime store where he bought everything he wanted and still looked at things hungrily. There, too, he said, "Why don't you buy me the whole dime store?" Whatever he laid eyes on made him discontented although he himself knew that his desires were so exaggerated they could never be filled. "Buy me all downtown Chicago," he said. "Maybe then I'll be satisfied." [4]

At the School we always keep a well-supplied candy closet. This closet with its stock of a wide variety of cookies, candies, chocolates, etc., is a source of security for many children, including Keith. Several times during the day Keith felt the need to supply himself with additional amounts of candy—often only to convince himself that the supply would never run out. He was particularly enamoured with the idea of a candy closet.

Before he came to the School, his greed for food had been partially held in check by his mother who was afraid of his overeating and tried to keep him to a diet. Nevertheless, he was sixteen pounds overweight when he entered the School. For the first year and a half of his stay, he took advantage of the unlimited food supply and overate constantly. During this time even the visible abundance of food did not lessen his greed in eating and at the height of the period he was more than forty pounds overweight.

Then slowly and without any move on our part Keith began to cut down. Over a period of three months (the 20th to 23rd months of his stay at the School) his overweight decreased by ten pounds.

Then came Halloween. For some time Keith had been at a loss as to how to dress up for going "tricks-and-treats." In general, we do not encourage the children to "dress up" in their ordinary play. We particularly try to avoid any costumes that would distort their appearance so much that they would be afraid of not being recognized, or unable to recognize themselves

[4] Participant observer: Gayle Shulenberger.

in the mirror. Our children already have a faulty sense of personal identity and many suffer from an outright fear that they may even lose their identity. Therefore, we prefer to avoid any experiences that might foster anxieties in this respect. But within these limitations they are free to dress up, particularly at Halloween.

On the afternoon before Halloween Keith's tension increased. The idea of dressing up revived his barely controlled violent aggressions, and with them his anxiety about things he might do, and things other children might do to retaliate. Not to dress up, to forego tricks-and-treats as some other children of his age group decided to do, was impossible for Keith because his greed was still too active to let him pass up this chance for collecting food.

In line with the aggressive phantasies which had finally led to his placement at the School he had first planned to dress up as Dracula or the Frankenstein monster.[5] The gory plans were known to one of his counselors and made it hard for him to retract them without loss of face—or what Keith considered necessary for maintaining his status. Therefore, from an appropriate moment on, Keith's other counselor began to help him exclusively with his Halloween preparations.

Here, as in other critical situations, both regular counselors and often additional counselors are made available to the children whenever possible. Of course, critical situations cannot always be foreseen, and hence it is not always possible to have more than one counselor taking care of a group at such times. But from experience we have some notion of when they are likely to occur. Halloween is one of the days we can plan for in advance. Hence both his regular counselors were available to Keith on that day.

As the afternoon wore on Keith became more and more excited and anxious. As he had learned to do in such moments, he fell back on candy for restoring his emotional balance. Then he asked his counselor to take him to the candy closet but when he got there, in addition to much candy, he also grabbed some empty candy boxes, put them on top of one another and said

[5] Participant observer: Clarence Lipschutz.

they would make a nice hat. He liked playing with the boxes so much that suddenly he decided to dress up as a candy closet. So he made himself a costume comprising a great variety of candy boxes and candy wrappers which he stuck on at odd places. As "Candy Closet," he enjoyed himself tremendously at our Halloween party and had no fear of going out for tricks-and-treats. When he went for tricks-and-treats, he was particularly pleased whenever people recognized that he was supposed to be Candy.[6]

Keith's dressing up as candy contained a measure of self-irony. Of this he was now capable, because although he was still extremely greedy, his overeating had been on the decline for the preceding three months.

His identifying himself with the candy closet that day was actually a turning point. This he revealed the day after Halloween when for the first time he admitted how he had always hoarded candy because he was so afraid that some day the supply might run out. He had kept it a secret, but now he showed his counselor a box in which he kept a large supply of candy "for emergencies."[7]

At about the same time Keith took to distributing some of his surplus candy to other children. From adults he still had to get a surplus of food, particularly candy, but he now enjoyed giving away some of the overage instead of hoarding it as before. This improved his relations to other children a great deal, and they became much readier to accept him. While before the sight of Keith's greediness was rather threatening to them, his new enjoyment of food became a social asset, and now eating, and life in general became more enjoyable for Keith.

Even after children are domesticated about eating we do not force them to join us at any meal. Usually they have a half hour's leeway about coming into the dining room. If they fail to make it within that time limit and if we feel, psychologically speaking, that they could easily have made it, they get at least the main

[6] Participant observer: Gayle Shulenberger.
[7] Participant observer: *Idem*.

course and as much milk and bread-and-butter as they want, but not necessarily the full meal. This holds, of course, only for those cases where we feel that the child should be ready to accept regular mealtimes, and that his rehabilitation would gain most at that point by his learning to conform in his eating habits.

Others are given whatever they want whenever they want it, so as to make them like being at the School (and like us), and to make eating so attractive that eventually they will join us at the regular meals. In order to do so it is often necessary for one adult to eat with a child alone. Eating with others has been so unpleasant for some children that they have first to relearn with only one other person that eating does not need to be a misery; only then are they ready to eat with a group. Some children mess so badly with their food that other children are revolted and cannot be expected to eat with them. With these children, too, an adult has to eat alone until their eating behaviour has improved. Incidentally, with the exception of Sundays, the children are served at the tables by maids so as to make meals as comfortable as possible.

It is much more difficult, while the children are eating, to help those who suffer from long-standing eating problems, although those are the times we can use most effectively with them. Children who have always fought with their parents at mealtimes, for example, are particularly slow about learning to enjoy meals at the School. To them, too, the enjoyment of eating must usually be restored outside of the regular meals. Once we have succeeded in that, they learn to follow the compelling example of other children, and slowly the enjoyment of main meals is established; then, as a matter of course, the need for much of the in-between eating subsides.

Eating problems appear even more forcefully at breakfast, the first regular meal of the day, than at other meals. There, before meeting the more mature tasks of the day, a symbolic return to early feeding habits helps the child to enforce his security. Some children combine this with a discharge of hostility by jabbing knives through the covering of their milk bottles to make holes.

for their straws. After thus demonstrating at one stroke either their strength or their ability to defeat enemies, or that they can provide themselves with the simple necessities of life, they then suck the milk through the straws. Some have to chew up or otherwise destroy many straws before they have discharged enough tension to be able to enjoy their sucking. Glasses are available for drinking, of course, but they are used only rarely at breakfast, even by older or more inhibited children who find it below their dignity to suck milk through a straw at other meals.

In general, we have found that even eating difficulties of long standing disappear very soon if they originally came about as an open defiance of parents, or a means of controlling them. Since there is no emphasis on eating or on table manners, and since the child may eat or not eat as he pleases, he can neither control nor provoke us through not eating or through his complaints. Moreover, other children set a vivid example by their enjoyment of food, although it is equally important to convince the child that he cannot control or deprive others of their pleasure in eating by his own misbehaviour.

Matters are much more complicated if the child's eating disturbance is not due to any conscious efforts at control or provocation, but has become an unconscious neurotic symptom, as in cases of anorexia, or of paranoid poisoning delusions.

Food intake represents one of the child's earliest contacts with the external world. It is the activity around which personal relationships first develop and around which they may first break down, with the most dangerous and far-reaching consequences. Hence, although an eating disturbance as such may disappear, the emotional problems originally connected with it may well persist. In this sense, our eating with the children often gives us easy and direct access to the disturbance and also to the working through of its origin in early upsetting experiences.

Paul's anxiety about not having enough food subsided only after he had provided his own reassurance by repeatedly inspecting the food supplies in the kitchen and storerooms. This was a compulsive activity of his that lasted for some time and gave him a great deal of security. One Sunday the milk truck was late in arriving. He was extremely upset as the breakfast hour approached, and he came back from his inspection trips to tell his counselor there was not enough milk on hand. She listened to his report but told him not to worry, that if the truck was really going to be late, she would just go out and buy whatever milk we needed at the corner grocery. In a little while, since the truck did not come, the two of them actually did that, although the regular milk supply arrived shortly afterward. This practical demonstration that we could always get whatever food was needed regardless of whether regular suppliers met their obligations or not, made a lasting impression on him and his anxiety and compulsive inspections subsided. It was interesting to note that as soon as emotional energy was freed in this way, he immediately applied it constructively to learning about the world around him.[8]

We have already noted the role of the milk bottle at breakfast. Here it may be said that sooner or later nearly every child has returned at least during mealtimes to sucking milk slowly through a straw out of the glass or the bottle. In addition, many children return to bottle feeding in the true sense of the word at one time or another, although this must be dosed very carefully if we wish to avoid permanent regression.

At one time, a group of six- to nine-year-old boys began to make speedy progress for some time after they had transferred the use of the baby bottle from the "session" rooms (in which they played or talked with staff members individually) to the dormitory, and for several weeks each of them took a baby bottle to bed with him. The value of the enjoyment of such regressive behaviour, when correctly used, is now widely recognized. But it is much easier to make good use of such a device and to dose it correctly in a setting where the total behaviour of the children is known, and where we can take best advantage of all of it, than in a treatment situation which remains apart from the rest of the child's life.

[8] Participant observer: Gayle Shulenberger.

In practice, however, matters are not quite as simple as they might seem, and many steps must precede any use of the baby bottle before it becomes beneficially useful. While its use is a valuable aid in a well-established relationship (which is a maturing experience), returning to the baby bottle outside of such a relationship may bring undesirable withdrawal from the world, may further regression into autistic isolation. The enjoyment of primitive pleasures within a more mature relationship can free the individual; the return to primitive pleasures to escape the challenge of socialization only restricts him. This is illustrated by the difference between solitary drinking or the escape into drunkenness, as contrasted with the social enjoyment of a drink that lends ease to personal relations.

A portion of Ann's history at the School may also illustrate first the asocial and then the personalized use of the baby bottle. Ann came to the School at the age of seven. She was a pretty child, hyperactive, delinquent, and basically an utterly confused little girl, unable to understand her own actions or those of the people around her. Her father died when she was three, and since that time she had lived in a variety of more or less unsuitable homes. Her severely disturbed mother had exercised a pernicious influence on the girl even before the father died, and since then even more so.

As a child the mother had received no physical or emotional care that was adequate and had often been exposed to severe physical hardship. From her only child she wanted the warmth, comfort, and companionship she had missed in her own childhood. Unable to give these things to her daughter, she even tried, when good physical and emotional care were offered to the little girl in a fosterhome, to compete for the fostermother's attention. Thus doubly deprived, Ann tried to achieve the impossible: she tried to provide herself with the comforts she needed, and to escape at the same time from an insufferable situation. To do the first, she tried to find comfort in, and to seduce others to comfort her through, provocative, conspicuous and prolonged masturbation. To achieve the latter she was constantly on the run. Often her abortive attempts at running away had the characteristics of pseudo-suicidal attempts, such as when she deliberately ran out into the street in front of oncoming cars.

At the School she soon returned to the point where human relations had broken down in her infancy, or had failed to develop at all. She returned to using the baby bottle intensively. As she had tried to use masturbation to satisfy herself and to gain satisfaction from others, she now used the baby bottle in ways that revealed both its autistic and interpersonal connotations to her.

In individual play sessions with her counselor she asked that the baby bottle be filled with milk. In this way she reassured herself that a return to more primitive autistic satisfaction would be available to her even if the personal relationship to her counselor should break down. For many months, at the beginning of each session, she would request that the bottle be filled, but would never touch it during the session. As soon as the session was ended, however, she would take hold of it, and as she and her counselor walked along the corridor, away from the room they had been talking in or playing in together, she would suck vigorously out of the bottle. Thus her behaviour indicated that at this stage she still had very little ability for maintaining relationships; they existed for her only while she was in actual contact within the seclusion of the room, and the relation had no permanency as soon as the very special setting was left. She needed the tangible assurance of the filled bottle to believe that infantile and autistic satisfaction was available to her should the contact with her counselor be interrupted, and she availed herself of it as soon as that particular contact was ended.[9]

Then came a time when these contacts with her counselor were augmented on a higher level of integration by her eating a great deal of candy. As the importance and depth of Ann's relation to her counselor increased she would occasionally and tentatively take up the baby bottle and suck out of it during the hour, but in doing so she seemed to need to put some distance between

[9] Participant observer: Joan Little.

herself and the counselor—greater distance than when talking or playing with her. All primitive pleasures still had rather autistic than social connotations for her, but at least she began to experiment with whether primitive satisfaction might not also become the carrier of personal relations.

Ann took a further step in accepting infantile pleasures on a personal basis when she asked the counselor to hand-feed her with candy. The final step in closing the gap between personal relations and primitive satisfactions was reached when she used sucking from the bottle as a means of coming close to her counselor: she then sucked her milk out of the bottle as she sat in the counselor's lap, happy and in very good contact.[10]

This relationship, now cemented by much needed infantile satisfactions, Ann set to immediate use in what was quite a mature step for her. Up to this time, Ann had been entirely run by several older children whom she had copied uncritically. Now, however, as she sat on the counselor's lap, she interrupted her sucking long enough to make some valid critical remarks about a painting that had been hanging on the wall for several weeks, a picture done by one of the older girls she had depended on entirely.

Thus, in her use of the baby bottle, she went through the various steps from primitive satisfaction in lieu of a personal relationship, to primitive satisfaction within a personal relationship, and finally to a personal relation enhanced by infantile pleasures—the last as her source of strength in a first bid for personal independence. Ann was able to make these steps more or less autonomously because although in her case the ability to form personal relations was blocked, the function of eating had not suffered severe interference.

When Grace came to the School at the age of nine she was withdrawn autistically most of the time; the rest of her time was filled by megalomanic and anxious phantasies. But there was no time when she was not totally disoriented, even as regarded time,

[10] Participant observer: Joan Little.

space, and her own identity. Unable to cope with the world around her, she tried to get what she needed or wanted by any means that came to her head, including utter destructiveness or stealing. Almost nothing is known about the first three years of her life, but from the little information available it can be assumed that Grace was never adequately cared for. Her father died when she was three. Shortly thereafter her mother deserted her and never again showed any interest in her. Grace was placed in a nursery where she remained till she was six and from then, until her coming to the School, she lived in various fosterhomes, none of which was able to cope either with her or her problems. In the meantime her disturbance became more and more acute and led, in addition to other serious symptoms, to a severe intellectual inhibition. Thus Grace's greediness, like Keith's, was due to a variety of severe and early deprivations.

For a long time Grace's greatest anxiety was that there might not be enough to eat and that she was going to starve. She, too, could only form personal relations—and through them develop the beginnings of a personal identity—after she felt assured that food was abundant and available at all times. And like Ann, she could only enjoy the baby bottle after her first greed and anxiety about food had subsided to some degree. The limited food supply of the baby bottle became pleasurable only after her starvation anxiety no longer interfered with the pleasure of sucking. As long as quantity alone was what counted, she found no real pleasure in eating, and no personal contact could be built up around it.

For many months Grace overate, remaining in the dining room after the other children had left and scavenging for food despite the large helpings she had already eaten. After every meal, she wrapped food in a napkin and took it with her for fear she might be hungry before the next meal. Whenever a course was put on the table, Grace jumped up and down excitedly and looked at her counselor for assurance that she would get enough. Frequently she ate directly from the plate without utensils in order to finish in time for a third and fourth helping although no limitations were put on the amount she ate. After a time she required fewer helpings of food. Then her eating habits changed from extreme greed to extremely infantile behaviour. She sucked her food, took it out of her mouth, looked at it and returned it to her mouth. Occasionally she spat things out. But slowly she gave up wrapping various foods in her napkin and began instead to carry a small jar about in which she kept a ration of candy.[11]

Like other children who have never before become truly socialized because they have early experienced severe deprivation of their most essential biological needs, Grace first learned to relate to others around eating. Progress in other areas of socialization also began around food or around eating. She learned to organize her life only after she had learned to organize her possessions; and she learned to be orderly about these things only after she had learned to be orderly about what was still of paramount importance to her: food.

She cleaned her candy box repeatedly, stacked candy bars according to colour and size, counted them and announced spontaneously as she handled them, "This is fun!" Later she began to clean her shelves, too. She arranged and rearranged her toys as she had previously arranged her candy bars and in the same pattern she wanted her clothes laid out neatly and exactly for the next morning. Her bed had to be perfect and she liked to sweep the floor around it and even underneath it. It was as if orderliness in the objects related to her had to follow the example of orderliness in regard to food, and both had to take place before inner order could come.[12]

With children like Julian, Keith, and Ann, the anxiety about food originated more or less directly in the severe deprivation they experienced as infants, and often for some time afterward. But these children are not the only group of children to whom eating, and all that goes with it, is of greatest significance. There are other children with whom it is much more complex to restore them to pleasure in eating. They are, in their majority, not

[11] Participant observer: Marjorie Jewell.
[12] Participant observer: Joan Little.

delinquent or otherwise asocial children. They are children whose early experiences led them to develop (or one might better say did not permit them to develop further emotionally) into children whose behaviour and thought patterns can best be compared to those of adult schizophrenics, rather than those of adult neurotics or delinquents. Some of these children came to the School as autistically withdrawn children (like Walter and Emily), others as children who were so totally out of contact with the world that they appeared feeble-minded (like John), or they were children who suffered from a variety of delusions of reference or persecution (like George).

Walter had been a feeding problem all his life. He suffered from loss of appetite, he vomited and had severe food allergies. At the School he remained a poor eater for some time. He lived almost exclusively on sandwiches of jelly and butter that only he was allowed to prepare. He was always deeply withdrawn into himself but this was even worse at the dinner table. All efforts to get him away from his daydreams or to establish contact met with failure, until one day his counselor explained where the various foods came from that the others were eating. Walter could be interested in such conversations only for very fleeting moments, but since they were the only ones he responded to at all his counselor continued her efforts without quite knowing why. After several weeks, she happened to tell him about the pineapple the others were eating, and which he rejected decisively as he did most other foods. She told him how it had been grown, and then prepared, canned, and shipped all the way from Hawaii for the children to enjoy at their breakfast. Walter was finally interested, but what interested him particularly was whether anyone could have tampered with the can between Hawaii and its being served at the School.[13]

From these and related questions it became clear that many of his eating difficulties were connected with a fear of being poisoned. His fears grew calmer as his counselor continued and enlarged on her discussions about how food that was served at the

[13] Participant observer: Josette Wingo.

School was safe from interference. But he had to prove this to himself by watching the food being prepared in the kitchen, to make sure that his delusional enemies could not get at it.

These talks and the observations he made allowed him to develop contact at least while he was eating, and with at least one person. The security he derived from the relationship then permitted him to open up about his traumatic experiences, particularly about the most consequential of several probably suicidal attempts.

It appeared that when Walter was three years old, he had swallowed a relatively large quantity of ammonia. He had had to be hospitalized, and from the hospital he was sent to an institution for retarded children because he was considered to be feebleminded. His stay among the feeble-minded children was very unhappy and he always thought of it as a punishment. The swallowing of ammonia he saw as an attempt by his enemies to poison him, and being kept at the institution as another of their doings. There, for one reason or another, he never got enough to eat, or so he believed. He was convinced that the plan was to starve him to death there, or to poison him.

For some time Walter would talk about these things only at mealtimes, when he was eating with his counselor and the other children. All efforts to discuss them with him in individual sessions, even when he ate there, had to wait until much later to succeed. Apparently he had to be tempted to eat by the example of other children, and to see that the food they ate was not poisoned, before he could afford to discuss his fears. Another reason may have been that this was the same situation—eating with other children—in which he had first developed the idea of being sent to an institution to be poisoned; or he may only have been able to talk at mealtimes because his counselor could not devote all her attention to him in the dining room since she also had to look after the other children. In this way he was free of the impact of her undivided attention, which was then a more intense personal contact than he could bear.

Later, and again at mealtime, Walter talked about experiences that took place still earlier than the ammonia poisoning. His mother had severely and frequently criticized the alcoholism of his father, to whom he was quite attached. She had also warned the boy repeatedly not to be like his father. At first this made him afraid of all liquids as being poisonous, and later he began to hate all foods, liquid or not. But underlying these poisoning fears were even earlier feeding experiences which expressed themselves in what can best be described as an aggressive biting or chewing or munching of food; this was a long-drawn-out process, combined with a great reluctance to swallow the food in the end. He behaved as if the swallowing itself was painful, and even a little frightening.[14]

As time passed and relationships were established at least between him and some of his counselors, he used his individual sessions with one of them mainly to bite and chew aggressively on the nipple of a baby bottle. Walter had to act out and work through his aggression in regard to eating or sucking before either of them could become pleasurable for him. For long time periods he bit at the nipple with almost no sucking of the liquid out of the bottle, and without swallowing. His expression during the whole procedure was one of greatest anger. After this had been going on for some time, he used dolls one day, to re-enact an elaborate story about a small child whose parents were either dead or had disappeared. The child was then sent to an institution until a new mother came and took him out. This mother was very nice and was appalled that the child knew so little and could neither read nor spell; so she arranged for him to go to school and learn. In his story, Walter stressed the fact that both school and home were in one building, showing how important it was for him—as for most anxious children—to have both combined, to have everything pertaining to his life taking place within one compact unit. As he worked through important elements of his traumatic past and became able to see the present more favourably, he also became ready to learn. Walter was then eleven years old, and although he had been tutored before coming to the

[14] Participant observer: Josette Wingo.

School, and we had made efforts to teach him all along, he actually learned to recognize letters then for the first time, and shortly thereafter began to read.[15]

Emily was eight when she came to the School. Her father had first had little time for his daughter, and was then away in the army for several years. A physical handicap prevented the mother from taking adequate care of her daughter. In view of the mother's difficulties Emily was entrusted to a series of nurses and maids who were instructed to adhere to a rigid feeding schedule, and later to equally rigid procedures as regarded her education to cleanliness and all other matters. From infancy on Emily's behaviour was autistic. She withdrew entirely from a world which offered too little satisfaction. Intense and prolonged rectal and vaginal masturbation filled her days and were interrupted only by the stimulation of her mouth by the same two fingers with which she preferred to masturbate. This oral stimulation, too, often had more of the character of masturbation than of sucking.

Emily had been threatened repeatedly about the consequences of her masturbation, and had also been punished because of it. For these and many other reasons her phantasies were filled with fearful images, both about what might happen to her and what she might do to others. Her dominant anxiety was that others were trying to kill her.

Emily had been an eating problem for years. Once at the School, however, she lost her general fear of eating rather soon. But any food that came to her from the outside, particularly cookies or candy sent from home (or whatever seemed to her to have come from home) was enough to revive her acute anxiety that people were trying to poison her. Our first indications of her poisoning fears came when she was given a box of cookies one day. She took one and ate it and then screamed at the top of her lungs that the counselor was killing her, choking her, strangling her. Finally the counselor understood that what disturbed her so

[15] Participant observer: Gayle Shulenberger.

much was that she thought the cooky she had eaten had been sent her from home.

It was only after a lengthy explanation about where the cookies came from, exactly, that Emily felt somewhat reassured. Then she checked with the counselor about what each of them had eaten all day. And again, it was only after she had satisfied herself that both of them had eaten the same food, prepared by the same cooks in the same kitchen, that Emily felt sure no one had poisoned her.[16]

Here, I might add a further note about School meals in general. Because of the children's poisoning fears—but even more so because of the feeling nearly all of them share of having been cheated out of their due by adults—they derive great satisfaction from observing the staff eating exactly the same fare that they do, and not only when staff members are "on duty" and would naturally eat with the children. It is particularly assuring to them to see staff members eating exactly what they do, and in their presence, even when they are "off duty." Almost every child has checked, at one time or another, to make sure that at the table where staff members eat together when they are off duty, nothing appears that is not also included in the fare the children eat. Quite a few children will check this for weeks until they feel satisfied they are not being cheated. For similar reasons we make it easy for them to check the menus. This permits them to feel sure in advance that there will be enough to eat and enough things that they like. In addition, the menu for a whole week is always posted in advance so that the children can check to make sure they get everything we have planned for them.

To return to Emily, it was some three months later that she described how she used to feel about all food that had been served to her at home being unsuitable for eating. A group of the children were eating cookies as they walked to the dime store, and some of them were talking about food at their homes. At this Emily began to talk to herself and said: "Father tries the food

[16] Participant observer: Joan Little.

and spits it on the floor. Mother tries the food and spits it on the floor. The child tries the food and spits it on the floor." These images she repeated several times.[17]

A short time later one of her counselors announced that she was leaving on a week's vacation. At first Emily pretended not to hear and remained totally withdrawn until the next meal. Then she finally made use of food to express her unhappiness about the impending separation. Being told that one of the persons to whom she had finally formed some elementary attachment was going to desert her made all foods seem poisonous again, or at least non-edible.

She took a little boat her counselor had given her the day before into the dining room with her. Once there she asked for cereal. The counselor served her cereal but Emily only filled her boat with it and dumped the whole thing on the floor. Then she asked for scrambled eggs and did the same with them. The toast she pulled into little pieces and threw down in the same way. She rejected all efforts by her counselor to feed her, but finally became less cross and consented to sit on the counselor's lap. Then she put her hand over her heart and said she had a pain there. The counselor promised her she was only going away for one week and described who would take care of her in the meantime. After a while Emily relaxed and finally cuddled up in the counselor's lap for the rest of the meal.[18]

In contrast to Walter and Emily whose early histories were free of any physical traumatization, John's schizophrenic-like behaviour could be traced back, in part, to a combination of physical and psychological injuries which occurred at the beginning of his life (as described on page 108). Here it might be added that in John's case, this was later reinforced by another injury to his mouth at a critical moment of his development. I might also add that John's mouth infection required artificial feeding immediately after birth, and that he had to remain at the hos-

[17] Participant observer: Joan Little.
[18] Participant observer: *Idem.*

pital for several months. The treatment involved was very painful so that eating became unpleasant from the very beginning.

When John finally left the hospital, his development had gotten off to a bad start. His mother was warned that she must feed him at all costs. But in terms of his unfortunate experience, John was unwilling to eat and this led to forced feedings, which he fought and resented. All this, together with the mother's anxiety, made their relationship distinctly unpleasant. John spit at her, and also spit out the food that she forced into his mouth.

Desperate because of the physician's warning, the mother was insistent about feeding him and every meal became a major battle lasting for hours. John's head was held firmly and the food was forced so deep into his throat that he could no longer spit it out. In order to accomplish this John was held down so firmly that neither kicking nor moving was possible; thus he was deprived of all outlet for his fear and his anger, and no discharge of tension through crying or movement was possible. The only way in which John could express his utter dislike of the whole process of feeding was to gag in anticipation of food, and to vomit once the food had been forced down his throat.

John's relation to his mother went from bad to worse. In desperation about his not eating and also annoyed by his resistance, she followed the advice of a physician and began to re-feed him what he had vomited. Under the impact of such a routine, not only did John's motor development remain slow and inadequate, but also his general growth including his intellectual progress. This, of course, only added to the parents' anxiety about John's not eating. At the age of three and a half, John finally began to show more activity in meeting the world. The parents tried to encourage his feeble efforts at exercising, and because of their insistence he prematurely and anxiously began walking the stairs. It was at this point that he fell down a few stairs and hurt his mouth and gums so badly that many stitches had to be taken.

This second injury to his mouth once again made eating a torture. Every movement of his mouth hurt. Moreover, he blamed his parents for the injury because he felt they had "forced" him to walk the stairs. The injury, his animosity toward his parents, and the painful forced feedings which were aggravated by the new injury made him hate life altogether. His loss of appetite and rejection of all food became so bad that eventually he was hospitalized with anorexia (inability to eat).

When John came to the School he showed a morbid and monomanic preoccupation with food. He was forever talking or having phantasies about it, and at the same time hated eating. He would talk about food by the hour. His feelings were best expressed in a story he made up for a TAT (a test of his imagination) in which one person said to another: "Oh, we must get some ice cream. Come, that's the best thing in the whole world. That's better than God . . . They didn't love God, they liked ice cream instead." Yet if John so much as saw food, even ice cream, he began to gag. When hunger finally forced him to eat, more often than not he would vomit up part of whatever he had eaten.

At the School, contrary to his previous experiences, his hesitation about eating led to no efforts on our part to force him to eat, his vomiting to no revulsion, recrimination or exaggerated expressions of compassion. Hence while vomiting and gagging, etc., were no longer adequate methods for getting even with or controlling his environment, such behaviour was still, on the basis of his past, an appropriate expression of John's reaction to eating. As with many other children and in many other situations we found ourselves caught in something pretty much like a vicious circle. So long as recollections of the past made his eating an ordeal for John he could never enjoy it; and so long as pleasurable eating experiences did not happen as often as unpleasant ones, eating had to remain painful for him.

Initially we had hoped that it might be best to establish pleasant contacts with John in some areas of living where he had not suffered so much, so that good relations established there might help to make eating more agreeable. But our efforts to get near him at the times when he was not eating got us nowhere. All his mental energy was so concentrated on his love for food and his hatred of eating that no energy seemed to be left for establishing rapport in any other situation. At play, when getting dressed or undressed, in his bath, or on walks, he withdrew into autistic isolation from which he emerged only when he wished to use human beings as tools or as servants. They had no other reality for him than the degree to which they submitted to his whims.

Although we continued our efforts to make him as comfortable as possible in all other situations, there was little or no progress. Hence, we had to concentrate our efforts on establishing personal relations where they should have arisen in the first place, and where whatever little of them that existed had totally broken down: when he was eating. Still, it was many, many months before John's vomiting and gagging began to decrease, and more than two years before they were given up entirely.

When John was at table, even after his gagging and vomiting had decreased, his hostility controlled everyone around him through quiet procrastination. It took him hours to begin eating, and usually he began only at the moment he became convinced—after one or two hours of exasperating waiting—that the adult who was with him was ready to leave; then in a few minutes he would gulp the food down so fast that, particularly at first, the result was another fit of vomiting.

In general, we find that with children who have been totally overpowered by adults the first freedom to retaliate reveals itself in hostile procrastination. They do not yet dare to be openly aggressive, but they hostilely inhibit our actions and movements by not getting dressed, by losing things for which we must then search for hours, by slowness of speech or movements, by endless and meaningless stories to which we must listen, by blocking exits, or by walking so slowly or so immediately ahead of us that they reduce us to standing still. Thus they block our freedom of action, of movement, as theirs was once blocked.

Again it should be mentioned that the small child finds (or tries to find) release for his tension by discharging it through motility. If the child was forced to internalize, to store up the tension he wished to discharge in movement, then his being quiet, his sitting still takes on the characteristic of "frozen" hostility. By becoming immobile he punishes us for having prevented him from moving. The particular way in which such a child expresses his aggression through procrastination or immobility depends in part on the area in which his desire for movement was most severely blocked. Thus John selected immobility (not eating) or procrastination around eating as his favourite form of punishing or controlling others, although in his, as in many similar cases, immobility or procrastination extended over all other life activities, if somewhat less intensely.

Still, we must allow the formerly overpowered child to control us in this way for a long time, because he must be allowed to reestablish some feelings of mastery wherever, and in whichever way, it originally broke down. After he has done so, and after his achievement has encouraged him to gain mastery in other areas of living, the time will come for slowly discontinuing the practice of allowing the child to control us by procrastination or otherwise. But by that time, most children will have become far too active and secure to rely on procrastination for control.

Just as John's parents once restrained him physically at mealtimes that lasted by the hour, and forced him to submit to their will, he now forced his counselors to submit to a similar ordeal of passive waiting. During this period, he continued to ignore them as persons. John recognized a counselor as a human being for the first time when he reverted from helpless vomiting and gagging to active spitting. He then repeated a phase of his earlier life when he had still been more goal-directed in his actions, when his spitting had indicated some interest in another person as a person, and in that person's reactions. As spitting had once preceded vomiting, it now followed the vomiting and heralded a newly revived interest in others. As he spat at the counselor he became interested in her reactions, his first recognition of her as a person.

After John had thus moved from passive to active efforts at

overpowering her, there eventually came a period of dependency in which he first accepted and then wished her to spoon-feed him. Finally John began to grow attached to the counselor and slowly formed a relationship to her at exactly the place where it had initially broken down: at meals. Without giving up spitting he moved on from there to messing with his food, getting it all over not only himself, but the table and the counselor sitting beside him. It was as if he had to deface the appetizing look of the food until he had made of it something similar to the vomit he had once been forced to eat.[19]

At a time when it slowly became more and more possible for John to give up his immobility, he had a conversation with the psychiatrist in which he expressed some of the reasons why he could now give up his stolidly hostile resistance to moving. Part of John's megalomanic disinterest in the world around him, and in adults, was his insistence that there was no difference between him, them, and other children. John said: "Grownups smoke and have a business, otherwise they're the same [as children]." When asked whether grownups did anything for children, John replied, "They give them plenty of fresh air and play games with them." Asked which games, he replied, "Who can do it faster, who can get dressed and eat fast." When asked whether things were the same at the School, John said: "At School there are counselors; they don't play the game about who's faster." This "difference" made it possible for him to recover at the School: nobody forced him to be fast. When he was asked a little later about what adults ought to do, John said: "Grownups should breast-feed children." Asked how he knew, he said, "I read it in mother's cook book. It's good for them. In the cook book is a picture of it, the baby— but I don't remember." Then he added spontaneously: "My mother doesn't make cakes so good," and after a pause: "You know we cook at School. We make fudge and pancakes. My counselor's done it for me very often."

The book from which important knowledge could be gained, including knowledge about child rearing (John felt) was the

[19] Participant observer: Betty Lou Pingree.

cook book. His mother didn't know how to use it well, her cakes were not as good as the ones his counselor made for him.

After food at the School had thus become tasty, eating became pleasanter in general for him. In a slow general process of unfreezing, the discharge of hostility which began when he was eating extended first over John's mental life and then also over his physical activities. This new freedom to act was used in the service of his hostility and his preoccupation with eating. John surreptitiously put salt in the sugar bowl, mixed plaster or soap powder into food supplies, and otherwise tried to spoil food for others (as it had always been spoiled for him). He also harboured phantasies about forcing poisonous concoctions into the mouths and throats of others. These phantasies about foods being poisonous then led to recollections of how he had been painfully fed, and how much he had hated it.

Only a few of the highlights of John's recovery have been mentioned here. It was in fact slow and tortuous and extended over years. But every step in higher integration, every advance in personal relations, in the speed and adequacy of his motor coordination, had first to be acquired at mealtimes or on other occasions when he was eating.

Oral difficulties, however, are neither the only ones that appear first around eating nor the only ones that are best handled at such times. Some children use the times when they are fed to express difficulties that originated in other areas. The reasons for this may be manifold: it may be that meals are less fraught with anxiety for them, or because eating was less disturbed for them than other experiences, or because feeding was the only process that involved pleasant personal contacts for them, or again because eating itself was the most pleasant experience they had had. Some of these children, for example, can reveal, or work through, certain preoccupations with elimination for the first time at the dinner table. In their tendency to smear and mess with food they may be reacting to a too rigid education to cleanliness, and though that experience took place around elimination they find it easier to deal with it while eating than when they are in the bathroom.

Charles, a nine-year-old boy of superior intelligence, suffered from various compulsions, tics, and inhibitions, including a compulsive cleanliness. The only instinctual satisfaction he could permit himself was eating. This he had done so much of that he was extremely obese despite his mother's year-long efforts to have him reduce.

Eating, the only pleasurable experience available to him, was also the setting in which Charles permitted himself to get dirty for the first time. While at first he ate compulsively and as if under great pressure, as time passed he became increasingly more sloppy as he ate, but also more and more able to really enjoy what he ate. He spilled his food all over his plate, wiped his fingers on his shirt, and very soon was the dirtiest and messiest boy in the School: but only when eating. He still did a meticulous job of being clean in the bathroom.

It was at dinner time that he revealed how fearful he was of being openly aggressive, and later also his preoccupation with elimination. After he had learned to permit himself to be as messy as he wished at the dinner table, he felt free there (but only there) to talk about the purpose of his hostile grinding of his teeth. When other children asked him about it, Charles said, "Oh, it's just one of my little habits." But as his relationship to his counselor improved, and particularly through her feeding him, he was able to accept her statement that to call something a "habit" was no adequate explanation, but just another way of avoiding one without admitting the intention.

At the dinner table, the only place where he really felt secure then, Charles was finally able to tell her his reasons: "When I do it," he said, "I try not to think about something else that's too unpleasant to think about."

While Charles thus established the connection between his unpleasant thoughts and his tics, some time later, and again while he was eating, he was able to recognize the connection between overeating and his preoccupation with anything pertaining to elimination. Once when the counselor was eating with him in a restaurant Charles ordered a large serving of navy bean soup. In a very confidential voice he told her that he had a secret: to himself he called this his "boo-boo soup." When asked why, he replied in an even more confidential manner and tone, "You know what beans do to you and I just love to do that [to pass flatus]."

Mealtime is also a setting which permits us to provide children easily and casually with those infantile pleasures they are anxious to receive but afraid to ask for directly. Children who do not feel secure enough to accept being babied as a matter of course, or to ask for it outright, will manage to create conditions which permit them to enjoy again those pleasurable services which are rightfully due every infant—services they were prematurely deprived of because parents forced them to "act their age" or "take care of themselves" before they were emotionally ready to do so.

At the dinner table, for example, Hank held his arm out very rigidly one day and said, "My arm is stiff. I can't get my hand to my mouth." On another day, after he had rejected the offer to be spoon-fed, he put his spoon in his mouth and pretended he couldn't get it out. "Help me," he said, "I can't get my spoon out of my mouth." [20] To ask to be spoon-fed would have made him seem far too passive. He wanted to remain in control of the situation and still have a chance to enjoy infantile pleasures. So he went through this sort of performance for some time: he rejected any offer to be fed, but pretended at various moments that he couldn't get the food to his mouth; or that he was unable to get the spoon out of his mouth without the counselor's help.

As mentioned in various contexts, food and eating are of great aid in restoring security in all moments of stress. They are a convenient distraction, they provide outlets for tensions, and most of all they are symbols of security. They demonstrate that satisfaction is available. Often the success of new ventures into

[20] Participant observer: Ronnie Dryovage.

more difficult achievements, particularly into as yet unknown areas of experiences (such as on trips away from School), depends on whether or not enough food is available and is distributed at the psychologically correct moments.

In general, we are very careful about taking children away from the security of the well-known setting of the School. But sooner or later they must learn that their fear of the imagined temptations and dangers of the outside world is unjustified and badly exaggerated. If we feel a child is ready to go on trips that to him represent much more an exploring of his fears and a test of his ability to meet the world than an excursion proper, we encourage him to take along whatever he likes. Holding on to some of his prized possessions then gives him a tangible and also a symbolic tie with the source of his security. Yet this is not enough unless supported by food.

To cite an example, a group of girls went on a ride in the School station wagon—a car they were perfectly familiar with. They took along dolls, comic books, and whatever else they felt they had to have. Nevertheless, as soon as the School was out of sight they became listless; some pretended to read their comic books, others that they were asleep, and in general the pleasure seemed to have gone out of the ride. But as soon as the counselor began to distribute candy and the children began to eat, they showed a new interest in the outside world, watched the sights and discussed them with one another or with the counselor in an animated way. Their only concern then was whether the candy would hold out for the whole trip. They were reassured only when they were told there was plenty on hand and if there wasn't, they would stop along the way and get more.[21]

[21] Participant observer: Marjorie Jewell.

8

rest and play

TRUE play is based on the pleasure of smooth physical coordination, and much of it has no other purpose except the child's enjoyment as he repeats some new mastery over his own movements; witness the small child's play of being a crawling dog or a running horse, where the phantasy is often little more than a pretext for running and jumping.

Rest, in the sense I shall be using it here, is something different from sleep which is normally the most restful of all experiences. For emotionally disturbed children sleep is often a thing to be feared, something fraught with emotional dangers. How sleep can be made restful for children is discussed in Chapter Twelve which deals with bedtime and night fears. Here it may be said that some very anxious children can rest only when they are fully awake. At no other time are they free of such fears as that terrible things may be happening to them in the darkness of the night, or even during the day if they do not watch for them. Even more frequent is the child's fear of committing some terrible deed in his sleep, when the ego is no longer controlling his asocial impulses.

If, in this chapter, rest and the development of coordinated movement loom much larger than actual play, it is because active play presupposes a coordination that is adequate in terms of the child's developmental age. So-called phantasy play which is not accompanied by action or a constant rearrangement of at least the toys and the play environment, has little play in it, but is mostly phantasy pure and proper. It is often a type of phantasy which lends itself easily to delusional escape from reality. As a matter of fact, the child who cannot learn to play ball because of his anxieties (expressed in his inability to move) is the child who spins phantasies about himself as the great ball player. But such delusions about his talents will make his failures on the ball field even more painful and he will give up playing in reality and escape even more into megalomanic delusions.

Eating, about which we spoke last, is, after all, only one of the basic biological needs which, when severely frustrated, may lead to emotional disturbance. Equally basic are the functions of rest and mobility. There, too, serious disturbances may result if the infant or child cannot enjoy proper rest, or if his need to move about is not adequately stimulated or supported, or even harmfully blocked. If we wish to restore an emotionally disturbed child to well-being, we must also restore his ability to exercise and to rest, and bring both of these faculties back into healthy balance.

Once a child has acquired the ability to move freely and to relate to others, he will be able to play, and play is no longer a great problem in his education to bodily, emotional, and intellectual adequacy. Therefore we shall concentrate mainly on the acquisition of bodily coordination and the ability to rest, rather than specific play activities in themselves.

Every child at the School has the freedom to rest or be active as he chooses. Children whose movements are inhibited, who are characterized not only by "frozen" personalities but also by "frozen" bodies, need considerable time and help before they can unfreeze, before they can move about freely, or permit themselves any emotions. They are like the infant who must first rest peacefully and pleasantly cuddled up in his mother's arms before he can develop the ability to move with pleasure and for a purpose (as opposed to the unpleasant random movements he will use in trying to deal with a frustrating experience). In the same way, some of these "frozen" children have to learn to rest before they can enjoy moving. After that, for the first time, they can learn to command their own movements enough to move about freely and with pleasure.

It is almost impossible for us to know when a child is ready to relax in this way. Putting him to rest before he is ready for it (as in rest cures, for example) would rob him of the last spontaneity he possesses—that of choosing the time or the place of his rest, or his returning to the crib, an action not always just purely symbolic. To be able to arrange spontaneously for the time and place of his rest is important for the child not only to enable him to enjoy his rest to the full; it is also the image in which he will eventually emerge from his rest and be ready for spontaneous action.

In particular, we have found that children who were prematurely forced into a pseudo-adequacy have learned to defend themselves against the anxiety and resentment created by pressure from their parents; they do it by exaggerating the behaviour they feel their parents demand of them: by being overly active. But while they show greater activity, they also defeat the parental intentions by acting without purpose, or in asocial ways. In addition, they also defend themselves from the temptation to rest by their frantic, though purposeless activity; some of them are runaway children, others delinquents, and again others just generally hyperactive.

Julian, when he slowly became ready to give up his hyperactivity, seemed to need warmth in the most literal sense before he could thaw out emotionally. For hours he would curl up on a bench that was built over a radiator. Interestingly enough—and in line with what has been said about in-between spaces—he selected a congruous place for his return to a neither-here-nor-there emotional state.

In the dormitory or on the playfield Julian was still the adequate self-sufficient boy, full of pep and always on the go: the all-American boy his parents wanted him to be. But in the cloakroom where the children keep their coats and overshoes he found his never-never land. This is the room in which our children stop between activities: when they are through playing outdoors and are going to play indoors, when they stop between classes to play, or between play and meals—the room in which no special activity goes on. The indifferent nature of this room of passage seemed to demand least from Julian by way of living up to the supposed need for being active.

On this bench in the cloakroom, sitting on the grill covering the radiator, Julian would gaze placidly through a window at what was going on outside on the playfield, or watch equally passively what went on indoors as far as his view would permit. Gradually he seemed to realize that others were being active while he was at rest, and that even so, nothing terrible was done to him. Slowly he relaxed more and more until he finally curled up in a ball.

For adults, after a short time, the heat emanating through the grill would have been most uncomfortable, but Julian seemed to thrive on it. For weeks he sat there, though if a child or adult approached he would uncurl and feign some frantic activity. Later he gave up the effort and remained entirely passive except for trying to growl them away. Still later, Julian permitted his favourite counselor to sit with him. Then he seemed to sense the warmth that was also in her. He would like her to put her arm around his shoulders and finally he really curled up to rest in her lap like a baby.[1]

In all other situations Julian's body was perfectly rigid and stiff, even when he slept at night. Thus he learned to rest only when he was fully awake, and established his first personal contact only when personal warmth was supplemented by its physical counterpart. The relations so established eventually carried over into other situations and finally Julian was able to loosen his rigid controls on the playfield and in many other settings. It took longest for Julian to become able to rest in his sleep.

While it was some time before Julian could rest at night or

[1] Participant observer: Ronnie Dryovage.

even when he just lay on his bed during the day, there are many other children who need to be able to retire to their beds in times of stress. This is particularly important for children who tend to develop somatic symptoms. We make it perfectly clear to them that they can go to bed any time they want to without having to be sick. Eventually this does away with their need to develop physical symptoms since they can reach their goal (safety in bed) without them. But once they have saturated their need for rest, or have grown strong enough to meet life more actively, we must begin to present the temptations of a more active life in correct dosage. Otherwise these children might spend more time in bed than they need to for regaining the emotional and physical strength for a life of normal activity.

To encourage the children to self-regulation in regard to rest, all children are free to rest or to sleep for as long (and whenever) they choose, particularly outside of class hours. But they can also stay in bed all day, and skip class if they need to, without much ado and particularly without having to be sick.

Walter, before he came to the School, had already spent a great part of his life sick in bed. He had always suffered from a large number of physical ailments—colds, allergies, disturbances of the gastro-intestinal tract, etc.—all of which, without being serious, were enough to keep him in bed several months out of each year. In this way he managed to find security in bed from a life that he never felt up to. In other ways, too, whenever life became unbearable, he took it out on his body, including several suicidal attempts. Thus, by a single technique, he was able to punish himself for the violent hatred he could never take out on others, and could also avoid the challenges of life and the unhappy fact of his inadequacy. Moreover, he had learned that he received tenderer care as a sick child than he ever got when he was up and around. Actually, those around him were discouraged by the autistic withdrawal from which he emerged for brief moments only to display massive negativism. Such behaviour on his part made it impossible for most people to be nice to him. It was only when he was (or seemed to be) physically sick that the withdrawal or negativism became somewhat more acceptable to others and hence did less to inhibit their well-intentioned efforts to please him.

Walter continued to develop physical ailments for some time after he came to the School. After it was pointed out to him repeatedly that he could always stay in bed without having to be sick he began to test us to see if that was true. When he was satisfied that it was, his illnesses became less and less frequent over a period of six months and finally subsided entirely. For more than a year, whenever he felt he was not up to even his simple and protected existence at the School he would choose to stay in bed for the day, but at least he remained in some contact with reality there, and played with his counselor, or some child. Then he realized that remaining in bed all day was unnecessary, and eventually he did as the other children did, flopping down on his bed for longer or shorter rest periods whenever he felt he needed one.

Usually it is relatively simple to ensure proper rest for the majority of the children who have retained from infancy some ability at least to rest, if not necessarily to relax. It is often much more difficult to restore disturbed children to adequate mobility.

All seriously disturbed children are characterized by an imbalance in their motor coordination. Some are so inhibited, that not only their psyches but their bodies seem as heavily "armoured," as medieval knights. They seem unable to move. It is almost as if they need all their energy just to lift an arm or a leg, and that achieved, there seems no energy left for further movement. Some children shuffle along stiffly as if they cannot lift their feet, others move only the whole arm, as if they cannot bend the elbow.

It took Peggy, who was nine years old when she came, and obese, about two years to shed some of her armour. She suffered from severe depressions which were only occasionally interrupted by temper-tantrum outbursts of hostility. These were usually as violent as they were brief, and after each one she relapsed into stolid isolation. In order to protect herself and those around her from her own violence, whose consequences she exaggerated megalomanically, she inhibited herself in every direction: intellectually, physically, and socially she was unable to budge. She was also close to forty pounds overweight, a consequence of her still clinging to the only pleasure she had known as an infant: eating. The overeating itself, incidentally, was by no means free of hostile incorporative tendencies.

Peggy's inability to move in a coordinated way she used cleverly for hostile purposes. She blocked the movement of others, particularly where it was impossible to get around her: in doorways and passages. She bumped into others, or planted herself firmly and immovably in front of them.

Later, as Peggy became able to show her hostility more openly which meant discharging some of it), the storage of the remaining hostility became less of a task. It also made her realize that her aggressions were not quite as devastating as she had always feared: nothing terrible happened to those against whom she directed her violent outbursts nor even to her, since the objects of her hatred, her teachers and counselors, made no attempt to retaliate. This helped to convince her that her heavy armouring was neither needed, nor an advantage, and she became freer in her movements. So Peggy, who for ten years had barely been able to move her feet, was now able to run and skip, and to enjoy it. This was quite an achievement in coordination considering her obesity.

At about the same time Peggy also began to recognize and take advantage of those socially acceptable ways for discharging hostility that were now open to her with her new abilities. She developed a near monomanic devotion to baseball for some time. As a player she hit the ball furiously and was able to beat the boys (representatives of the hated and admired sex, and of the particularly hated and feared brother). As long as she had been afraid that her hatred would bring about severe injury to her brother unless she inhibited herself totally, she had been too afraid to move. But now she could see that neither her hatred of boys nor her beating them in competition had any bad after-effects. On the contrary her victories raised her status and permitted her to form relations which had previously been out of the question for her. Success in freeing herself from her physical armour also gave her the courage to unfreeze intellectually and she began to make academic progress almost simultaneously.

While Peggy, and children like her, are inhibited from moving, other children move their limbs and joints continuously, a hyperactivity which often extends to involuntary muscles or those which do not usually move independently from others. These children, in addition to their hyperactivity, show a continuous twitching of the small muscles, and a wide variety of tics. They seem to have so far lost control of the movements of their limbs or other parts of their bodies that they appear spastic or disjointed. Sometimes a combination of extremes can be observed in the same child: a heavy armouring of those parts of the body which are normally subject to conscious control (particularly of parts used for meeting the world, such as the arms and legs) and a continuous movement of other parts of the body, such as a twitch of the mouth, a shaking of the head, or a grinding of teeth. In still other children the hands, which are generally used for mastering the world or for expressing aggressive tendencies, are in continuous motion but are kept from giving vent to the child's hostility by being occupied with restraining the individual.

Tom, for example, was in continuous motion when he entered the School. With one hand he was forever clutching his genitals and with the other he was hitting himself on the forehead in a continuous rhythmic movement. Thus with one hand he was busy enacting against himself the sexual attack which he originally intended to direct against a parent and then feared that the parent might inflict on him. With the other hand he was punishing the head which thought up such incestuous and hostile ideas. Of course this, as do all other complex symptoms, had other meanings, too. By touching his genitals, for example, he was also convincing himself that his sexual organs were still intact and had not been damaged in punishment for his desires. In any case, he prevented his hands from attacking the parent by keeping them busy on himself all the time.

Peter, when he entered the School at the age of eleven, was a typically "disjointed" child. He was continuously on the run, both in movement and in speech. By talking incessantly he tried to hold his mother's attention without pause, while at the same time hiding his incestuous desire for her as if behind a smoke screen of words. He also hoped, through his incessant high-speed talk, to prevent his father from discovering how he hated him. In addition, Peter's fast talk was an effort to ridicule his tongue-tied father, an effort to seduce the mother with his agility and to show up the father as slow witted.

The speed factor was also present on a physical level. By running like a race horse (the animal with whom he identified even to his frequent "horse laugh") he hoped to escape from his father's retaliation should the father ever realize how aggressive his son's phantasies were. The possibility of such retaliation seemed likely enough to Peter, since his father was a butcher and slaughtered many animals, including horses.

At the time of which we speak, Peter had begun to realize the meaning of some of his own "queer" behaviour and had empathy with another child who seemed to be suffering under similar handicaps. Observing the schizophrenic-like behaviour of Chris who was then a newcomer, and quite shaken by his own observation, Peter remarked to his counselor: "When he acts dirty [when he hyperactively exposed himself], his screws should be tightened, so he won't; and when he's so quiet all of a sudden [when Chris went into a stupor], that frightens me even more. Then they ought to be loosened so he won't be so scared. Like last night, when the counselor used some knives to fix the snacks, and Chris started to act as if he was going to commit harakiri, and then the counselor took the knives away, and Chris stopped moving altogether. I wish he could act o.k." [2]

[2] Participant observer: Marjorie Jewell.

Peter's observations, incidentally, also revealed his insight into the fact that mental health (as also true freedom), is a middle area between license and inhibition. But it is a long way from recognizing the connection between physical and emotional imbalance (which even a child can detect), to undoing it and restoring the total personality to a more even ability to perform. Charles presented such a problem, with the great disparity between his motor and intellectual development. This nine-year-old boy had the intelligence of "genius" (I. Q. over 160) but was as heavy and "stupid" in his movements as though he were mentally retarded. Since he constantly felt rejected by his mother he had turned to his father for warmth and affection. But Charles' father, though he was fond of his son, was himself a cold, intellectual person who knew of only one way to establish contact with the boy, and that was through intellectual talk.

Like Peggy and many other emotionally deprived children Charles found comfort in the most primitive satisfaction, in food. And like Peggy he felt he could better protect himself from the impulse toward physical aggression against a parent by becoming so heavy that he was virtually unable to move. Overpowered as he was by unintegrated hostility, he felt safe only when he was perfectly still (they said he was "such a happy, placid child, always playing quietly by himself"). If he could not move, he could neither hurt nor kill. Thus from infancy on all his movements were severely inhibited. But anxiety and hostility pressed for some sort of relief.

The blocking of motility cut Charles off from the more frequent avenues for discharging tension and even as a small child his enormous hostility destroyed every personal relation he might have formed with other children. All this merely increased his unhappiness, hostility, and withdrawal from an all too unpleasant world. On the cues his father gave him, he tried more and more to make up for other pleasures by exploiting his marked intellectual abilities, but reality proved that impossible. His playmates resented his aggressive flaunting of knowledge and his hostility increased even more. Superior intelligence thus applied in the service of hostility just increased his isolation and made his life more and more miserable.

At the School he felt secure from the threat of his mother and unable to harm her since she was never around; in addition, he was no longer exposed to the father's intellectual overstimulation nor did we offer praise for his mental gymnastics as his father and his teachers used to do. Here at the School we were slowly able to help him unravel the thoughts that obsessed him.

As Charles described it, he felt himself a powerful steam engine (his intellect and body strength) which it was safe to turn loose only because it was strictly controlled, and because the path for the discharge of power (his aggressions) was predetermined by others.[3] The engine could move only on the tracks that were set for it and any deviation on the basis of Charles' own desires was impossible. It was safe to go full steam ahead on the intellectual tracks his father had set down for him without having to fear he might act of his own accord. To do otherwise was to run the risk of acting on his hatred, and this, with his superior intelligence, might be most dangerous to the people he depended on most—to his parents.

When Charles first came to the School he used the freedom it affords every child for spending more time than ever in studying his major obsession: railroad engines. But intelligence used so delusionally cannot lead to knowledge that reassures, not even in a setting like the School.

He learned everything he could about engines, but his intellectual preoccupation gave him no understanding because it never went beyond the most minute details of what supposedly made one type of engine more powerful than another, one type of engine or track more secure against the engine's leaving the roadbed, etc.

No amount of studying could bring him to trust that the engines would stay on their tracks. But eventually he used the freedom of the School to explore more directly into his domi-

---

[3] Our first insight into the nature of this obsession came from one of the children themselves. For an account of that incident, see p. 272.

nant anxiety. What may appear to be too much freedom, I might add, is not always given out of any inner conviction on the part of the staff that too much of it is always good for a child, but more often because we have to wait for the child to provide us with leads on how we can best help him. Such leads are much more apt to come if we let the child follow his own inclinations. Once we understand the cue the child gives us, we may then very well decide that what the child needs is not more, or as much freedom as we gave him but rather well-planned restrictions.[4]

Charles gave us our lead in due time. Sitting fascinated and motionless by the hour he watched the trains go by on the Illinois Central tracks where they run over a viaduct two blocks from the School. He was always in fear that an engine might jump the tracks, in which case his whole system of defense would have seemed to collapse.

These prolonged and anxious watchings of the trains were what helped us to understand better Charles' specific anxiety about engines, an insight we never got from his preoccupied studying of engines and railroads. Conversations with him while he sat there watching the trains revealed that Charles not only identified his own hostile tendencies with engines, as we already knew, but that he also identified them with parental hostilities. After his obsessional defenses had begun to disintegrate he remarked, as he heard a train whistle one day, "It sounds like a wife yelling at her husband." (There was much bitter quarreling between his parents.)

The dissolution of Charles' fear of his parents, and of his personal hostility, had to make considerable progress before he could be freer in his movements. But the dissolution of his compulsive preoccupation with steam engines, those symbols of his rigidly

[4] In the case of Harry, for example, we could not have known a priori whether, when and why to restrict his incessant visits to the movies. Only by following his leads and letting him go to the movies as much as he wished, and also by accompanying him there, were we able to learn what they meant to him. The leads we got then and there were what suggested how to wean him of the habit. (See Publications on the School, no. 9, pp. 243-44.)

controlled power and hostility, was needed before he could acquire freedom of movement, and freedom of movement was needed before Charles could free his superior intelligence for any constructive purposes.

The first real progress Charles made was when the relative security he experienced at the School encouraged him in his first efforts to acquire some freedom to move, and soon afterward to rest and relax (because this unmoving child was never relaxed). He began by playing at being a train conductor. This also implied progress in becoming more active, because he had never really played at being an engine, he had only phantasied it. The play of being a conductor involved no movement as yet—he was a motionless train conductor—but that he was able to imagine himself as a person signified progress. He now imagined himself to be the person who controlled power instead of believing he was a senseless and inhuman power himself.

After a while the train conductor became more active, and began to move in his imaginative game; he would run along the train, checking to see that everything was in good order. And a while later the ability to rest followed the newly acquired ability to move. Charles then fitted his bed out as a train station, a terminus, where all engines must come to a stop. In this way "the trains won't crash in the middle of the night and wreck everything." With this frightening possibility under control, he was able to rest peacefully in his bed and could slowly unlimber his body while he slept.[5]

At the beginning of his stay at the School Charles found it virtually impossible even to walk up an incline five feet high. Later he claimed it was hard work, but that it was probably healthy exercise and he supposed he ought to try it. To encourage him to do so at that time would have been ill-advised. It would only have replaced the father's pushing for intellectual achievement by our pushing for achievement in exercise and motor coordination. On the contrary, we advised him not to try to manage it if it was too hard for him. We explained that exer-

[5] Participant observer: Gayle Shulenberger.

cise that was no pleasure seemed pointless, and encouraged him not to worry about his health.

Later his counselors pointed out to him that other children seemed to enjoy running up and down the little hill; that they did it not because it was healthy or good exercise, but just because it seemed like fun. Considerably later we mentioned that it was too bad he had to miss out on such pleasures, though we always qualified that it was up to him to decide whether he wished to participate in such activities or not. This idea seemed to surprise him and he began to reconsider his attitude. Charles still expressed the fear that he might fall down; or that in running down the incline he might get up so much speed that it would carry him away and he would be powerless to stop where he meant to. But this he now connected spontaneously with his fear of what might happen if an engine did not stay on its tracks.

By this time Charles had also established a fairly good relationship to his counselor and (for him) was feeling little hostility toward her. This counselor explained to him how engines, when their brakes happen not to work, are always stopped by buffers, and she promised to stand at the bottom of the hill and if necessary to catch him like a buffer if he found he couldn't stop himself. With her, he felt safe enough to try this and he ran down the hill, throwing himself against her with aggressiveness and tremendous force. Fortunately, she managed to withstand his onslaught.

It was only after this concrete demonstration that there was someone to stop him even if he turned loose his aggressive motility that Charles dared to move a little more freely, since he knew now there were people who could stop him. For some time, however, before moving any more freely he insisted that his counselor stand ready to stop him and catch him if he found he couldn't do it himself. After this experience was repeated often enough, he began to run more freely, and soon he rolled down the hill, ran and fell very much like a two-year-old. It was as though he were developing from scratch not only his motor coordination, but the enjoyment of bodily movement. Slowly, after that, he arrived at the conviction that there is pleasure in moving one's body. From rolling down the incline he proceeded to going on walks, and finally even to playing ball with his counselor, but this process took more than two years.

Before Charles was able to apply his new freedom to playing with other children he had to repeat with them the experiences he had had with his counselor. First he ran aggressively into any child who happened to step on his imaginary tracks. Later, he took to chasing after the children, his head lowered, charging straight ahead and puffing like a powerful steam engine.

But the day came when he suddenly stopped dead in his tracks, went over to the table and got a cardboard train which he had built the night before. Carrying it in his outstretched arms he ran after another boy, saying, "I'm going to run my locomotive into you."

Thus, here, too, Charles became the carrier of the train—the conductor as it were—rather than the powerful but dead engine under rigid control. A back and forth movement between the use of the cardboard engines to express his aggressions, and being himself the powerful engine on tracks, continued for weeks, until he finally gave up acting the engine and began running after the objects of his anger as the boy, Charles.

As one might expect, when Charles was being the engine, he could only charge blindly and straight ahead; but when playing the conductor, he could run with his cardboard engine in most any direction. The children recognized the difference, though it was never explained to them. When Charles was playing engine they would cry out, "That steam engine is chasing us again;" when he was after them with his cardboard engines, they would accept it matter-of-factly or say, "Charles is after me again." [6]

Thus for Charles, as for those children who must re-establish ego control on awakening (see Chapter Four), some hostility must be discharged before they can follow a more socialized pattern of behaviour. They must first demonstrate to themselves (to their egos) that coming to some terms with the world

[6] Participant observer: Gayle Shulenberger.

is useful even for serving unconscious, or partly unconscious, hostile impulses. In the motion-inhibited children, a hostile use of motor abilities has to precede any constructive use of them. Very often the ability to move more freely has to be acquired in the service of asocial instinctual purposes before it can later serve social or rational purposes.

Parallel with Charles' growing ability to humanize his aggressions (which meant controlling them to some degree), was his ability to humanize his movements. First his stiffness changed into robot-like movements (charging, head down and straight forward) and then at last came a steadily improved motor coordination. Slowly this permitted Charles to accept playing with toys, to participate in games and thus to form pleasant relations with other children. Then with his growing freedom of movement came a gradual neglect of his intellectual preoccupation. While he now made less of a show of his intelligence, he used it more constructively. He became more and more able to apply it to matters more closely related to the interests of his age and his age-mates. Freeing his movements and restoring the ability to rest had been the necessary steps in closing the gap between his intellectual superiority on the one hand, and his inability to apply it constructively or to relate to human beings, on the other.

The final adjustment came when Charles began to apply his intelligence toward an understanding of those problems from which he originally sought to escape: the bad relationship between his parents, his fear and hatred of the mother, and his resentment against the loved father for being more interested in his intellectual abilities than in satisfying his more legitimate childish needs.

At the same time he also learned to understand and accept as normal such bodily functions as eating, digestion, and elimination—functions which until then had been so full of secret meanings to him that he was too afraid to explore them. He now applied the newly won freedom to use his intelligence purposefully toward understanding these physiological processes. His comments revealed how he had also gained insight into another cause of his overeating and his monomanic preoccupation with steam engines. What he had set out to learn was how strength can be gained in the process of turning matter into energy—as symbolized for him by the burning of coal in a steam engine. After he came to understand that even the greatest of food intake would not appreciably increase the amount of energy available to him, he was able to give up some of his overeating. Such knowledge his preoccupation with steam engines could never have given him, even had he learned all about them.

Charles' initial inability to acquire true knowledge, i.e., knowledge related to life problems and their resolution, had to be mentioned here, because in a way this motion-inhibited boy of superior ability (as measured by I. Q. and success in rote learning) was actually no more able to deal with his life problems than Peggy, or other children whose motor inhibition is accompanied not by high intelligence but by intellectual blocking.

It is generally recognized that the child becomes active in mastering the world, in recognizing and in understanding it, only as he develops the ability to move deliberately and purposefully. Until then, the infant remains completely dependent on the adult and acquires no understanding of the world. As he begins to move on his own, and with purpose, the infant acquires a modicum of independence which for some time increases exactly at the rate that the child becomes more and more able to move freely, to use his body organs for exploring.

Similarly we were able to observe in our motion-inhibited children, even in those of high intelligence, that independence of thought, and finally the ability to develop personalities of their own, came only after the ability to move freely and without support, just as with infants.

No child can enjoy an adequate social life unless he has acquired the ability to play with other children. Play, much more than adult-imposed learning, is the area where the child tests and develops his independence, where he learns to hold his own with his peers. Therefore, Charles' superior intelligence became a social asset only after his emotional need for relations to children could be satisfied through his learning to move and to play. Then he no longer needed to exploit his intelligence to compensate for his hostile isolation and could use it to gain pleasure in a social way of life.

While Charles had to be freed of his motor inhibitions, other children, as I have mentioned, have to acquire control over their disjointed, random movements. Previously I described how John's vital energies had to be freed around the eating situation. But freeing energy is only one step in rehabilitation; using it constructively is still another one, and the more important one in the final analysis. For John, it was a matter of beginning at the beginning. Like a baby in his crib, any inner or outer stimulation led to non-purposeful waving of hands and arms, to a rolling of the head, and whenever he wasn't actually standing, to a kicking of the legs.

John had given up all hope of ever learning to hold his own in games with other children. Unlike Charles he could never even compensate by intellectual superiority. From an unpleasant reality he escaped into grandiose daydreams about an imagined superiority which supposedly forced everybody into subservience to him. Thus he tried to make up for the constant defeats he experienced in fact.

Our problem was to restore him to action and thus to show him that he could succeed at least in some games. Actual success in competition, we hoped, would make it unnecessary for John to believe that he was so wonderful about winning games that none of the children dared to play with him. (That was the way he megalomanically explained why he never had anybody to play with.) The experience of success in games, we felt, John should gain preferably through a skill that would also encourage him to try for some bodily coordination. Obviously it had to be a game where coordination could be practiced without any exertion, since he was incapable of any. It had also to be a game that would force him into some personal contact, an occurrence he usually dodged if he could, to avoid realizing his inadequacy.

Another qualification was that failures had to be part of the game. Given John's inadequacy, frequent failures were unavoidable and the first failure would have led to a total abandonment of effort and a withdrawal into autistic phantasy.

This happened, for example, when very simple puzzles were presented to him. He would rarely fit the pieces into their proper places and was always frustrated. When we offered him crayolas or paints he would draw a few lines, but remain in autistic isolation. He was satisfied with the worst scribbles, which he interpreted in megalomanic detail as the planned expression of his artistic talents. In coloring books he could never stay within the lines. But while they left him free to withdraw into isolation, they added to his frustration because he could never fill out the spaces. Cutting with scissors was generally rejected as too strenuous and soon led to defeat whenever he took it up because he could never cut as he intended to, and the result was again the same—a frustrated return to angry isolation.

The game which finally served the purpose (it was pick-up-sticks) required two persons to play it, and temporary defeat was part of the game because otherwise the partners could not take turns and the game would be stymied. It required the coordination of only one hand and of only two fingers, and this he eventually learned to manage. No exertion beyond this was involved, because lifting the sticks could not be said to have required energy. Finally, defeat being part of the game, it meant no loss of face, particularly since the other partner had to make his mistakes sooner or later and this must visibly show John that his defeats were only temporary and not total.

John played pick-up-sticks regularly for more than a year and a half. He played it for prolonged periods of time with one adult in several sessions each week. Later, he returned to it each time he experienced defeat in other efforts toward greater coordination.

John, and like him many other children who are similarly handicapped, though not necessarily as severely, cannot afford to make efforts at higher motor achievement if they feel they are being observed by other children. They have known failure too often to be able to risk it again in the presence of children whose superiority they envy. Thus, John, who had never learned to swim, also avoided the pool and the beach under various pretexts such as colds, coughs, and other imaginary ailments. Not until he was finally sure that there were other children, too, who had never learned to swim, and that he was not expected to learn unless he wanted to, could he give up imaginary ailments and the protection they offered against defeat in the eyes of others. Then he at least began to play in the shallow end of the pool.

It took nearly two years of just playing in the water, and of getting more and more familiar with and less afraid of it, before John felt any desire to learn to swim. This desire he expressed not in the water or close to it, but in the safety of the room where he had his private session with a favourite person. There he asked to be taught how to swim and there he learned one separate movement after another, and then their combination. Secluded from the observation of others, and with much patient help, he mastered the coordination needed for swimming and this knowledge he then transferred to the pool. Similarly he had to learn to catch and throw a ball with one trusted person in a situation where he knew he was unobserved by other children before he dared to play ball on the play field.[7]

The attempt to establish only later in life the motor control which was never acquired in infancy is so important, and usually so difficult, that another example may illustrate the wide range of approaches that are possible and necessary. It also illustrates how the ability to enjoy proper rest has to precede the ability for normal coordination and purposeful movement. For actually, even the infant who has acquired the ability to direct his movements will revert back to random movement when he is lacking in rest or whenever he is tired or tense.

Tony's impairment of vision had been so bad that for all prac-

[7] Participant observer: Florence White.

tical purposes he was nearly blind as an infant, though his parents remained unaware of the fact for several years. So long as he remained in his crib he was a happy baby, but when he began to crawl and walk he was constantly hurting himself, could not estimate distance correctly, and yet was obviously not blind. The parents' irritation at his continuous wailing and lack of development only made matters worse. After several years, the nature of Tony's visual defect was discovered and corrected by glasses. But by then it was too late to do much good as long as the correction of vision was not accompanied by the resolution of those emotional difficulties which sprang up because of it.

Tony had acquired the ability to control his movements in the security of the crib. But contrary to normal development, his later experiences prevented him from using that control to keep on acquiring motor abilities. His continuously bumping into things and hurting himself forced him to use this control to inhibit all motion, rather than develop it. His object, of course, was to avoid the unpleasantness that resulted from most of his movements.

By the age of seven Tony had virtually stopped moving, and all his efforts were directed at having others move him, or move for him.

Yet his stillness was never a relaxed resting but simply a tense avoidance of motion. Before we could help him in directing his muscle control toward purposeful movement rather than the inhibition of motion, we had first to restore his ability to rest. His fear of falling, of hurting himself at every move, had to be eliminated, and he had to be freed of all pressure to be active. In the past his parents had tried to encourage him to walk and run about and play because they understandably wanted him to be able to do all those things. To their pressure had been added the ridicule of age-mates, so that in terms of his total experience Tony responded with greater and greater tension and immobility. Life had taught him one thing for sure: to move is to hurt oneself, either physically or emotionally.

At the School we made it clear to him that he was not expected to move; he was first carried and later guided carefully up and down the stairs. When he walked, someone held his hand, and in this and many other ways it was conveyed to him that we made no demands toward activity, but that when he did move we took every precaution to make it perfectly safe.

His ability to rest was very slowly restored, thanks to this regime and to the fact that he could rest or lie down at the School whenever he wanted to. Tony's muscles became more and more relaxed when he was lying down and the tenseness of his features decreased. He, incidentally, like other children in terror of falling, preferred to stretch out on the floor instead of a couch or a bed. On the floor there was no place to fall from and there he felt free to relax; the bed was something he might roll out of and for some time he could never relax on it. Finally, with enough safety behind him, he became ready to venture activity again. At that time he began to walk up and down the stairs of the School by the hour, first holding on to the railings for dear life, later without touching them.

Next, Tony explored his ability to achieve even more difficult tasks of coordination. He took to carrying rubber rings on his head to see if he could balance them while he walked. At first he just walked around the dormitory and was very excited about the fact that he could keep the rings balanced on his head. Then he began to walk up and down the stairs, first just to the second floor, then to the third, then all the way down to the basement. That first time he walked up and down the stairs for about an hour, always returning to his counselor and reporting his successes, how far he had gone, and at last telling her with pride how when he got to the basement, he had walked twice around the post "just to prove I could do it."

From that day on he continued the exercise daily, and to his counselor he talked of nothing but his new achievement. Frequently (and astonished about it himself), this child who had rarely sucked his thumb before also told her: "The only way I can do it is to hold my thumb in my mouth when I'm going down the steps." Or "I can't do it if I don't have my thumb in my mouth." When asked why, Tony replied very clearly, as if he had thought about it a great deal, "I don't know why I have to have my thumb in my mouth, but I always have to, or I can't do it." [8]

Tony's behaviour, and incidentally his remarks, demonstrate how close a connection there is between higher achievement in one area and regressive behaviour in another. Tony could afford to leave babyhood in regard to coordinated movements only by clinging at the same time to some tangible evidence that more primitive pleasures were still available to him despite a more mature control of his movements. While thumb sucking itself is not exactly rest, it is certainly experienced as restful, as one can observe in any small child who grows quiet and contented when he can return to his thumb sucking after tension. In this sense Tony's behaviour demonstrated the intimate relation between the two opposites—rest and motility.

For many of our children the most integrative experiences they have are the ones most directly connected with some tangible achievement, some newly acquired skill. Many of these successes are never directly referred to as such. Others find verbal expression only in the way in which the self-confidence enjoyed after a new step in achievement permits the child to reveal some of the pressing fears he was previously unable to speak about because he had never even dared to face them. Success in one area gives the child hope that he may also be able to do something about his fears, or their causes, and this enables him to bring them out in the open. It is only natural that the child should be quicker to reveal such a fear to the person who has helped him to achieve in some other way. This was true, for example, of Ann.

Ann, although in perpetual motion, was most inadequate in her physical coordination and intellectual achievement. Among her anxieties was the dread that if she should learn to behave and succeed in more grownup ways she would no longer be

[8] Participant observer: Betty Lou Pingree.

loved, for she would lose her position as the baby. It was her babyishness and inadequacy, she felt, which enabled her to control the adults around her.

Another reason for wanting to remain infantile, as mentioned previously, was that from the beginning of Ann's life, her mother had depended on her for emotional satisfaction and for giving meaning to her life. For that and other reasons, the mother could never permit her any independence, treating Ann as if she were still part of her body. Her mother's emotional needs Ann could meet only in her role as a baby. So to defend herself from any possible loss of love from her mother, and in order to satisfy the mother's desires, she remained immature. But by doing so, she paid the price of all those fears of the incomprehensible world which characterize infancy. She could never learn to understand because a baby is not supposed to understand. She was dependent and unable to take care of herself but at the same time disappointed because while her mother forced her to remain dependent, her need to be adequately taken care of was never satisfied.

The relative security Ann experienced at the School permitted her to make her first efforts to achieve in more mature ways. At first, she wanted most of all to have better physical coordination. Above all she wanted to be able to ride a bike but this was beyond her for some time because of her poor coordination.

Finally, with the help of her counselor, Ann learned to ride. This gave her the courage, on the very same day, to attempt the deep-water test in the swimming pool, a test she could have passed many months earlier had she dared to try. That evening Ann was very much elated and wanted to ride the bike as long as she could before bedtime. She and some of the other girls were taking turns on the bicycle, and while waiting for her turn Ann spontaneously started to clean up the front yard by picking up papers and raking the leaves away, a constructive social move she had never before made, even when asked. Thus the self-confidence gained by her new achievements was immediately set to use in socially mature ways she had never even considered before. Over and over again she exclaimed: "I can do two things now, I can swim and I can ride," and to herself she sang happily for a long time: "I did it, I did it, I did it."

This double achievement in controlling her movements seemed to have given Ann the courage to attack some of her other fears, particularly her sex anxieties; perhaps because she now hoped that she might be able to master them with the help of the counselor who had helped her in other recent achievements.

Specifically, one of the other girls was riding the bike a little longer than Ann felt she should, and Ann was impatient for her turn. Raising her voice more and more in complaint, she exclaimed: "What's she riding so long for? She thinks she's a queen, she thinks she's a princess, she even thinks she's a man!" [9]

While Ann thus revealed her general envy of boys, she was even more specific about her sex fears that evening as she was preparing for bed. At that time she asked her counselor: "Does it hurt when the baby comes out of the vagina?" [10] With the answer to this question all talk of her sex fears was over for the day.

But these and similar thoughts seemed to continue to occupy Ann's mind and her real new achievements gave her the confi-

[9] Participant observer: Dorothy Flapan.

[10] When children enter the School they don't usually know the proper names for the various genital parts. They either point, or use childish or obscene names. We try to teach them the correct names to avoid both the obscene and the pussyfooting euphemisms. The child soon learns to use the correct expressions, although often there are misunderstandings that need to be ironed out.

Harry used a common enough expression to designate his penis, whose use he offered freely, particularly to female counselors. I mentioned that what he was talking about is usually called a penis in more polite language. This struck him as being funny. So with the help of one of his more literate friends he looked up "penis" in their dictionary. There they found that it was "the male organ of copulation." But the older boy, in terms of his own neurosis, misread it as "the male organ of completion." This aroused great excitement and required more explanations which were constructive for both boys. From then on they not only knew the correct name for an important part of their bodies, but had also acquired a better understanding of its function.

PLATE 9: He is so afraid of his own aggressions that he thinks if he throws the ball to another child or a counselor he will hurt them. So he has to learn that it is safe to play by actually handing the ball over to the counselor. The other boy is further ahead and feels free to play ball. He can even stand not having the ball at the moment and can look on, content with his newly acquired ability to play freely and enjoy it.

PLATE 10, FIGS. 1 and 2. *Above:* Some children who are afraid of reading can only learn to recognize letters within the security they derive from a fully trusted adult. But even then, they can tackle mature tasks only if more primitive satisfactions are immediately available, such as toys, a box of candy. *Below:* This ten-year-old girl is torn between too many desires. She wants to play house, like any child her age. She started to—but she's never had a decent family life, and she doesn't know where to begin. Only when clutching some pleasure she has missed (in this picture, the bottle) does she find the courage to do the grownup thing: learn how to take care of babies. The doll play has to wait until she has learned about that.

PLATE 11, FIGS. 1 to 8. She began by trying to play house. She asks the adult to fix one of the children in the doll family and continues her play (1-2). Then she recalls that she was never adequately taken care of as a child, becomes anxious, and to reassure herself asks that the baby bottle be filled and put right in the play house (2-3). With the bottle within reach (and as the most important part of her house play) she can continue even more actively (3-4). She becomes frustrated again when her family play reactivates thoughts of her infancy. Anxiously she looks for help in understanding how children are born, and asks the adult to open the book of diagrams showing the baby in the womb, and including pictures of how babies should be taken care of (*facing page, bottom*). When she realizes that she can understand what is explained to her, she begins to relax, sucks pleasurably, and listens with attention (5). She interrupts her sucking only to point to a picture in the book, asking for further explanations (6) and from then on follows the explanation while drinking out of the bottle (7). She has taken in—intellectually, emotionally and orally—what she was ready to absorb, relaxes and returns contentedly to her play. Should another moment of stress arise, the now empty bottle is still within reach (but now outside of the doll house) and can be refilled immediately, or she can help herself from the candy box on the table behind her.

PLATE 12. This girl never permitted herself to be touched, nor did she ever dare to touch anyone else. But here, surrounded by warm water and further protected against too much closeness by a water ring, she reaches out for her counselor and holds on to her, concentrated on this relation and untouched by what is going on around her.

dence, on the next day, to push further. Then she asked her counselor: "How old are you?" and to the answer, "twenty-four," Ann exclaimed in an angry voice, "What? so old? and you're still menstruating?" thus revealing her fear of menstruation by her hope that it would stop soon. This she followed up with a statement indicating a much more pressing anxiety than her preoccupation with birth and menstruation—namely her concern with masturbation.

After she had received assurance about masturbation the conversation went on for a while until Ann finally asked her counselor: "Do you touch your vagina?" But at this one of the other girls exclaimed: "That's her own business, god damn it," in an effort to protect her own privacy and that of the counselor. A third girl who had been at the School for some time put an end to the interchange by stating in such an authoritative way that "some people do and some people don't" that the matter rested there as far as the children were concerned. Nevertheless, the shift to generalization on the subject of masturbation permitted the counselor to talk about it in general terms rather than in relation to herself or to any specific child, which proved reassuring to Ann and also to the rest of the girls.[11]

Whenever successes in physical coordination restore courage to children who have always been fearful, they are likely to be used for some time in aggressive and asocial ways. The brand new self-confidence will apply not only to real tasks and achievements, but also to illusions about the self. Bodily coordination in particular, when acquired in infancy as it should be, is normally accompanied by exaggerated notions on the part of the infant about his own body, power, and strength. Hence it was reasonable to expect that Ann would apply her novel self-confidence not only constructively, in bodily coordination, but also in a delusional way by developing exaggerated ideas about her body.

Ann's elation continued. Most of her free time she rode happily on her bicycle, but she also began to play ball more effec-

[11] Participant observer: Dorothy Flapan.

tively and in class attacked learning problems she had always been afraid of. But three days after she learned to ride the bike she showed how her new self-assurance had also increased her delusions about her body. While undressing for her bath on that evening she asked her counselor to help her take off her under-pants and while the counselor was doing so she said: "Now you can see my penis." This permitted the counselor to assure her that she had no penis, and never did have one, and both this and further conversations helped Ann to be more accepting about being a girl, although this topic continued to come up in various contexts.

Thus, although the new strength gained through real achieve-ment did not decrease Ann's illusions about her body, it at least gave her the courage to state them. After that, since the counselor had proved her value by being able to help Ann with a difficult task, and since the new mastery had increased Ann's security considerably, the counselor's realistic statements about girls' never having had penes carried considerable weight. This, together with her greater adequacy, made it possible for Ann to cling less strongly to her megalomanic delusions about her body and constituted an important step toward their eventual disintegration.

The connection we have drawn between acquiring control over one's bodily movements, and higher emotional maturity, is fur-ther supported by Ann's subsequent behaviour after visiting for two weeks with her mother. This visit took place some seven weeks after the events here described. We realized that such a visit would be detrimental for Ann, since her mother had previ-ously shown how she used any contact with her daughter to exploit her for her own neurotic needs. (Efforts at treating the mother herself had proved unsuccessful.) The only hope for Ann—since the mother had the law on her side in insisting on visits, as destructive as they were for her child—was to protect her as much as possible from the mother and to continue, be-tween the infrequent visits, to build her up as a person so that once having reached emotional and legal maturity she might be able to strike out on her own.

Ann's progress, at the time of writing, seemed to justify the hope that this plan held much promise of final success. But what happened after Ann's return to the School may incidentally demonstrate how our work is made up of a long series of ups and downs, but that by and large each new low is less deep, and each high that follows is both higher and better than the one that preceded it. Only for the sake of brevity are the ups and downs which are countless in number not told in detail.

During the visit Ann's mother had again forced her into the role of the baby. Only this time, such a role seemed less satisfying to her than ever because her recent experiences had taught her what the true satisfaction of childish needs could be like. In addition, her efforts to gain approval from the mother for her new and more mature achievements were met mostly by severe criticism. Ann returned from this visit emotionally insecure, asocial, hostile, unable to learn in class, and again in continuous motion without purpose; she had also lost the ability to ride a bike.

On the day after her return she reduced to complete wreckage some of the tools of her last great achievement before going on vacation. These had now acquired threatening meanings. They were symbols of the challenge to maturity, a maturity she now feared since it had brought her into conflict with her mother. Ann went to the place where the bicycles are kept at the School, threw some of them on the floor and by stepping on them wrecked two of them. But the bicycles she wrecked were those of the older children, not the smaller one, not the one she had learned to ride; this one she did not touch. Thus she symbolically satisfied her mother's demand not to achieve along adult lines by destroying the bikes that represented just such achievement to her. But she also managed to make sure that such higher achievement would still be open to her, if and when she might again be ready for it, by preserving her own bike. Actually after three days she was happily riding again and slowly the effects of the visit wore off.[12]

[12] Participant observer: Joan Little.

Each of the various activities we offer at the School have particular meanings for particular children. Swimming, for example, is as often a source of terror as it is of pride. Normally, the sensation of warm water on the skin, the narcissistic pleasure of a smooth and easy flow of movement possible only in the water, the way it gives way and envelops, all this and much more makes the water, our first medium of life, a particularly rich source of enjoyment and integration.

Sooner or later playing in the water becomes a satisfying experience for all of our children; also learning to swim freely for those who have never learned before. The value of play in the water has long been recognized, and warm baths from time immemorial have been a means of casual and natural sedation. In addition, the falling or jumping into an element which so cushions the fall that it becomes enjoyable rather than painful, is an experience that gives most of our children great pleasure. Contrary to their anxious falling phantasies, they now fall and are caught pleasantly not only by the soft element, but also by the protecting counselor.

As with every other activity we have described, the use of the pool and of swimming have their own particular beneficial propensities. To be able to swim, for example, goes a long way toward mitigating some of the child's fear of drowning. Learning to swim has the emotional connotation of having gained independence from the all-engulfing liquid while still feeling it softly all around one. On still another level it has the reassuring meaning to the child of: "I was afraid of being hurt when I fell through the air, but now I fall, it is pleasant, and nothing bad has happened to me." Or it may mean: "I was afraid of drowning, but now I know how to swim." This is similar to Freud's discovery that the examination dream (in which the dreamer is afraid of failing an examination he has already passed in reality) has the reassuring meaning: "Do not be afraid . . . think of the anxiety which you felt . . . yet nothing happened to justify it."

But each activity may also have specific meaning to a particular child and hence offer particular openings for help, as in Eddie's case.

Usually, Eddie approached his various fears in such roundabout ways that it was most difficult to help him. True, the protected life we provided for him did not lend itself well as a suitable image for his prevalent anxieties. All he got from our protection was the freedom to indulge undisturbedly in his delusions of persecution and intense hatred. Eddie, who was then twelve years old, had almost drowned when he was three. At about the same time he had nearly been run over by a car. (His mother was also pregnant at the time and soon afterward a sister was born.) When he was ten years old, he acted out against another child by pushing him in the lake with homicidal intent. This act landed him in court and thereafter all his numerous anxieties and delusions had to do with his killing or getting killed. He was particularly afraid of accidents, of being destroyed, and of his dangerous powers to destroy others. Incidentally, such fears and imaginings are quite typical for many of our children, although not always quite as violently as with Eddie.

Eddie's anxiety about drowning (either his own or someone else's) we could handle more directly when the presence of the water revived them, and when he felt he was protected at last from the possibility of drowning. He was first able to speak of his fear in this respect after his counselor had helped him to acquire the skill that seemed to offer that protection: namely, swimming.

Initially, Eddie was afraid even of going to the pool. When he finally went, he made no effort to learn to swim but remained at the shallow end of the pool where he would splash at the other children violently. When this became too bad, he had to be taken out of the pool but as his counselor lifted him out, he would apply to the other children his favourite technique for gaining magic control over persons and things: he would stare at them aggressively and make clawing movements at them with his hands.

One day, on such an occasion, his counselor felt he was ready to talk about his fears, particularly since Eddie seemed friendly that day toward his counselor. As they sat on the edge of the pool, the counselor asked, "Why do you do that, Eddie?" (meaning his clawing) and the boy said, "Because it makes them go away." He repeated the movements and stared in the general direction of the other children who weaved backward and forward in their play, which may have given him the impression that he really controlled them and could force them away.

The counselor asked if he really thought it did and Eddie said, "Yes. It's a ray. I turn it on somebody or something and it makes them go away." Then his counselor said, "Why don't you try it on me, Eddie?" So Eddie clawed at the counselor two or three times, making a growling sound, and also staring at him violently. The counselor did not move, so Eddie continued the clawing movements, but now he closed his eyes. Quietly his counselor said, "Don't be afraid, Eddie. Open your eyes, I'm still here." Eddie opened his eyes and stared at the counselor who smiled at him. Then he smiled back and seemed relieved. "Yes," he said, "you're still here," and they continued to sit there in friendly contact.

A few minutes later, Eddie asked his counselor to get him a ball and said he wanted to get back in the pool. His counselor got it for him and Eddie held on to it and began to push himself around the pool by kicking. This was the first real effort he had ever made to learn to swim.[13]

It took three more sessions in the pool before Eddie could actually swim, although still only in the shallow end of the pool. At the first session he also gave up splashing at the other children for the first time, and when his counselor pointed that out to him he was thoughtful, and said: "Today I really enjoyed myself. As a matter of fact, I didn't even notice the other kids."

At their next session Eddie decided to try to swim the length of the pool and succeeded in passing his test. Now that he was sure he could take care of himself, even if he were again pushed, or fell into the water, he was ready to discuss what was really in his mind, and the following conversation took place.

[13] Participant observer: Roderick E. Peattie.

Eddie asked: "If a man had a fight with another man on a cliff and the man pushed him in, he would drown if he couldn't swim, wouldn't he?"

Counselor: "There are too many 'ifs' in that, Eddie. I really don't know exactly what you want to know."

Eddie: "But if you got knocked in the lake, you ought to be able to swim if you want to get out, shouldn't you?"

Counselor: "No one's going to knock you in the lake here, Eddie. As long as you stay at the School, you're all right."

Eddie: "But if you fell in the water you should be able to swim, shouldn't you?"

Counselor: "Yes. If you fell in the water and you could swim out, you'd be safe."

Eddie: "Well, once when I was a little boy I was lying on the edge of the pool, and I fell in. I don't even know what happened. I don't think anybody pushed me, but all of a sudden I fell in the water."

Then the counselor asked Eddie what he would do now if he fell in the water and Eddie said: "I would swim."

Eddie now felt he had learned to protect himself, at least in some respects; he felt less threatened and more in control. Now, too, he began to feel some desire to control himself, particularly in his aggressive tendencies, as was demonstrated a few days later. Another child had just annoyed him and he reverted to his clawing gestures. This time, however, he stopped himself almost immediately, looked at his counselor, smiled, and then slapped his hand, saying, "It's a bad hand. I'll have to slap it."

Of course his counselor told him there was no need to slap himself, that hands are neither good or bad but simply do what people make them do. But this, Eddie was not quite ready to accept yet. It seemed as if, like a very small child, he had to view himself separately from a hand which did unacceptable things, so that the rest of his personality could exercise control over it. But we felt that this effort to control his aggressive tendencies was a result of the security he had gained in learning to protect himself from drowning.[14]

[14] Participant observer: Roderick E. Peattie.

In this and other instances of reality testing, great care must be taken to protect the child from having to face situations that resemble the upsetting past too closely before he is able to face old anxieties in a realistic way. Nothing is more damaging to the child than being forced into situations that he cannot yet master, that would simply re-enforce old traumata.

Eddie was helped to work through some of his anxieties about drowning in a setting which was close enough to the original disturbing situation so that success in the pool could effectively relieve it. But this was possible only because the setting was at the same time controlled enough, in terms of life guards, counselors, and the security of the child's personal relation to his favourite counselor, to permit him to deal safely with anxieties based on past experiences. Here, as always, it was important not to force the child to face his recollections of the past or to test reality prematurely, but to handle the situation so that the child could independently regulate how he dealt with his past memories and resultant anxieties in the present.

Another emotional factor directly connected with the ability to move, and opposed to the security derived from it, is the anxiety which is particularly aroused in emotionally disturbed children when they move about freely. For example, girls who wish to outdo boys will insist on dangerous activities; boys who are trying to live up to true or misinterpreted parental expectations want to behave like "real he-men" while others try to gain status with their age-mates through foolhardy behaviour. Then exercise is no longer a pleasure, even in well-coordinated children. Instead it becomes an occasion for anxiety which may add to already existing difficulties. Although we have not yet had a child in our School whose principal difficulty was the anxiety created by the daring exploits he felt called upon to perform, we have very often found it a complicating factor. Often, however, it provides us with one of the easiest openings for relieving the anxiety of the child, and for opening up to him the pleasures he can enjoy in his own smoothly functioning body.

Children who in general feel inferior, either for valid or in-valid reasons, try particularly often to compensate by daring. Most of their dangerous activities they also regard as a challenge to fate. It is as if they must demonstrate to themselves that they cannot be bad children after all, or fate would take advantage of the many chances they offer it to punish them by making them have accidents.[15]

Eddie, for example, when first taken to a public playground, would compulsively climb up a ladder that led to a double bar slide. In doing so, he showed enough signs of anxiety for the counselor to tell him each time that he didn't have to climb up, and if he did, he didn't have to slide down. The counselor also told him that he'd prefer it if Eddie stayed away from the slide altogether, or if he insisted, that he at least let the counselor help. But Eddie felt he had to establish his courage with the other children, and thought this was a good place to show off. Since he insisted, the counselor climbed up with him, and holding onto him, they slid down the bars together. With his counselor's protection Eddie was able to complete the show of daring that he needed.[16]

In this particular situation it was best not to prevent the ex-ploit. All we could do was lower the anxiety connected with it— one of the reasons being that this was a public playground, espe-cially outfitted with equipment for children's use. Hence by im-plication it was clear to the children that society expected them to be able to handle such equipment. Frequently, however, a child's efforts to show off by daring can be prevented in such a way that his need for status is nevertheless protected.

The counselor takes the initiative in holding the child back when he wishes, for example, to jump into a swimming hole, walk on a high ridge, or climb out on a limb, etc. The child's insistence on performing the stunt, an insistence that grows louder and angrier the more convinced he becomes that the counselor will prevent him from doing it, permits the child to

[15] See also Publications on the School, no. 9, p. 234.
[16] Participant observer: Clarence Lipschutz.

236 • *Love Is Not Enough*

feel perfectly safe and still to establish or maintain his status with the other children. They witness his desire to do the daring thing and they see, too, that only the insistence of the adult, and not at all the anxiety of the child, is what prevents him from going through with it. Moreover, all possibility of defeat is also excluded.

New children usually test the counselor for some time with their insistence on daring behaviour until their status in the group is so well established that they no longer need to impress others with pretended courage. Only when they are finally convinced that the counselor will prevent them from going dangerously too far do their movements become free of anxiety and a source of genuine pleasure.

It is well known that a significant step in socialization is made by the child when he gives up imagining himself in the role of the robber and prefers instead to play the policeman. He has not yet given up acting out his aggressive tendencies, but he no longer needs to do so in asocial ways. He is willing and able to discharge them in socially approved manners. With many of our children we cannot afford to wait until they themselves take such steps toward socialization, because their egos are too weak to do so without our support. In order to strengthen the child's ego it is best if he is helped to make the transition to social behaviour by himself. Therefore it seems preferable if the adult stops the child's asocial behaviour and lets things rest there. It is then up to the child to decide if he wishes to take the next step.

In a way we function like the law which mainly prohibits violence and only rarely enforces decent behaviour. The latter is the prerogative of the individual, a prerogative he must exercise on his own in order to "find himself" as a self-respecting citizen. Putting a stop to asocial behaviour is our right and duty as adults; but it is the child's privilege to make the transition from discharging aggression asocially to doing so in socially constructive ways.

For example, one day Louis was roller skating wildly around our indoor gymnasium, narrowly missing the walls and pillars, continuously risking injury to himself and other children by skating into them. The counselor stopped him, explaining that he wasn't going to permit Louis to hurt himself or anybody else. Thus prevented from discharging his aggression asocially, Louis spontaneously decided to be a policeman. He got himself one red and one green ping-pong racquet with which he successfully regulated the roller skating traffic so that everybody could enjoy it and nobody get hurt. For Louis this was an important experience with controlling his asocial tendencies in constructive ways. What made it easier for him was that the transition of roles within the game was so immediate that it required very little repression of his aggressive tendencies. The new role increased Louis' status in the group considerably, and also his self-respect. Immediately afterward his counselor had a really animated conversation with him for the first time in many months. Whereas before a conversation with Louis had to be kept going with effort by the adult, it was Louis himself who kept it going and alive this time.[17]

Matters are more difficult in the case of games which are superficially harmless and seem perfectly legitimate activities. Still, because of the phantasies some child may connect with a particular play, it may seem full of danger to him, and the game will create only anxiety without relaxation. Ralph, for example, seemed to think, dream, and live only for baseball. On a superficial level he seemed to do this firstly because he thought it was the only tie he had with his father (his mother, he thought, had no use for him), and secondly because it was the only activity in which he was more than adequate for his age. In most other areas of living he was seemingly inferior. Thus for some time we thought Ralph should be permitted to continue with his monomanic devotion to baseball so as to enjoy all the status it gave him; at the same time we hoped he might utilize the

[17] Participant observer: Roderick E. Peattie.

strength of this status to build up other areas of achievement, intellectual and physical. But as Ralph permitted himself to show us more of his true emotions, it became obvious how anxious he was whenever he played baseball. Despite encouragement to give it up, he could not seem to relinquish what for such a long time had been so important to him. As he matured along other lines, and particularly after he became fascinated with chemical experiments, he began to be clumsy about catching the ball so that this once excellent player not only fumbled but hurt himself several times until finally one of his fingers was dislocated by an awkward catch.

Ralph insisted of course that he meant to continue to play with a bandaged finger, but things had then reached the point where we felt baseball could be declared out of bounds for him without loss of status. He was told that we wanted his finger to heal without interference, and although medically such precautions were not indicated, he was told that he would have to quit baseball for at least a two week period.

Protected for at least two weeks from having to play he opened up for the first time about his anxieties. He enlarged on the terrible accidents that may happen in baseball, winding up with the story of how in a school he had previously attended, one of the children "got his head all smashed up by a baseball till it was all gooey. Boy, it was horrible!" That this fear of what might happen to him on the baseball field was connected with unconscious emotions about his younger brother also became clear at this point. After elaborating for some time on the horrible accident, he continued without any interruption, "And when I go home I'm going to play with my little brother. He'll come into my bed, and boy, am I going to play with him!" [18]

Changing a game from the threatening to the assuring is a device well known to most educators. In working with emotionally disturbed children this device is particularly important because it is another way of showing them that what they interpret as threatening can be viewed equally well as reassuring

[18] Participant observer: **Fae Lohn.**

without loss of pleasure in the game. Of course, such changes from anxiety to security can be achieved only after the child feels secure within the School, and within his relationship to his counselor. Typical of such incidents are the changes from gangster to cowboy or sheriff, from firesetter to firefighter, and so on. But these changes are possible only if the particular game (or the role) is not part of the delusional system of the child or his specific anxiety. Hence some games, as innocuous as they seem, are so directly connected with specific anxieties through their content or connotations, that no direct approach will eliminate their threatening meaning to a particular child.

One preadolescent boy who for years had been suffering from serve learning difficulties wished more than anything that he could live on a ranch. Either openly or in phantasy he was constantly playing at being a cowboy. His parents concluded that since he resented city life and academic matters so much, it might be a good idea to have him live the simplified life of a cowboy. When we were able to penetrate to the true meaning of his phantasies, it became apparent that his games were far from innocuous. His phantasies rotated around the idea that he would lasso the cattle and then burn them with his initials, the place chosen for the branding being invariably the animals' genitals. Thus even the universal play of being cowboys may acquire a meaning for a particular child which is quite different from its meaning for most children. What we have to do in such cases is to stop such a game since it cannot, psychologically speaking, be changed into a reassuring game and only takes the child farther away from reality, deepens his anxiety. His annoyance at the counselor for doing so is less delusional than his aggressive daydreams; it is part of a real relationship and hence is often a good lever for approaching the deep anxiety. In these and similar situations strategically correct interference with an activity is the best way, in the last analysis, of handling a situation.

9

alone and in the group

THUS far we have mentioned a number of ways in which children may receive help with their difficulties: help given on the spot, help in mastering tasks, in testing reality in overcoming fears, help through marginal conversations, through non-verbal contact and so on.

Much of this support is given when the child is with his group (if not always part of it) and this conditions, to some degree, the nature and effectiveness of adult support. For most of their lives, the children whom we serve have either been too far away, or too close to adults for their emotional well-being. They have become, for example, either defensively and precociously independent of adults (as delinquents) or have never gained any true emotional independence (as with anxiety-ridden children). As a matter of fact, most of them show both tendencies: at one moment they are defensively independent, at another they are clinging to us anxiously.

Personality development proceeds parallel with the forming of an independent ego. The development of an ever richer, more independent ego should coincide with a greater and greater ability to relate freely to others. A free and spontaneous interplay between dependence and independence on others should be the high point of personal development, at least as far as personal relations are concerned: a freedom to establish close emotional

240 >

contacts while preserving, for most of the time, an independent ego. Although in close relations, the emotions (the ids) may seem to merge and the superegos to become similar, yet mature persons, even in emotional closeness, will retain some measure of ego distance from one another.

Such a mature attitude is not possible for children, and particularly not for severely disturbed children. It is especially difficult for them to maintain their individuality while relating in a one-to-one relationship to an adult. Either the child does not relate at all, is unable to establish and maintain contact with any of the adults whom he hates and fears, or he establishes so close, so dependent a relationship that he gives up his independence entirely, never forms more than a parasitic relationship. But while the latter seems to offer the child at least some momentary relief, it also stunts his growth as a person. In either case his ego is prevented from developing.

The need for correct dosage of ego distance in the therapy of adolescents was only recently illuminated in a paper by Dr. Gitelson.[1] In younger children it is even more of a problem than in adolescents, because the maturational state of the adolescent makes some measure of independence easier for him. Buxbaum,[2] Redl,[3] and others have further discussed the need for group living in the case of smaller children. Therefore, the following remarks are mainly an elaboration of what they and others have already implied in their writings. For the rest, it is not my purpose here to spell out in detail the difference between group relations as compared with adult-child relations.

Suffice it to say that while a group may have adopted a com-

[1] Gitelson, M., "Character Synthesis: The Psychotherapeutic Problem of Adolescence," *The American Journal of Orthopsychiatry*, XXVIII (1948) 422-31.

[2] Buxbaum, E., "Transference and Group Formation in Children and Adolescents," *The Psychoanalytic Study of the Child*, Part I (New York: International Universities Press, 1945) 351-65.

[3] Redl, F., "The Psychology of Gang Formation and the Treatment of Juvenile Delinquents," *ibid.*, pp. 367-77; and "Group Emotion and Leadership," *Psychiatry*, V (1942) 573 ff.

mon superego, a group ego, at least in modern society, seems a contradiction in terms. Even a coherent group can at best offer its members something like a common group climate, to use a Lewinian [4] term, a climate which supports the individual as if his ego were in accord with the prevalent group tendencies.

On the other hand, a coherent group will either disregard the individual whose tendencies are not in line with the group climate, or try without pressure to draw him into its orbit. But it will always permit the individual to maintain his separateness. In the group, the severely damaged individual gains support for his weak ego. At the same time the group prevents him from giving up his independence entirely because there is no one person whom he can arrogate to himself and therefore no one he is forced to emulate. Not that some children do not try to do so, but the convergent demands of other members of the group on the individual make it almost impossible for a child to maintain total isolation forever. Similarly, total dependence on the group leader, the adult, is not possible when the demands of other children, and his response to those demands, is ever present.

Thus the group not only supports the weak ego but also stimulates it to experiment with independence. All levels of ego distance—with the exception of total independence or total dependence—are thus constantly possible. The child may submerge his individuality in the group at one moment, and experiment with various degrees of ego distance, of independence, at the next. What is even more important for many of our children is the fact that for some time they can live relatively satisfying lives without any emotional relations to adults because the small emotional involvement they are capable of they can get through the group. On the other hand, while the child can experiment with a close relation to an adult, the presence of the group reassures him that it need not engulf him as he may fear.

---

[4] Lewin, K., *Principles of Topological Psychology* (New York: McGraw-Hill Book Co., 1936); and *Resolving Social Conflicts* (New York: Harper & Bros., 1948).

While it is thus most important for a child to be living within a coherent group, somewhere along the line of his rehabilitation he must learn to form and manage more lasting, more intense and mature relations than those he can form within the group, be it to the other children or the group leader. Precisely because the child's ego matures within a group which allows him to experiment with ego distance and ego closeness, a point will be reached where he no longer wishes to submerge himself in the group but to experience privacy. Then he no longer needs the group to hide in immediately, should a conversation with the adult lead him out too far; by then the group's presence may actually interfere with his desire to explore more deeply into his emotions and the recesses of his mind.

Therefore, the children also need longer, uninterrupted individual contacts with adults which are not necessarily centered on immediate activities. Merely helping them to understand their present behaviour, or how the past interferes with their present would remain incomplete in freeing the child from old anxieties, if it were not also accompanied by an actual clearing away of the residues of the more distant past which still interfere with his present behaviour.

At the beginning of his stay at the School, and often for a long time afterward, the group's pressure for, and concentration on, the immediate present is a great relief to the child who is only too painfully involved in his past. It shows him that, contrary to his fears, the present can proceed relatively independent of the past. Nevertheless, there comes a time and a need for a more extensive working through of past experiences.

There are also certain types of acting-out behaviour which can only be permitted in situations that are somehow more controlled and more circumscribed. The working through of certain experiences or emotions can take place only when outside interferences are at a minimum and when the child feels free to act out without fear of reactions by others. And again, there are some children who can only develop close relationships in a relatively intimate personal setting. Therefore, all children have the chance, if they want it, of meeting with a staff member in private, so-called individual sessions.

Much that happens in these individual sessions is similar to what goes on in any other form of child therapy based on psychoanalytic principles. Ample publications are available on the purpose, nature and content of these therapy sessions with children and on the particular problems they pose, or how the adult-child relations they involve may be handled. Hence I shall here disregard what is common to both the sessions at the School and to therapeutic sessions with children in general. Instead, I shall concentrate in the first part of this chapter on what seems specific to sessions that take place within a setting such as the School.

To begin with, the frequency of sessions is not set once and for all, but may change or be arranged in line with the child's own desires or his needs of the moment. They vary in frequency from one to five times a week. Approximately half of the children are seen by their own counselors; the remainder are seen by staff members who are not their counselors.

The first arrangement is preferred if we feel that the child cannot afford, at the moment, to form more than one close personal relationship, or if we think that all central life experiences should be kept as compact as possible for him. In such cases the counselor who sees a child is one of the two counselors regularly assigned to the group whom the child has singled out as his favourite. Of course, we are not entirely unlimited in making such decisions. For example, one of the two regular counselors for a group may be unable to take on any more children for individual sessions, while the other is not yet far enough ahead in training to be able to help a child in individual session. Then, too, another staff member has to see the child individually.

While the therapist in most child psychiatric work does not actively participate in the child's life outside of the treatment situation, our procedure follows the classical first case of the psychoanalytic treatment of children—the case of little Hans, where the father himself was the therapist.[5]

These sessions have a continuity of their own, despite the other close contacts the child has with the adult in question. Quite often they proceed independently of what is going on between counselor and child during their common group life. For example, a child may be discharging massive aggression toward his counselor in a series of individual sessions, but may nevertheless relate himself in a very positive way to that counselor within their daily group life. Another advantage of this identity between group worker and individual therapist may be seen from an example below, in which feelings of sibling rivalry having their origin in the group situation, as well as in the relation of a child to his individual therapist, were worked through with the latter in an individual session.

On the other hand, it is important for some children that the person with whom they work through some of their more pressing problems should not also be the person who eats with them, dresses them, and bathes them. These children are seen by staff members who do not participate directly in such aspects of their daily life—and this will also be illustrated below.

Here it should be stressed that even when the staff member who sees a child in individual sessions is not his own counselor, he is nevertheless very definitely a part of the School. He knows in broad outline what is going on, and he is informed of the child's difficulties or preoccupations as they arise. The child is well aware of this, and often uses the staff member who sees him individually as an intermediary between him and his counselor, or between him and the director.

Thus, there are several major differences between our individual sessions and what is commonly practiced in child psychotherapy. One of them is the close contact between the sessions themselves and all the rest of the child's activities at the School.

[5] Freud S., "Analysis of a Phobia in a Five Year Old Boy," *Collected Papers*, III (London: The Hogarth Press, 1925), pp. 149 ff.

Another is the fact that the adult is a person who is closely integrated with the total School life, and hence also with the life of the child.

Since the sessions take place at the School, we do not have to call for the child, nor does anyone else have to send him or bring him. In this way, either attending or avoiding the individual sessions remains the responsibility and the privilege of the child. Even our most disturbed six-year-olds are well able to come on time if they really want to. For the first two or three sessions, the adult calls for the child; after that he waits for the child in the play-room. If the child cannot tell time, he may be given a drawing showing the hands of the clock which are set for the time of his session; he can then watch the real clock till the two look alike; or, in some cases, the teacher will remind the child. But it is always up to the child whether he wishes to go or not.

All sessions take place during class time. We have found that it creates too much conflict for the child if he has to choose between sessions and after-school play. If a child comes to sessions, well and good; if he does not come he may later be asked why he chose to stay away, or his not coming may be disregarded, depending entirely on the situation. This policy has the advantage of not burdening the sessions with what preceded it: the coaxing or the forcing of a child to attend, or the distractions en route to the session.

At the same time, in a setting such as ours, the individual session is particularly important. It has functions in addition to those usually inherent in psychotherapeutic sessions with children such as ours. For example, by trying, at the School, to make activities as attractive as possible, and life as pleasant as possible, and by taking the initiative in doing so, we deprive the child of many outlets for his negative feelings. Some children find relief through their early morning pestering or by refusing to learn, or in one or another of the various ways mentioned in previous chapters. But for others, it is the session which provides them with an opening for very massive aggression or negativism which is not readily available to them in group situations, or might have undesirable consequences for the child or the group life. Some children express their negativism by letting the counselor wait fifteen minutes before they appear, or by leaving the session just a few minutes after arrival. In addition, they show all other types of negativism which are found in all psycho-therapy.

One boy, for example, spent many sessions reading quietly with his back to the adult. Other children spend whole sessions, or several sessions in a row, making grunting noises, or accusing us of every crime under the sun. By discharging such massive ag-gression against the adult, some children are simultaneously enabled to build up relations to their age-mates unburdened by accumulated tension and hostility. For them it is more impor-tant, at the moment, to be able to establish relations to children than to adults, and their sessions make it easier for them to do so.

How a freedom to attend or be absent from sessions is used by the children may be exemplified by Teddy, whose fear of his mother, and of women in general, led to particular defenses against his anxiety. One of his defenses was seductiveness and another, the practice of assuming the role of a girl. Both defenses he revealed at his very first session; the first, by coming with the front of his trousers unbuttoned; the second, more explicitly, by stating that he disliked playing with boys because they fought so much, and if he got into fights his mother got mad.

By being so freely seductive and girlish in this first session he could afford to behave more boyishly in the group, and thus to establish himself there more securely. At the second session he admitted, "I don't like to be myself." But these and other frank statements created so much anxiety that he was too frightened to come to his third session. When he was asked why, he re-plied that he was all confused. His counselor questioned him gently and at last he burst out, "I didn't come because I'm scared," and he began to shiver.

His counselor tried to assure him there was no reason to be afraid, that it was entirely up to him whether he came to the sessions or not. The friendliness she maintained for the rest of

that day, and on the following days when the two were together in group situations, convinced him that this was a mother-
figure who did not punish him for staying away when he felt
he was expected to appear. This freedom to avoid coming to
session, with which he experimented repeatedly, plus his counselor's reaction of acceptance, proved a very reassuring experience for Teddy.[6]

Jealousy is another of the problems which lend themselves
well to being worked through in individual sessions. Jealousy is
unavoidable, of course, in a setting where children must often
share the attention of one and the same adult, a person who is
important to all of them. Moreover, sibling rivalry has already
aggravated the difficulties of most of the children so seriously
before they came to the School, that they are driven to re-enact
it in their new relationships. This acting out permits us to deal
with it constructively, but in order to do so we must be able to
help the child recognize it immediately. Otherwise, it can interfere so much with his relation to a significant staff member that
the child is no longer able or willing to recognize the origin of
his difficulty in the relationship.

Sibling rivalry must be accepted as a legitimate expression of
natural emotions. But at the same time, the child must be helped
to understand that his jealousy of another child (whom he views
as a competing sibling) becomes exaggerated if he bases his relation to a staff member mainly on the fact that the adult also
has a relation to another child. We must help the jealous child
to understand that having to share the attention of a counselor
does not mean he himself is rejected.

In the School this common emotional problem is not reserved
for sessions with a therapist who is remote from the center of
rivalry; neither is it re-enacted solely by means of dolls, nor expressed only in hammering or kicking games which can at best
release nonspecific, unintegrated tension. Instead, we try as
much as possible to deal with these emotions within a personal

[6] Participant observer: Josette Wingo.

relationship, and in exactly the settings in which they originated.

Richard, for example, felt rejected all his life by a mother who he thought favoured his older brother. He had been seen in individual sessions for some time when he learned that his counselor was also to begin seeing Jerry (another boy in the same group) in individual sessions. We knew it would be difficult for Richard to take, and expected some reaction, though we could not know when or how it might come. It might be while the group was together, or when he ran into his counselor by chance, or perhaps in his next session with her. As it turned out, it was when she saw him the next day, individually.

Richard came on time but as soon as he walked in he turned his back. Then, without speaking to her he edged over to the candy box in a round-about way, stuffed his pockets with candy, turned his back on her again and began to eat the candy, strewing the wrappers all over the floor. Since this brought no reaction, Richard pretended to stagger about the room and then began to grumble, though his counselor could not make out what he said.

After waiting for some time, hoping he might be able to say what was bothering him, she finally asked, "Richard, why don't you tell me what you're angry about instead of acting this way?" "I'm not angry," he said, but he turned away roughly and looked out of the window. After another short pause he walked toward her very quietly, grabbed the chair over which she had hung her coat (though there were other chairs in the room), pulled it forward as if he meant to sit on it, and managed to have the coat fall to the floor. Once it had fallen he stepped on it heavily and deliberately.

His counselor said, "I wish you'd tell me what you're angry about. You're stepping on my coat but I can't tell from that what's really the matter." He looked up at her, and after a moment's hesitation, he picked up the coat and put it back on the chair. Then he blurted out, "You don't like me anymore, you never do anything with me, you never take me any place, you never give me anything." When she asked him why he thought that, he said, "I don't know." So she asked him again what had made him so angry, and again he replied, "I don't know." She asked what had happened that made him feel he wasn't liked—what had happened that week, the day before. . . . When they came to the preceding day, his "I don't know" was less sure. Then he said, very slowly, "Well . . . I don't know."

By then his counselor felt that he himself had come close enough to the real source of his anger, and had also convinced himself that she still liked him since she hadn't been cross about his ignoring her at the beginning of the session, about his not wanting to have anything to do with her, or his stepping on her symbolically by stepping on her coat. (She was able to accept these things so sympathetically partly because she herself felt bad about starting to see another boy individually when she knew how it would make Richard feel.)

At any rate, it was here that she asked, "What about me starting to see Jerry yesterday," And now Richard was very sure of himself. "Yes," he said, and when she asked what about it, he replied, "You don't like me." But she assured him that her seeing another boy didn't affect her relationship to him, that she liked him just as much as before.

Then Richard asked if he could use the baby bottle again. His counselor said he knew he could, and he asked her to fill it for him. (Previously he had always filled it himself, but he had not been using the baby bottle for some time.) She filled it, put the nipple on for him and he sucked on it for some time, very content, and very much in contact with her. Then he said, "It's a long time since I started seeing you, isn't it? It's been over a year and a half," and he went on sucking the bottle. A few minutes later he said, "Patty, I never had one of these when I was a baby," and he looked at her provocatively. "That was a long time ago," she said, "and pretty hard to remember." He dropped that line then, and said, "Yes, I suppose so. I did use one when I was a baby but I can't remember very much about it."

Richard went on drinking out of the baby bottle for the rest of the session, and before he left he said a very friendly "so long" [7] to her.

It was as if, after first having convinced himself that his counselor was still fully accepting of him in spite of her also seeing Jerry, and after Richard realized that his feeling of no longer being liked was due to his own emotions and not to her actions, that he recalled the many pleasant times he had had with her in individual sessions.

He had convinced himself that even the most primitive satisfaction was still available to him with her and yet he had made one last effort to provoke her; this time not into rejecting him, but into providing him with a very special satisfaction; that is, by pretending that he was much more deprived than anybody else because he had never been allowed to enjoy sucking as a baby, and therefore had very special claims to indulgence.

When she dealt with this last remark realistically, he dropped his provocative behaviour. He was convinced, then, that she accepted his drinking out of the bottle not because she felt guilty about also seeing Jerry individually, or because it was a particular measure that her job obliged her to, but just because he enjoyed it. He believed now that she still liked him and he felt secure again about enjoying childish pleasures in close contact with her.

As I have said, it is best for some children to be seen individually by their own counselor, but it is equally important for other children to be seen by someone other than their counselor. Louis, for example, had formerly felt seduced by his mother around most of the bodily help she had given him. He therefore expected seductiveness from any woman who performed similar services for him and could not work through with them his particular anxiety. In order to do so he had to be seen by a woman, but one who did not also attend to his bodily needs. Therefore, he was seen not by one of his counselors, but by our social worker. After a long period of getting acquainted with her, he told her one day at the beginning of the session, "I like

[7] Participant observer: Patty Pickett.

to come in here." And when she asked him why, he said, "Because I like to do things in private."

But even what he did "in private" was conditioned by his fear of direct bodily contact or of being forced into personal involvement. Some children use this privacy for their first experiments in regressive behaviour, such as curling up in the adult's lap while they suck out of a baby bottle; only later, if at all, can they transfer such behaviour into less private situations. But Louis, who was incapable of any relatively mature activities and who always acted the frustrated, and helpless small child, used this privacy to experiment with boyish activities more in line with his age. In this way he could test out the dangers of more grownup activities and also see if he could master them, while still playing the small child in the dormitory and classroom.

Similarly, this boy who had been looked on as seriously retarded by both teachers and parents, later used the privacy of the individual session for explorations which encouraged him to learn printing and spelling with a toy printing set, long before he could engage in such "dangerous" activities in the classroom.

Much later, when skills acquired in individual sessions were so well established that he dared to use them with his group and in the classroom, he experimented in the individual sessions with regressive behaviour. He dared to investigate whether "babyishness" in a private situation and with a mature mother figure, could be practiced without danger of overstimulation or seduction. After experiment convinced him that this was indeed possible, he knew he was free to enjoy both infantile satisfaction and mature achievement.[8]

Quite different was the situation with John whose motility was so seriously blocked that he couldn't even catch a ball. For adequate growth, at a certain stage of his development, he needed a relation that went on in semi-privacy, but one that was nevertheless closely linked to the School, because any adjustment to the outside world would have overtaxed his very limited adjustive capacities.

[8] Participant observer: Florence White.

All efforts at psychotherapy outside of the School had failed with him because the energy he used up on the way to the therapist, and the adjustment to a different environment were such overpowering experiences that no working through was ever possible. On the other hand, the structure of his disturbance drained his counselors of emotional energy to such a degree that it was actually impossible for them to meet him successfully in individual session. They had to serve him in so many menial tasks and to help him in so many difficult situations, he reduced them to the position of such infra-human tools that it was difficult for them to accept him without some adverse emotional reaction in individual sessions. Thus he needed closeness to a person who, while still closely connected with the School, was yet not his counselor.

For a long time he used this person for acquiring those skills which are the absolute minimum for social interaction among children, such as learning to play jacks; and after he had mastered the jacks he learned to catch and throw a ball. With her he acquired the skills he needed to enter the play of other children on the playground. Similarly, as noted in Chapter Eight, he could never learn to swim in the pool because others were present. He had to learn the swimming movements in the privacy of the play-room, a room in which he felt secure not only because of his relationship to the particular adult, but also because the room itself was part of the School.[9]

One problem that arises sooner or later, and one which is often handled in individual sessions, is the child's bewilderment or anxiety about our keeping of records. We wish, of course, to give the child the conviction that he is fully capable of understanding the world he lives in, at least as it pertains directly to him. Yet the children's records, which concern them very directly, are kept in the office under lock and key.

The office is the only place at the School which is kept locked when no adult is present, although the children are free to visit

[9] Participant observer: Florence White.

and explore it in detail when it is open or when an adult can accompany them. Nevertheless, although they are familiar with the office and its equipment, what transpires there arouses their curiosity. We tell them truthfully that the reason the office and particularly the files are kept locked is that no child would wish others to learn what his own records contain, and hence we must prevent all children from seeing any but their own records. But while they accept this as a reasonable explanation, it of course, only increases their curiosity.

Otherwise, every effort is made to give the children all the freedom they want to familiarize themselves with the office and its paraphernalia. For example, Max's conviction that the director owned a mind-reading machine ended only after repeated experiments with the dictaphone and after he had convinced himself that this mechanical device had no secret powers of divination or control over his thoughts. It gave back only what was spoken into it. For similar reasons all children experiment not only with the dictaphone and the adding machine, but particularly with the switchboard. This last is the mechanical gadget that most frequently arouses suspicion and is also the item of greatest interest.

Newcomers are usually too perplexed about life at the School, and how it differs from their previous experiences, to worry about anything as complex and un-immediate as their own or the other children's records. Moreover, they are still so convinced that the world of adults and what they do is beyond their comprehension that it never occurs to them to try to explore it.

Sooner or later, though, there comes a time for each child when he grows curious about his own record, a curiosity which is willingly satisfied, but only within the context of a firmly established relationship. Without such a relationship that security would be missing which is not only necessary for exploring, but also for understanding the content of the records. Only this relationship, moreover, permits us later to work through the possible misunderstandings or distortions the child may have created to satisfy neurotic needs of the moment.

When the child expresses what we feel is a genuine desire to inspect his record, or when he seems to be testing our intention of living up to our promise that he can do so if he wishes, the procedure is usually to encourage him to open the books at random, and to select any passages he wishes to read; whenever necessary, he is helped in his reading.

It is not the intention to have him read the transcripts in their entirety, but no child has ever asked for the reading of more than five or six passages. Thus far all children who have inspected their records have been much amazed to find that they consist mostly of a running account of events the child has participated in, and ones he can usually remember. The common reaction to this experience is typified by the child who concluded, "There's nothing here I don't know."

These and similar comments provide a good starting point for explaining that we have no secret knowledge, that we know very little about them that they do not know themselves. It is pointed out that one of our purposes in keeping the records is to help us to remember what happens, to help us see from the child's behaviour where we have made mistakes we can avoid in the future. Moreover, over a period of time they help us to see what is bothering a child, and that makes us better able to help him along.

Almost all children who read parts of their records are impressed by the care with which they are kept and derive security from this proof of how much effort is made to understand the child and to improve the way we handle our living together.

I might incidentally mention that as far as possible our records are observational and free of interpretations. We feel that efforts to commit ourselves in writing to "on the record" interpretations might interfere with the spontaneity of our personal relations. While we cannot avoid interpreting the child's behaviour to ourselves in our efforts to understand it, we feel that such tentative and often inadequate interpretations have no place in the permanent records; they tend too much to prejudice feelings and actions. Interpretations of the child's behaviour may be made after the treatment is finished, but by then the personal relation to the child has subsided in intensity by force of circumstances, and interpretations cannot then interfere with the spontaneity of our feelings and evaluations.

Certain parts of the records are attractive to all children. It is amazing to see how much comfort they derive from looking at the charts of their height and weight. The tangible evidence of their physical growth is always reassuring to them. This is, therefore, the type of data we even volunteer to show a child who is perturbed, for example, because he thinks that his body is not developing adequately, whereas with other parts of the records we usually wait for the child to take the initiative because we feel he knows best when he is ready for such an experience.

The initial inspection of records and the discussion of their contents always takes place in the privacy of an office or of the session room. Naturally, each child reacts differently to such an important experience, but allowing for individual differences, Teddy's reactions are as typical as any that might be described.

Among Teddy's major problems was an intense hatred for his younger brother, to whom he felt vastly inferior. After he had been at the School for more than a year and a half, he had his first truly pleasant home visit during which, for the first time, he no longer saw his younger brother as a superior, or even as a rival among equals. During an individual session with his counselor on his return, he told her how his brother used to be a "kind of a bogey man to me and now he's just a little punk." [10] For the first time, too, he had an idea that he himself might amount to something in life and with it there emerged for the first time some pleasant recollections of the past.

It began with his saying he would like to become a garage mechanic, and when encouraged that this might be a good idea (actually he had excellent mechanical abilities) he said, "There used to be a nice guy at the Pontiac garage near my house, and

[10] Participant observer: Josette Wingo.

he used to show me how to fix things. There was another nice guy there, too." This was the first event out of his past that Teddy had ever mentioned with pleasure. Before that he spoke only about his delinquent escapades, about how big guys used to beat him up and how unpleasant things had been in his family.

It was after this visit, too, when he was talking about his little brother, that he mentioned how his brother got a nickel every time he didn't wet his bed. By his tone of voice and the expression of his face, Teddy showed what he thought of the immaturity of his brother and what he now recognized as "foolishness" on the part of parents who paid children for not wetting their beds instead of ignoring it as we do at the School. He added that his brother had offered to buy him a present with the money, but Teddy had refused, saying, "Why should I take your money?" To the counselor he added: "Why should I take a little kid's money? I have money of my own and I get more allowance than he does."

This conversation took place during his session in the morning. That evening at bedtime he had another spontaneous recollection of his past: "The kindergarten I went to," he said, "had a nice little slide," and saying so, he laughed happily.

This ability to evaluate his home realistically, combined with pleasant recollections of the past, seemed to give him the courage to explore his life further, and one day soon afterward he asked to see his records. It was obvious that it seemed possible to him now that their contents were not nearly as bad as he had feared before the emergence of his pleasant recollections. He requested that his counselor bring the records along for their next private session.

Teddy, too, wanted first to look at his height and weight charts. But when he looked at them he became confused and said, "Oh, that's scary." His counselor asked if he really meant that, if it really was scary, and he admitted it wasn't, that it was only confusing. They had a conversation then about his tendency to interpret everything he couldn't understand right away as being scary, after which they went over the charts together and he was relieved and happy when he could finally understand them.

As always, a reading of the various observations on his behaviour at the School proved nothing but reassuring to Teddy, and his curiosity about that part was soon satisfied. And now his ability to learn about and understand his present and immediate past at the School became the starting point for exploring further with his counselor into his more distant past.

First Teddy asked a number of questions about his parents, questions he had never had the courage to ask about before. He was very pleased to learn in detail about his father's having come here from a European country, something he hadn't known before, and for the first time he saw his father in a new and better light.

Further talk about his past led to a discussion of his not having wanted to leave home for school. In a tone indicating that this was a revelation to him he said he had refused to leave his mother and his baby brother alone and added, "Maybe that's why I didn't get such a good start in school." His counselor agreed that that might very well have been the case but that only he could know if it was actually the reason.

Immediately after his inspection of the records and the talks that grew out of it Teddy was very thoughtful, but shortly afterward he underwent a change of mood and seemed happier than we had ever known him to be. This mood persisted for some time, and Teddy behaved as if a great weight had been lifted.

He had requested that his counselor bring the records to their next private session together because he wanted to read more of them. Accordingly, she brought them along and placed them in a conspicuous place on the table, but he barely glanced at them. Instead, he and the counselor played with a rather complex kaleidoscope, experimenting and exploring an enjoyable present in preference to a more or less unpleasant past.[11]

[11] Participant observer: Josette Wingo.

While some children need the privacy of the individual session with an adult to work on their immediate problems of the moment, other children are better able to state the feelings which are most perturbing to them when not only the counselor but the group, too, is present. This is particularly true of children whose relationships to adults have been damaged so severely that even in the one-to-one relationship with a relatively trusted adult they are unable to reveal their most important emotions.

The presence of others, particularly of children they feel are "in the same boat" as far as adults are concerned, gives them the courage to state their problems to the adult who is then more of an observer than a participant. Also, while engrossed in the play with other children, they are less on guard, and their defenses are likely to crumble more easily.

Grace felt very badly at one time because one of the counselors for her group was being replaced. Although she had never been too closely attached to the counselor the leaving of any person revived her deep fear of separation and particularly of death, which had brought about the most traumatic separation in her life—the loss of her mother. Her own counselor tried repeatedly to discuss the event with her in individual sessions, but Grace was silent and retired to seemingly innocuous play.[12]

One afternoon (following a morning session in which Grace had refused again to discuss the counselor's leaving) Grace and Mary played house together for quite a long time. Then Grace took over the play and the character of the game changed. First she took all the furniture out of the doll house and put pieces of Kleenex around in the corners, saying they were cobwebs. But Mary objected to their playing in such a desolate house and left the game, so Grace carried on by herself. She then proceeded to put cobwebs (pieces of Kleenex) on her hands and said she was dead, that the spiders were weaving cobwebs over her, and finally that she was a ghost.

At this point, it became possible for the counselor to start a conversation with Grace which was steered toward the other

[12] Participant observer: Joan Little.

counselor's leaving, toward Grace's known fear of separation and how she had dealt with this problem in the past. She assured Grace that she (the counselor) was staying with her and with the School and with that promise given, Grace was able to talk freely about her fear of separation and loneliness, although she had been unable to do so in the individual session.

When the counselor finally convinced her there was no question of her leaving, Grace took the cobwebs off her hands and out of the doll house. She replaced the furniture and the dolls, and in a little while Mary and other children joined the play with the doll house which continued along less morbid lines.

There is thus such a close inter-relation between the treatment value of a child's experiences in session or with the group, that there is little point in generalizing about which of them is finally most effective. Of the various devices we employ, some are more effective at some times and with some children, others with other children and for different psychological reasons.

Among others, the influence of the children on one another is one of the most effective devices at our disposal. This factor, however, as it operates at the School is so all-pervasive that there is hardly a chapter in the book in which it does not enter. Moreover, it has already been described in a separate paper and will therefore be dealt with more briefly at this point than its importance would otherwise warrant.[13]

Jack was a child who suffered from delusions of persecution and various compulsions. For some time after he came to the School he interpreted all suggestions made by counselors or children in terms of his own compulsive tendencies—to him their suggestions were never less than rules which he felt he must either break or obey strictly.

During the early part of his stay the other children felt uneasy about his inability to make contact with them and objected particularly to his expressions of pretended emotions. Once when he asserted in a kind of ventriloquist's voice how much he was

[13] See Publications on the School, no. 1.

enjoying a party which the children had arranged for themselves, the boys commented about it to one another. Then they proceeded as if they knew it might be easier for Jack to change his behaviour if they tried to make him join without the threat that might be implied in a direct challenge. When this didn't work, they became more direct and finally one of them said: "You sound like you're far away," to which Jack replied, "I am." So the children objected and said they refused to have anyone at their party who wasn't there.

This made quite an impression on Jack. For one thing he really wanted very much to be "in," and for another their threat to exclude him, much more than their friendly (and later their critical) remarks convinced him that both he and his emotions—which had always been neglected at home—were important to them. All this wore away his defensive isolation and the results were a pleasant surprise both to him and the others.[14]

It was a few days after this that Jack was present when another child was pretending to be a bear. The counselor looked askance at the game in view of the other child's tendencies to avoid reality, and told him he wasn't a bear at all, or even an animal, but a human being. Jack, who had never admitted that he, too, imagined himself to be an animal, became very incensed and said, "Aw, that's another of your damn rules. That rule is so filthy it needs a bath." His angry explosions continued for some time until another boy finally told him, "Now shut up. You're not an animal, you're a human being," at which Jack complained, "I always made believe I was an animal, but you and these damn rules around here won't let me."

Thus, for the first time, and due to group pressure, Jack not only admitted to phantasies he had previously hidden, but also conceded the possibility of having to give them up. The argument was concluded when the other boy announced with an air of finality, "Well, you are a human being, and if that's a rule, it's a damn good one." [15]

14 Participant observer: Josette Wingo.
15 Participant observer: *Idem.*

This episode, incidentally, is an example of a very frequent occurrence: The group, or another child, exercises a restraining or interpretative function, leaving the relations of the children to the counselor unencumbered from some of the need to restrain or interpret. It also permits the counselors to remain more positively supporting in their relations with the children.

In this, as in many other cases, the group asserted a reasonable attitude, and succeeded in exercising a reasonable control. But the motive which prompted the group to assert its influence in the first place was the unreasonable behaviour of a child, which seemed to threaten the integration and security of other members of the group.

Delusions are not the only threat against which a group or its members will defend itself and by so doing exert a helpful influence on the individual. Almost any coherent group of children will feel threatened by the sulky, withdrawn individual, and make efforts to draw him into its orbit. This makes it much harder for the withdrawn child to resist the temptation to form positive relations. The imaginary pleasures of social intercourse are more easily withstood by the sulking individual in the loneliness of his room, where he is at liberty to point out to himself that others are hateful or hateworthy; it is quite another thing to disregard them when they are present in reality and when others are visibly friendly.

The group also serves as an agent of therapy when it becomes an object for the discharge of hostility that might otherwise have to explode more asocially and result in severe counter-aggression—or engender more guilt feeling than occurs when aggression is directed against a group that feels secure in itself.

Among other reasons, the group permits the individual to express his emotions more freely because one of the main fears of the hostile individual is that his aggression may carry him too far and may lead him to commit dangerous acts. This fear is mitigated by the presence of the group which is better able, as such, to restrain the individual than anything he can do to restrain himself.

Moreover, while aggression directed against a group may provoke counteraggression, the counteraggression of a coherent group—though not of a mob—will never be as violent as the counteraggression of an individual might be, because the coherent group feels its strength, but also its obligation even to those of its members who at the moment are turned against it. Therefore, the coherent group feels less threatened by the act of the aggressor. It makes both the aggressions of the child and his fear of retaliation more manageable, and the process of living can proceed much more easily in spite of the act of aggression than it could if the individual were not living within such a group.

All this holds true, of course, if these living experiences take place among a group of children who otherwise live contentedly, or at least peacefully together, for most of the time. With emotionally disturbed children it is true, moreover, only if the presence of a protective adult gives them the security that he will step in, in time, if things threaten to get out of hand.

On the other hand, a non-coherent group of disturbed children will feel threatened by an individual's hostility and may react to the aggression of a stranger with greater violence than an individual might because their number gives them the strength and the courage to act out their anger.

In general, the less coherent a group is, the greater violence it will show in responding to the aggression of an outsider. But matters take on a very different colour if the aggression originates with a member of what is otherwise, and for most of the time, a coherent group of friends. The strength they usually derive from one another permits them to ignore aggression, delusions, or otherwise aggravating behaviour. Secure in their mutual relations, they do not feel threatened by it. They may deal with it by telling the aggressor to "quit that" or "lay off," or by addressing the rest of the group as if to reassure them (and in this way themselves) that such behaviour is of no import, by saying knowingly, for example, "There he goes again."

The offender who gets such reactions slowly gets the conviction that despite his aggressive outburst, he does not permanently lose the good will of the group, as he has feared, and that even when he discharges his tension following an inner need, he does not permanently lose the security that his relations to the others provide.

While this at first tends to increase the frequency and intensity of a child's hostile behaviour, in the long run it decreases it. The counteraggression which he used to dread after each act of aggression will now be absent, and will mitigate his fear and tension; hence, fewer aggressive feelings will accumulate. While the need to discharge aggression is thus lower, the behaviour of the group cannot fail in the end to create friendliness in the individual; feelings that persuade him to control his aggressions so as not to ask too much of the group or risk the loss of their friendship and esteem.

The group asserts its influence where its own general interests, or that of some of its members, are involved. Otherwise, the security which the members of a well-knit group derive from cohesion permits them to be untouched by behaviour which in other social contexts might arouse violent reactions. This is of great significance in the treatment of children who suffer from various delusional ideas.

It is interesting to observe how birds of a feather flock together at the School. A delinquent newcomer will immediately attract the interest of all other delinquents; a paranoid child, that of other children suffering from delusions of persecution; and so on.

In the chapter on learning, I mentioned how the defensive needs of the delinquent who has outgrown his acting-out stage may be set to good use in the rehabilitation of a delinquent who is still acting out. Here it may be added that the same holds true for paranoid children, or for children suffering from other delusions. But a word of caution also seems necessary. Two or more acting-out delinquents may well re-enforce one another and succeed in placing both beyond reach of the teacher, counselor, or other children. Similarly, two paranoid children may re-enforce one another's delusions and thus defeat all our efforts.

For example, two boys who for good reasons were very much afraid they might lose their still tenuous control over asocial emotions and be carried away to destructive (or self-destructive) actions, were both fascinated by the sight of drunkards, persons who had obviously lost control over their actions. Together, they played at being drunk themselves, and often claimed to be seeing casual passers-by who were drunk. In such cases a strange and vicious circle of behaviour would begin. One of them, having already lost partial control over his actions with delusional remarks and uncontrolled movements, would call the other boy over and point out a man he could see from the window whom he would describe as being drunk.

His calling of the other boy seemed to have meanings on several emotional levels. There was some hope that the other boy might deny that the man outside was actually drunk, in which case he could feel safe. This defensive goal, however, he could better have achieved by calling almost any other child, who would be much more likely to correct the misapprehension. But doing so would have meant that he would stand revealed as a person who misinterprets reality in terms of his delusions, in a word, that he was "crazy," as the children would say. To avoid being shown up, he preferred to call a child he felt sure would understand his anxieties because he had empathy with them, since they were also his own. For this reason he called the child who he knew was most likely to also misinterpret the visual experience as he had: namely, to agree that the man was drunk.

Thus, the effort to test his experience against the observations of a second person re-enforced his own fears, the more so since the other child was reacting with the same fear of losing self-control when confronted with what both children interpreted as a proof of how easily control can be lost. That they were both frightened only made the fear and the danger more real and hence increased their anxiety. Seeing the second child's anxiety grow then increased the first child's, which in turn doubled the other's anxiety, and so on ad infinitum.[16]

[16] Participant observers: Anna Lukes and Patty Pickett.

In the case of these two boys, a different grouping was technically impossible at the moment. Since neither could be helped as long as both of them continued to live at the School, one of the two had to be transferred to another institution to prevent the mutual re-enforcement which made treatment progress out of the question.

For these and similar reasons, it is often impossible to have more than one violently acting-out delinquent, or more than one child who is suffering from a given type of delusion, in the same group or even in the School at the same time.

The addition of another child with the same symptoms, if not the same disturbance, must then wait until the first child's defenses are so well established, that while he may still feel the newcomer's difficulties as a threat, he will not succumb to them. Then, and only then, does the threat of the newcomer become an integrative experience, because the child who is better adjusted can test his integration against the newcomer's unintegrated behaviour and come out encouraged. Then, too, the better integrated child offers the newcomer the most suitable object for emulation, for identification, because he recognizes that the other child has conquered his difficulties and that heartens him to believe he may be able to do likewise.[17]

In contrast to the mutual re-enforcement of delusional behaviour is the way such behaviour is ignored by a coherent group, as touched on above and as may be illustrated here by an example.

One evening Jack and his group were listening quietly to a story being read to them just before bedtime. The lights had been dimmed in preparation for their falling asleep, and all the

---

[17] This remark barely touches on the critical problems of grouping or admission policies. Perhaps after we have much greater knowledge about grouping, about the advantages and the handicaps that the various groupings imply, we will be able to make far better progress in the management of institutions, and particularly in mental hospitals. But the study of these problems is important not only for the handling of emotionally disturbed persons, it is equally important for the grouping of normal individuals, whether in schools, in the factories, in offices, in the army, etc.

children were absorbed in the story when suddenly Jack yelled, "There's a dead man there under the table." Quite forcefully and almost in unison the other children exclaimed, "There is not and shut up; we want to hear the story."

No reassuring statement by an adult could have been so impressive; in fact, Jack would never have listened, for adults at home had always denied the validity of his delusions, and otherwise convinced him that they never understood what perturbed him.

At home, children, too, had usually reacted to his delusions with so much emotion (as had also his parents and other adults), that he had never believed their assurances, since their emotional reactions clearly indicated there was more to the matter than they said. Other people's distress over his delusional statements, as well as their effort to reassure him, he was wont to interpret not as due to his distortions of reality but as an admission that there was good reason to be upset. Therefore, that the children should this time discredit his fearful imaginings without even the mildest of interest made him very uncertain.

He made one more try, though the ring of conviction was gone from his voice, and perhaps also from his mind: "But it looks like a dead man," he said. To which the others replied: "Well, it might look like it to you, but it sure doesn't to us. There are no dead people in the School."

Jack was apparently reassured for a while, but some fifteen minutes later he said quietly: "There's a man sitting on my bed." (It was no longer a dead man.) By now things had narrowed down enough so that a short investigation with the counselor convinced him there was nobody around to be afraid of. After that, reminding him where he could find her during the night was enough for Jack to fall asleep on without further ado.[18]

Of course, Jack was neither freed of his anxieties or his delusions, but for once he fell asleep early and peacefully, which at that stage was a rare and encouraging experience for him.

This example may incidentally illustrate how the compactness

[18] Participant observer: Josette Wingo.

268 » *Love Is Not Enough*

of life at the School, and particularly how the living within a coherent group, tends to help in disintegrating a child's delusions. While Jack lived at home his delusions were naturally upsetting to those who were close to him. They were upsetting both because they pointed up Jack's suffering, and also the degree to which he misinterpreted, and even turned into their opposites, all the well intentioned efforts of parents, friends and relatives. At home obvious efforts were made to humour him, and to give him the feeling of being protected. But these he only interpreted as proof of the validity of his beliefs, and also as being spied upon. If he mentioned his delusions to casual acquaintances, to classmates at school or to children he met on the street or on the playground, they made fun of him or wanted to have nothing more to do with him. In either case their behaviour added new fuel to his conviction of being persecuted by everyone.

At the School he was no more humoured or watched over than any other child. Hence, it was impossible to maintain for very long that he was being singled out for special attention, whether to be spied upon, or to be watched because he was so dangerous or so uniquely exposed to danger. The compact living arrangements at the School made it difficult for him to wander from adult to adult, or from child to child, looking for people to intimidate by his behaviour. Although he tried that at first, he soon exhausted those who were living or working at the School. Moreover, as time passed, opinions and attitudes that outsiders might have had about him lost importance when compared with the attitudes and opinions he encountered at the School. As indicated above, neither children nor adults at the School were particularly upset by his delusions, nor did they reject him permanently on that basis. Yet this in itself would never have been enough if outside influences had still supported his notions of being spied upon, or of being persecuted. Thus it was the healthy attitude of the group toward his delusions, plus the compact arrangement of life at the School, which together reduced the influence of outsiders to a minimum and helped Jack in overcoming his delusions.

The example of the cohesive group and its reaction to neurotic defenses is a strong incentive for the individual to change his own neurotic behaviour once he convinces himself that he must live with the group and cannot permanently escape from its impact. It forces him to adopt a more natural behaviour; and even if he does this defensively at first, as though to "escape into health," the more normal surface behaviour permits better reality testing which may then lead to truly better health, and the giving up of neurotic defenses.

For example, many children on entering the School, are very much afraid to undress in front of other children, though rarely is this due to a feeling of modesty. Usually the motives for what they explain as modesty are their own neurotic fears. Either they feel there is something wrong with their bodies, particularly those parts which their parents have taught them to keep covered, or they fear that their nudity will arouse uncontrollable sex desires in themselves or in others; they fear either that their nudity will be taken as an invitation to sexual aggression, or that being nude in itself will arouse them to becoming the sexual aggressor.

But whatever the source of their fears about showing themselves, the experience of seeing other children behaving with relative freedom about dressing and undressing is a challenge to the child's low opinion of the looks of his own body (or parts of it), while the experience that his nudity arouses both them and himself so much less than he had hoped for (and feared) proves most reassuring.

It would be too simple to assume that just the sight of their different behaviour suggests to the child that he follow their pattern. If a child feels inferior about his sex organs, for example, the process seems to be that while he himself is distinctly aware of his own feelings of inferiority, the sight of what he interprets as the freedom of others soon forces him to think about how strangely they behave while at the same time it brings into relief how his own feelings differ from theirs.

The conviction of the strangeness of their behaviour will force him, often for the first time, to view his own behaviour as odd. Once this point is reached, his next step may be to arrive at the conclusion that if they act so naturally and seem odd to him, he must seem even odder to them who are so free where he is inhibited.

For the first time nudity also appears as something that is accepted by others as being natural on certain occasions, another challenge to his old beliefs and anxieties. Actually, the others are not quite as uninhibited as he thinks—they only act out their anxieties differently—nor do they think him as odd as he believes.

Of course, freeness in dressing and undressing seen in one or another of the children would never be really convincing. They would only be looked on as "bad" children, or children who never knew any better. But the child cannot easily dismiss a group pattern of free behaviour which is followed in a matter-of-fact way and in the presence of an adult who is more or less experienced as a parent; this is a challenge to freer behaviour that cannot be totally ignored.

Again, undressing freely in front of others is itself no solution to the child's anxiety. As a matter of fact the child who is first shy and then begins to undress easily in front of others does so with even greater anxieties than the fears that originally made him want to hide parts of his body. But without it, the anxiety that reveals itself in not daring to expose oneself before others could never disintegrate through reality testing, because the "modest" child would never have experiences that might one day convince him that his body is as good as anyone else's, that it arouses neither disgust nor any outlandish sexual desires in others.

True, the challenge of the group often forces the child into behaviour that, at first, is at least as asocial, if not even more charged with anxiety than any of his former defenses—such as when he exhibits himself. But it soon becomes possible to plan his experiences in such a way that the new and more open behaviour will eventually lead to the disintegration of feelings of genital inferiority which originate in his low opinion of the looks of his sex organs, and this in turn may lead to a more rational view of his own body and the consequences of exposing himself.

It is not only the image of freedom in others which makes it possible for the individual to afford to be freer himself, but much more the feeling of security that he senses in the actions of others. It is not nearly so important that the other children act freely, as that they seem to be secure when they do so.

The child who is fearful of exposure or of the sexual feeling it may arouse, is induced by this general spirit of security to dare to be freer himself. This freer behaviour, while still fearful (because it is positive behaviour and not just avoidance of action) eventually allows for reality testing which may then have its chance to disintegrate the anxiety.

All this presupposes, of course, skillful handling by the adult. If the child, on initial or later exposures of himself, should experience ridicule or arouse too much interest, either turn of events would discourage any further reality testing and in its stead lead to under- or overevaluation of the impression that his genitals create. Similarly, if exposing himself arouses sexual aggression in others, the effect may be most damaging. Thus, independent of overt actions, it is always the casual way in which the cohesive group conveys its security to the individual which makes it an agent of therapy.

The security derived from the group also permits one child to interpret another child's action. In the one-to-one situation a child might not permit himself to realize or to verbalize the meaning he senses behind the actions of another child because he might be too fearful of retaliation. But secure in the support of the group, the individual child can afford to be daring about having, and expressing insight into, the unconscious motivation of another child.

One day, for example, a group of boys were returning from the beach with their counselor when a thunder shower broke in the distance. The children saw the lightning and could hear distant rumblings of thunder, at which Charles became very frightened and began grating his teeth. As the shower came closer the grating increased in intensity. Bob, another boy in the group, complained first to Charles and then to the counselor about the disagreeable sounds he was making. But Charles only grated his teeth louder and faster until Bob broke off, saying, "Just because you're afraid you don't have to bite our heads off," at which others joined in with similar protests.[19]

Since the group obviously understood some of the feelings his behaviour expressed, Charles no longer denied his hostile anger and admitted the truth of the interpretation. He was forced, in addition, to realize that others understood the meaning of what he had explained away lightly to his counselor as a harmless "habit." But Bob had been able to say what he did mainly for two reasons: firstly, he was part of a coherent group, and secondly, the presence of the counselor gave him the feeling that he was protected from any counteraggression from Charles, which he knew could become rather violent. In addition, the tooth grating was much less of a threat to Bob while the group was around than it would have been if he and Charles had been alone at the time.

These interpretations by members of the group take place under various circumstances. Often we get our best insight into the meaning of a child's strange behaviour through the comments of another child.

Charles' preoccupation with engines was discussed in detail in Chapter Eight. But that he identified himself with the blind and destructive power of a steam engine was first brought to our attention one day just after he had once again "run into" another of the boys. We had seen him do it before and had viewed it as an expression of his violent aggressions. But this time the victim exclaimed: "Here comes that steam engine again, running me down."

Questioning then revealed that Charles was imagining himself to be running on tracks, running down everything and everybody that obstructed his right of way. But the fact that from then on the other children understood his behaviour made it pointless for

[19] Participant observer: Gayle Shulenberger.

Charles to keep his phantasies secret, as he had done up to then. Once he had admitted them openly, once his behaviour was understood and hence no longer a source of irrational anxiety to his playmates, other children were able to enter the game.

Here again it is the compactness of living at the School which allows such interpretations by other children to come to full fruition in terms of a child's treatment. If Charles could have believed that there were still some children who weren't "wise" to the secret meaning of his game he would have continued to keep it secret, or have switched his associations to another group of children. But at the School Charles had to face the fact that all the children he could possibly play with or (what was currently more important to him) who could become victims of his aggressions, now understood the nature of the phantasies he was acting out when he bumped into them.

After that what had long been a form of isolating, asocial behaviour (and might have remained so forever), was transformed by another child's interpretation and the help of the counselors into a socializing game that drew Charles out of his isolation and reduced his hostility toward the world.

Children will interpret another child's actions or feelings not only to one another, but also to a counselor whom they trust. In this way, the members of a cohesive group will often explain the child's behaviour to himself in the most unobtrusive way by pretending to, or actually explaining it to, the adult.

Bert, a relative newcomer, was testing out counselor and group one day by trying to annoy Hank. First, he put his foot up on the table where Hank was trying to play, until Hank moved away. But Bert followed him and again put his foot on the table so as to prevent the other child from going ahead with what he was doing. At that the counselor took hold of Bert's foot and put it gently but firmly on the floor.

Bert sat there quietly for several minutes and then began to cry. He hid his head under the table as if he hoped that no one could see he was crying and tried to separate himself from the group. The counselor asked him if she had hurt his foot but Bert shook his head and went on crying hopelessly. At this point, Ralph spoke up and said, "Of course you didn't hurt his foot, Gayle. You hurt his feelings." And then Bert, who had been crying to himself, began to cry openly, raising his head and looking around at the group whose understanding and support he now seemed to sense.

While previous efforts by the counselor to console him had had to be rejected, he could see for himself now that the group understood and respected his feelings (although he had actually been the aggressor), and he was ready to accept her consolation. Pretty soon he stopped crying and curled up in her lap, and shortly afterward he entered the play of the children as a member of the group.[20]

This last is an example of the interaction between the direct help the child can get from the group and the marginal help of the counselor. In such interaction it is often important that the adult (the counselor) should represent attitudes pertaining to the reality of the situation, such as in preventing one child from annoying another. The task of the adult is to explain the world to the children and to help them understand it, while the application of this new understanding to the child's emotional problems is best provided by the child himself, or by other children who are closer in age and can better interpret it on his own level. This makes the application of any newly won understanding of his emotional problems less threatening and hence more acceptable to the child. In this connection it should be stressed once more that all seriously disturbed children live at war with the world of adults far more than they do with the world of other children.

If the children take up and discuss an adult's explanation, it is no longer something that the adult, for unknown and possibly selfish reasons, wishes to impose on the child, but something that he himself could (or has) figured out for himself. In this way the new understanding does not remain something extraneous, ego-

[20] Participant observer: Gayle Shulenberger.

alien, but becomes part of the child's outlook on the world and himself. In this, two examples may illustrate.

George got very angry one day because some of the children were being quite critical of his nasty remarks. By way of reply he announced that he was going for a walk by himself. In general we do not stop children from isolating themselves when they feel uncomfortable in the group, but in this case the counselor felt it was not to George's advantage to let him annoy the other children and then run off to dodge the consequences of his hostility. She felt that by now he was well enough ahead in development to learn to give up discharging random hostility against others without any connection to their attitude toward him, which in this case had been very friendly. But George insisted, saying in a grandiose way that he was going off and that he didn't wish to be bothered by what other children felt about his remarks. He added that he didn't care how the counselor felt about them either, at which she shrugged her shoulders.

But now Paul, one of the other boys took over and said: "Your wanting to take a walk is just like a man who drinks. You know some people go and get drunk when they have lots of troubles, and they think they'll forget them that way. And then they go and sleep it off, but after they wake up they find that they have the same troubles and didn't get rid of them. It's just like that when you want to take a walk."

Paul's reasonable approach changed the whole situation for George. It gave him something to think about and he began to wonder if his efforts to always evade issues by just going away by himself was really such a successful way of dealing with reality.[21]

In quite a different way the attitude of the group was a help to Morton when his anxiety prevented him from seeing world affairs in their true perspective. Morton, like many other children, used newspaper stories, as well as comics and what he called scary movies, as additional phantasy material for his anxieties. He also

[21] Participant observer: Gayle Shulenberger.

used them as a means of rousing anxiety in other children in terms of his own neurotic needs.

At the time of this incident, the newspapers were full of the danger of an impending war with Russia, and Morton used the headline "U. S. Plots War Say Russ" to go around excitedly telling other children that there was going to be a war. His counselor used this behaviour to explain to him once more the meaning and purpose of newspaper headlines, and also his misuse of headlines without investigating the story and the facts.

Some of the children joined the discussion and said they wished the newspapers weren't allowed to print such headlines. This was taken up by the counselor to again discuss with the group that while everybody has a right to state his opinions, one shouldn't just accept them but should investigate them, talk about them, and particularly what seems frightening or of concern to oneself. In the case of the headline, she showed them how easily others can be attacked and how quickly a fight can get started if opinion is taken for fact—and how little can be done if one's anger or anxiety are not spoken about. She then pointed out how a specific statement about the future—because it was presented as fact instead of opinion—aroused great and unjustified anxiety, and perhaps even aggression.

This stimulated interest among those children who were prone to state their fears about possible aggression by others as actual fact, and who then used the "fact" to justify aggression or asocial withdrawal on their own part.[22]

The result of this conversation was an acceptance by the group of the counselor's offer to help the boys read newspapers more accurately, and to learn how to separate opinion from fact. At this, Morton, who was excitable and paranoid, spontaneously provided an example of how a headline he had seen on a newspaper stand, had upset him. The headline he referred to read: "Mr. Bennett Found Dead in Room." And he laughed in an anxious way and tried to excite the others. But they said, "Who's Mr. Bennett, anyhow?" and "They talk about people you don't

[22] Participant observer: Patty Pickett.

even know and that's how they get you to buy the paper like that. Just like scary comics."

The counselor told the boys that while it was true that some newspapers try to get more people to buy papers in this way, there are others that print only the facts and give the people a chance to think for themselves. She told them that just the other day the staff had decided to order a few papers like *The New York Times* (Sunday edition), so that the children could have them and see for themselves that there are newspapers which can get along without unreliable opinions and flashy headlines about crime. The children, and particularly Morton, were very interested to learn that we talk about such problems at staff meetings.

The next day the counselor put a local newspaper on the table before the group entered the dormitory. The boys looked through it and found that the first three pages were taken up with murder and divorce stories, all of them about people unknown to them. They discussed it among themselves and decided that since none of them knew any of the people the papers talked about, the stories really had nothing to do with them.[23]

This was the first time Morton was able to look at a newspaper without getting anxious, and without feeling that every murder story he saw might pertain to him or his family. He repeated to himself several times that he didn't know any of the people the papers reported about, that they meant nothing at all to him. And while he had not yet fully accepted the truth of his own statements, he was seriously thinking them over because he had arrived at his doubts about whether all frightening news pertained to him by discussing it with other children, and not merely because an adult had delivered an opinion.

This kind of interaction between children and adult becomes particularly important when they are exposed to events which are removed from our control, when they come into contact with the outside world. But more about this in the following chapter.

[23] Participant observer: Patty Pickett.

10

the world outside

AT THREE o'clock on a weekday, school is out bringing with it the longest in-between period of the day. Whether the counselor is waiting for the child at the door of the schoolroom, or in the dormitory, she has prepared herself for the onslaught as best she knows how. Things are arranged nicely, and on the table she has set out ample snacks, games, and material for activities. But from past experience she knows that at best this will satisfy children who have been at the School at least a year, or longer. So it will help some, but not too much.

The children leave class full of pent-up tension. No matter how much at liberty they have been to study what they like, to move around freely, to talk things out, no matter how actively they have played during recess, they will still quit the classroom with a load of accumulated tension, if for no other reason than the strain they have felt in learning or the fear of now having to decide how to fill the next hours.

Some children come in, flop on their beds and want to do nothing at all. Others are raring to go, but as soon as another child or the counselor opens his mouth to make a suggestion, they shout, "No, no, I don't want to do that." And even if one of these negativistic children makes a suggestion and finds it accepted he may still change his mind, because what he really wants is to find reasons to feel persecuted.

In various ways we try to cut down some of the tensions created by this kind of indecision. For example, on four out of five weekday afternoons we have one prearranged activity extending over at least a few hours. Although these activities are regularly planned, the children don't have to participate if they don't want to although we try persuasion whenever we feel a child is ready to benefit by taking part. Still, even these events only extend over a limited period and the rest of the day is still free to be filled by the child himself. It would be easy to schedule further activities, but that would cut down on the areas of spontaneous living and the opportunities for choice-making, both of which the children must eventually learn to master.

As far as the planned and repetitive activities are concerned, experience has taught us that it is best to use the University swimming pool twice a week, the University gymnasium once a week, and one of the University's machine shops once a week. In the machine shop the children use mainly the woodworking machinery, although other machines are also available. The University's gymnasium and machine shop offer much more elaborate equipment than our own gymnasium and craft shop. Our own facilities at the School are used by the children freely, without any prearranged planning as to hours or days.

Once a week is allowance day, which means that going shopping for things they want to buy is likely to appeal to many children as a logical activity. With the exception of swimming, all other planned activities are arranged on any one day for only one, or at most two groups. This means, for example, that a child who didn't want to go shopping when his own group went, can join another group on some other day, and so enjoy additional freedom of associations.

Saturday and Sunday remain almost entirely free of planning although counselors are prepared to offer several alternatives if the children run out of ideas. Throughout most of the year the Saturday movies at the Museum of Natural History, or the story hours at the Public Library are preferred activities, as are ice skating in winter, and going to the beach in the summer. In this way, each of the five weekdays and Saturday morning hold out to the child one activity that he knows about in advance. But each of them stretches at most over two hours, leaving some three or four additional hours each day that are free to be used as the moment suggests.

Within pre-planned activities the child still has a wide freedom of choice, such as where to go shopping on allowance day, and for what. In this way, each child in his own good time can explore with varying degrees of freedom and with his ability to make choices. He can stick pretty much to what the School or the counselors have arranged for him, or he can decide to strike out on his own. But even the most insecure child has to make some decision such as whether he wants to stick to his bed, or join what the group wants to do; whether he wants to do something all by himself, or with one or two companions.

The following remarks will pertain mainly to those children who wish to have contact with the outside world, but they will also apply to all the children, because sooner or later they must all learn to deal with the world. Even those who would prefer to have nothing to do with the outside cannot always be protected. Shopping for shoes, for example, could be done for the child, but we prefer not to eliminate all taste of the outer reality.

It has been said before that we try to create an environment for the child which is so arranged that it does not present him with challenges he cannot master. But this we can do, if at all, only within the confines of the School. Our doors are always wide open, at least as far as a child's leaving the School is concerned. During the day, the child is protected by adults against outside intruders; at night, the doors are locked on the outside but may be opened from within. Thus the child is always free to leave the School grounds, but in doing so he exposes himself to an environment which is not controlled by us.

When a staff member is with him, it is understood that it is the duty of the adult to mediate between the random, everyday environment and the special needs of the child. But the counselor is not the only cushion between child and environment. Other children, too, namely the group in which the child moves, will protect him to some degree, always provided that he does not stray off on his own.

Children who come to the School fall roughly into two groups as regards their desire for contact with the outside: those who wish to roam in it freely, and those who wish to avoid it entirely. It is usually a long time before a child takes an intermediate position. Even runaway children who used to "escape" to the outside eventually lose this desire and want to stay put. It is only after they come to feel genuinely secure within the School that they slowly get ready to face the outer world once again. At first they will dare this only with their counselors as mediators. But as they grow more secure, they eventually make small excursions by themselves.

First, they may want to venture on their own to the corner drugstore, then to the branch Public Library three blocks away, to the dime store, to the nearby museums, and finally they may even go downtown all by themselves. The chief thing is that the child is always sure he does not have to go out by himself, that we are ready to accompany him at any time. If he insists that he wants to go out alone we try to arrange it so that it does not happen too early in his stay, or too often. After all, our major tools in helping the child are the impact of a planfully controlled environment and of personal relations; if both are absent, there is little we can do for the child except pick up the pieces afterward.

Therefore, the newcomer who wants to roam by himself, the runaway child, presents a difficult problem because he is not yet attached either to us or the School. He does not venture out from a basis of security to test how well he can deal with the unexpected in everyday life. The less he is around, the more time it will take him to benefit by the security which the School can provide. In his case—as with George's progress in domestication described in Chapter Six—we may have to follow where he runs. But then it is less to mediate between him and the world and more to protect him from at least the worst consequences of his own asocial behaviour. Yet even for these runaway children there comes a time when they want to stick as close to the School as they can, even more so than children who right from the start wanted never to leave the School grounds, or only rarely. Hence, for them, too, comes a day when they have to learn that the outside world is neither as dangerous, nor as hostile, nor even as threatened by their destructiveness as they fear.

In short, all children have to learn by slow and gradual steps that they can master those unpredictable events that every one of us encounters in the normal process of living. This they learn on their excursions into the world, be it on casual walks, on trips to the museum, to the forest preserves, to the zoo, etc.

Fortunately for our purposes, we are in a particularly good position for mediating between the School and the outer world, over and above the planning of trips and the presence of protective adults. We happen to be part of an institution which is larger than the School itself and which, without being part of the School, is still so closely connected with it that it stands as an area closer to "home" than the strange world at large. It is the smaller world within which the School functions: The University of Chicago.

Sooner or later every child derives great security from, and takes pride in the fact that the School is part of the University. They realize then that when they step outside the School door, everything as far as they can see are University buildings and grounds, and to the child, the immediately visible is pretty much the whole world. It is mostly the physical extension of the University campus that first impresses them as another source of security and then gives them a feeling of status, of belonging, when confronted with the open world.

It would be nice to think that it is also the intellectual character of the University which impresses the child, but this is not so. What he longs for is protection and security, and at his level of integration such abstractions as the world of letters mean little to him. If and when they become important, and eventually they do to at least some of our children, then the School has accomplished its task and the child is about ready to leave.

Things are different as far as the reputation the University enjoys in the community is concerned. This does add to the children's security. But as always the human element is much more important than anything else. It is the various strands connecting the staff of the School to the University that do most to make our children feel at home in it. That many of their counselors and teachers received, or are still getting their education there (some of them take courses at the University while working at the School), makes it a friendly, familiar place.

It is also important to them that the whole larger community in which they live is devoted to learning, which means they are not the only ones who are expected to learn and grow. This fact sets them less apart from the adults around them. That is, while most intelligent parents will tell their children that nobody ever stops learning or growing or rendering service to the community, parental reality usually indicates that these things are a sideline, an embellishment to life, and not part of its essence.

Teddy, for example, after he had been at the School for some time began to wonder how it happened that he was changing and how the School had accomplished this. One evening some of the boys were discussing improvements that had been made at the School since their coming, and wondered what made the staff interested in arranging for them. Then Teddy called his counselor over to his bed and asked her, "Patty, how does Dr. B. make you like the School?" (Dr. B. is the abbreviation of my name used by children and staff.) She replied by saying that neither I nor anybody else could make a person like the School, but that she hoped, from what he observed and what happened to him there, that he would eventually form his own opinion. "Well, like what?" Teddy asked. And his counselor told him to think, for example, about what had happened that day and on the previous day, about whether things had happened that he liked and were pleasant to him; and if that had been the case and if such days were repeated rather often, he would probably like to live at the School; conversely, if he had unpleasant experiences during the day, and if they were repeated, he would probably dislike the School. Teddy nodded and said, yes, there were lots of things he had liked.

Then he thought for a moment and added: "But the School isn't here just for the kids. The counselors get something from it too, don't they?" His counselor asked him what he meant and he said, "Well, a long time ago, when Josette started being my counselor, she didn't know what to do with a boy like me and then she learned how, so the School did something for her too." The counselor told him that was very true, that one of the main reasons the counselors worked at the School was that they felt it taught them a lot, and that to help them learn more was one of the purposes of the staff meetings he had recently been questioning her about. And Teddy said, "You mean where you talk about certain kids and not just things what to do around the School?" The counselor nodded and Teddy asked: "Well, how many meetings like that do you have—you have almost one every day, don't you?" The counselor said yes, we did, but that we discussed our work not only at meetings but whenever anything came up that anybody wondered about, or found interesting or important. Then Teddy asked, "Well, is that why Connie is visiting with us? Is she going to be our counselor?" (Connie was then a beginning counselor who had just started her training.) The counselor said no, that Connie wasn't going to be his counselor, but that she was observing with some of the counselors who had been at the School for a while to learn about their work. "You mean," Teddy asked, "she's supposed to learn something from watching you and then she'll be a counselor?" and his counselor replied, "I don't know if she will or not, but that's the general idea." [1]

Thus it is important for the children to see that even the staff members working at the School learn and grow just as they themselves are expected to do.

[1] Participant observer: Patty Pickett.

At the University, everybody clearly considers learning and maturing his main task, and the obvious purpose of the University is service to the community. These examples, and the spirit of the place are a valuable help in further socializing the child, but only after he is emotionally ready for it. Before then, such concepts would only overpower him, and therefore we don't bother him with them.

The University is also of direct service to the child by introducing him to the value of the community around him. It changes it from an indifferent or alien place to a friendly one. Through its clinics, the University looks after the child's physical ailments and protects him as much as possible from disease. Walks on campus, visits to the various University buildings, make it a place where he belongs. Since children appreciate most what is done for them tangibly, they like the fact that so many of the services that make life easier or more secure for them are provided not by outsiders but by the University to which they belong. University crews repair the buildings, University shops (which they visit) send the men who fix the furniture, and so on. All these things help them, in time, to understand that they are part of a greater universe which takes an interest in them, cares about them and for them.

While adults at the School mediate between the child and the outside world, the University, in a way, mediates between the School and the community at large. Depending on his need for security, the child can move exclusively in the small world of the School, in the larger world of the University, or finally, when he has learned to move about successfully in this relatively protected world, he can move out into the city at large.

It might be said that these observations have little general validity, because it is a unique advantage of the School to be part of a large university. But while it is true that the particular setting is not easily duplicated, it is by no means true that the underlying principle is not valid. Sound education anywhere in the world must proceed step by step. The child first grows acquainted with his own small family. From there he must go on to relate to his other relatives, to the family at large. After that he must develop the courage to explore the block he lives on and make it part of his life, and so on to the local church or public library or whatever other facilities for living the neighbourhood may offer. The seriously disturbed child is either totally withdrawn from the world, or is battling it. In any case he has never established, or has lost all contacts with, the community. These contacts have to be re-established in a slow, step by step growth.

The outside world reaches out even to the protected environment of the School. We cannot and do not wish to eliminate all communications that come from the outside; after all, the child must eventually learn to live in it. Therefore, as with other factors of reality, we try to dose stimulations correctly rather than eliminate their challenge altogether. Thus while we censor some of the magazines and newspapers to rout the worst of the gruesome pictures and stories that might be more than a child could bear, we can only do this within wide limitations. We cannot prevent the children from seeing magazines on the newsstands, and not to let them have any would arouse unmanageable curiosity. So, by and large, we must be satisfied with deleting the worst of their stimuli, and for the rest, pick up the chips as they fall.

But here again we hope that the security we offer the child will help him at least within the School to get the feeling that his anxieties play him tricks when he sees accidents everywhere without reasonable cause. Later, this may slowly make him less fearful about the dangers that seem inherent in everyday living, as in the case of Eddie's fear of cars.

In addition to his fear of drowning, Eddie was also very much afraid of cars, an anxiety that began when he was nearly run over by a car as a small child. Then and later he interpreted the accident partly as proof of the dangerous power of his enemies, and partly as a punishment for hostile phantasies and desires. Like Charles, he tried to conquer his fears by learning all about cars. At first, he questioned people incessantly about the merits of the various makes of autos and about which cars they liked best. On the basis of this knowledge he hoped to be able to figure out how dangerous each person was that he talked to.

Secretly, he believed that if he knew enough about automobiles, he would never be run over. For hours he played with little toy cars, moving them back and forth before his eyes or watching fascinated as he bent down to follow the turning of their wheels. As though in a magic effort, he tried in this way to control their movement until they should no longer endanger him. All direct reassurances were a failure, and we had to concentrate on more peripheral fears for decreasing his anxiety in general. For example, by providing him with more than ample food and toys, etc., we tried to counteract his feeling of present deprivation, and the way he constantly expected to be deprived in the future.

Since we preferred not to deprive Eddie of newspapers and magazines, and since we could not deny other children for his sake, it was unavoidable that pictures of accidents should reenforce his anxieties. But even if we could have eliminated all pictures of crashups it would have helped very little since even car ads were enough to activate his fears.

We assured Eddie over and over again that he was not likely to be hurt or endangered by accidents if he was reasonably careful. To ease his anxiety about his dangerousness to others, we also pointed out that we would never tolerate his hurting others, that the counselors were there to prevent such things, and that we were well able to protect not only him but other children and ourselves from whatever he might do. For a long time, though, he had little faith in what we said.

One day, after he was considerably more secure, he sat leafing through a magazine looking for pictures of cars or car ads, as he often did, when he saw something that apparently unnerved him. At any rate, he turned the page quickly without looking at it again. What he had seen was an advertisement for an oil company showing a car "riding" on a canoe, to convey the idea of how smoothly cars run when they use the company's oil.

Speaking casually, the counselor told Eddie that the ad on the page he had just turned was not a picture of a car running over a canoe but of a car riding on top of a canoe. He then explained the purpose of the ad without alluding to the boy's fears.

This discussion of an ad, rather than of cars and their dangers, created a feeling in Eddie's mind that perhaps his anxieties were exaggerated. It also gave him the assurance that there were ways to discuss his anxieties without getting at the root of them, a step which at this time would have created unmanageable tension. Other children, too, became interested in the purpose of ads and of how symbols are used in presenting ideas, and these things also helped Eddie in approaching his fears more objectively.

As a next step, Eddie gave up relying exclusively on a magic control of cars, and began to act his aggressions out openly by hitting them with snowballs—again something he could never have done if we had tried to separate him from the outside world. That we allowed it, and that we assured him there were no consequences to be afraid of, further lightened the tension he felt every time he saw a car.[2]

After this he became less afraid to leave the School grounds. When he was on the street it was no longer so necessary to concentrate on his magic control of cars. (He used to do that by staring at them, because he thought that if he let them out of his sight they might suddenly turn on him and destroy him.)

One day, after he had been pelting cars with snowballs for a while, he suddenly began to speak about the source of his anxiety about cars. Following the opening he gave us, the next time he began to throw snowballs at automobiles his counselor suggested to him not to hit windshields or windows because they were breakable. Instead he suggested that Eddie concentrate on the metal parts.

In time, Eddie had discharged enough of his aggression to be open to reason and he took up his counselor's suggestion. As a next step the counselor advised Eddie not to hit moving cars, because there his aim might be spoiled; the snowball might land

[2] Participant observer: Victor De Grazia.

on the windshield, blur the sight of the driver, and an accident might result. This also seemed reasonable to Eddie and then he told his counselor how he hated cars because they ran people over as he had once come near to being run over himself. This was the first connection Eddie made on his own between his near accident in early childhood and his present fear of cars.

A long conversation followed which also, for the first time, helped Eddie to understand what had often been explained to him before, namely, that cars have no will of their own, are controlled by drivers, and that if accidents happen it is the driver's fault and not the fault of the car. Slowly Eddie began to understand that his fear of cars was really a fear transferred from his father onto cars, a father who seemed particularly destructive (to Eddie) when he was driving a car.[3]

Originally Eddie had transferred his fear of the father to a fear of cars because automobiles seemed less able to control or to threaten him than his father. But since there are no streets without cars, this transfer had made it impossible for Eddie to relax on the street for an instant. Once he had gained some understanding of the psychological meaning of his fears they became less intense and he began to concentrate on one part of the cars. In line with the anthropomorphic thinking of children, Eddie was no longer afraid of the unmoving parts of the cars and stopped hitting them with snowballs. Instead, he concentrated on the wheels, the moving parts. Later he hit only at cars bearing license plates from his home state, i.e., cars that might possibly be driven by his father.

After a while Eddie became free enough on walks to stop concentrating on a magic control of cars and began to look around him and observe. Only then could he begin to understand and enjoy his walks, as well as himself and those with him.

Like Eddie, many of our children have particular anxieties which not only keep them from enjoying walks on the street or trips away from the School but also, which is much worse, pre-

[3] Participant observer: Roderick E. Peattie.

vent them from gaining an understanding of the world such as normal children get from their casual observations. As mentioned in the preceding chapter, people who are intoxicated, people who have visibly suffered an injury, who are spastic or who in some other way have lost control of their bodies, are very threatening to many of our children. They seem to be living proofs of how easily control can be lost, and the children are afraid that they, too, may suddenly find themselves minus a part of their bodies (as when they see persons who have lost an arm or a leg) or lose control over their bodily movements (like the spastics), or over their minds (like the drunkards). On walks, these children concentrate on looking for disabled people to the exclusion of observing the world, or enjoying activities that might have been fun.

Nevertheless, walking with a child offers many occasions for marginal talks that help him to understand his own behaviour, to overcome fears through reality testing, and to correct false impressions he has gathered about the world at large or about human relations. Often these contacts are non-verbal in character, and therefore hard to describe convincingly. It is difficult to say precisely why it is so much more meaningful to a child to have his hand taken hold of at a certain moment than any verbal effort to dispel his conscious or unconscious fears might be. Tentatively, it may be suggested that non-verbal contacts reach into the deepest or earliest layers of the personality, layers that were developed before speech. At any rate, moments in which the ego has little contact with reality, is less well integrated than usual, or suddenly falls down on its function to perceive correctly (as when the child suddenly views a casual passer-by as drunk), are the times when non-verbal contacts are by far the more useful. Then non-verbal communication, or non-verbal but reassuring conduct on the part of the adult is most constructive in bringing the child back into contact, in restoring control to his ego, in helping him to interpret what he sees more in line with reality.

In a printed account which must necessarily rely on words, it is difficult to describe this kind of non-verbal support and I must more or less limit myself to quoting verbal contacts that take place informally during the day. But it should be borne in mind that these are always accompanied by non-verbal gestures and expressions of emotions to which the child is also responding, and often this taking hold of a hand, or a "well, well," having the nature of a reassuring noise, does more to restore the ego and encourage reality testing than any articulate exchange could have done.

Contacts of this kind which are so incidental to what is nominally going on, are particularly important in making the "uncontrolled" outside world seem less threatening and more manageable. They preserve the intimacy of personal relationships in the very midst of the strange outside world, and make it easier for the child to recognize how irrealistic his anxieties are. They also convince him that we accept him as a person whose emotions are always valid even if we may also try to show him that his reasoning is not always valid, or may have to interfere with some of his actions because they may lead to trouble.

One evening, a group of boys were returning home from ice skating along the Midway—a wide parkway on which the School borders, which is partly flooded in winter for skating. It was already dark when Jack, who was walking beside his counselor, looked ahead and saw a man approaching. "There's a killer," he said. "He's coming to get me. He's going to kill me."

The counselor took Jack's hand and told him nothing was going to happen to him, that he was there to protect him. But as the man passed Jack tightened his grip on the counselor's hand. After a moment the counselor pointed out that nothing untoward had happened and Jack let go of the counselor's hand. But his anxiety was not over.

On the way back to the School, the children passed a traffic signal control box whose clicking was audible at close range. Jack heard it and began to shout, "It's a time bomb. It's a time bomb," and broke away from the group. He ran in wide circles around the box, and as he ran, he waved his hands wildly, screaming, "Look out! It's a time bomb." He was about fifty yards away when his counselor called to him, promising to explain what made the box click. Jack came back, and his counselor then explained that the box had a motor in it that changed the traffic lights. He asked Jack to listen to it and watch the lights at the same time. Then he would see that when the box clicked the lights also changed. Jack was very interested and the two of them stayed to watch the lights change a few times. Jack said nothing at all, but he was obviously very relieved and soon hurried ahead to catch up with the other boys.[4]

Fear of strange things and persons is so typical for our children, and it is so important that they learn how unjustified their fears are (and incidentally learn to trust others and feel secure in this world) that a second example may be added.

This incident, like the preceding one, took place while a group of boys were out walking with their counselor. At one point, Mitchell, an eleven-year-old boy who was rightly afraid of his own violent aggressions and of losing control over them, dropped behind to look in a shop window. A few minutes later he came rushing up to his counselor to tell him that a man with a cane had pointed a knife at him.

The counselor first gave him some reassurance and then took him by the hand and told him that they would go back to find the man and have him arrested. As they retraced their steps, they passed a man with a cane, and the counselor asked Mitchell if this was the man he meant. Mitchell said no, but he turned his head aside without daring to look at the stranger. They walked on a little further until Mitchell said, "He isn't around anymore." Thereupon the two turned back to rejoin the other boys.

On their way they again passed the man with the cane and the counselor asked Mitchell again if he was sure this wasn't the man. By this time Mitchell dared to look at the stranger and

[4] Participant observer: Victor De Grazia.

repeated that this man wasn't the one who had threatened him. But now, after passing the man for the second time, Mitchell's grip relaxed, and the counselor let him drop his hand. He had tested reality and convinced himself that his anxious imagination had played him a trick. There was no need to admit his error to others. But later, on the way home, the counselor used the incident to reassure both Mitchell and the other boys that the police were always there to protect them if they were ever in danger.[5]

Often, when our children venture into the outside, we have to rely on and stress the protective functions of the police, the fire department, and so on. As mentioned above, some of our children are frightened by drunkards. Once it happened that a drunk made his way into the School and the children were impressed when they saw how easily he was removed by the police who arrived less than five minutes after we telephoned.

Similarly, visits to the closest fire station, and seeing for themselves how near and how well equipped it is, has done much to reduce night terror among the children, and their common fear of fire.

Depending on circumstances, reassurance about the care society takes to protect its members may take varied forms. For example, the children were on a visit to the zoo one day, and Eddie became filled with anxiety when he saw the genitals of the big gorilla. It was some reassurance that the animal was safe behind bars. But the excitement of observing the large genitals and the conversation that sprang up among the children created so much anxiety that they began to run in various directions until two of them, unfortunately, got lost. Then Eddie's tension reached a peak.

Yet before the day was over he derived great and lasting assurance about society, and about his safety in moving freely within it, because firstly, the lost children were found within a relatively short time, and secondly, the counselor looked for

[5] Participant observer: Clarence Lipschutz.

them at the police station to let the police know that they were lost. As it turned out, it was at the police station that they turned up, which accentuated the protective functions of society.[6]

Contacts with the outside world, or just being outside the protective setting of the School, often reactivates neurotic types of behaviour that have disappeared for some time within the School or have never even come to the fore there. Temptations of the outside world may also revive instinctual desires that have not yet been integrated, or defensive attitudes that have not yet disappeared. Two incidents out of the lives of Tom and Ellen may illustrate these two opposite phenomena.

After three years, Tom accepted the fact that within the School all his sexual attempts to provoke a mother-substitute fell flat. Nevertheless, the uncontrolled outside world tempted him to give his old seductive devices another try.

Tom and a group of boys were out at Jackson Park and Tom decided he wanted to play hide-and-seek. The other boys agreed and they started a game up, one boy hiding and the rest hunting for him. Tom ran and chased with them for about twenty minutes, getting more and more excited. Then he ran up to his counselor, saying, "Will you chase me?" Her simple "no" took the steam out of him for a minute, but he made another last try. "Will you play 'hide-and-peek' with me?" he asked. And again she said "no." Tom was quite aware of his slip of the tongue but he did not correct it. Nevertheless, the excitement was over.[7]

With Tom, the greater freedom of the outside world was a temptation to see if he could seduce mother-figures as he used to think (and be afraid) he could. With other children, the world at large makes them fall back on old defenses. Many children then feel they have to test us again to see if they need to placate us by "good deeds." They explore to see if we don't still expect them to adopt socially accepted, although pretended, emo-

[6] Participant observer: Josette Wingo.
[7] Participant observer: Gayle Shulenberger.

tional attitudes. They also want to find out if they can afford to act according to their own true emotions, even if they are outside the protection of the School.

A great deal of such testing takes place around the birthdays of parents or siblings, on Mother's and Father's Days, and similar occasions when the children want to see if we expect them to buy or make presents, write congratulatory letters and so on. Usually this crops up not when the children are at School, but when they are out with their counselors on walks or on shopping trips at about this time. Outside, the ads remind the child of Mother's Day, for example, and he will remark about something in a shop window and say he wants to buy it as a present. Most comments of this kind are attempts either to test out the counselor or to provoke the support they need before they can follow their true emotions rather than make the gesture of good will devoid of meaning. If they were encouraged to carry these out, they could never satisfy themselves that genuine emotions are preferable even to the nicest gestures.

Ellen's behaviour in a store one day was typical of this kind of testing. The counselor had bought her several toys and also some candy. Ellen was intensely jealous of her siblings, a jealousy which she transferred to the other girls in her dormitory. But now, after feeling so indulged by her counselor she also felt guilty. So in terms of her mother's insistence on being nice to her siblings, she asked, "Now can I buy something to bring back to the other girls?" The counselor told her there was no need for that but Ellen insisted, so the counselor said if she really wanted very badly to take something back it was up to her to decide. Then Ellen, who could generally make very quick decisions, took a long time in deciding what to get for the girls. Finally, she picked out the cheapest candy, which was also a kind she disliked.

The counselor pointed out again that she didn't have to bring the girls anything, but that if she wanted to bring something, it oughtn't to be something she didn't like, something she knew the others wouldn't like either. The counselor added that she would much prefer it if Ellen didn't bring anything at all to the other children and that she'd like it much better, if Ellen still wanted to get something more, that she get it for herself. So Ellen chose a kind of candy she liked, still on the pretext of getting it for the other girls. But after picking it out, she said: "I'm not going to give this to the other girls, I'm going to eat it myself." Then, seeing the counselor did not answer immediately, she added, "Of course, I'm only joking." But the counselor said she wasn't joking, that Ellen didn't really want to bring candy or anything else to the other girls, and that that was understandable and perfectly all right. This statement sealed the success of the excursion for Ellen, and she ate her candy to the last piece.[8]

Shopping for wearing apparel is not exactly a daily occurrence, but it comes up quite regularly since we like to make each such trip a pleasant occasion and therefore do not buy en masse. This alone often goes a long way toward making children feel they have some control over their own affairs.

Chris, for example, began to recognize that we never took him shopping for more than one or two things at a time, and went to small stores where there were no crowds to push him or hurry him. One day, on the way home from a shopping trip, he began to talk spontaneously about how he had always resented going shopping when he lived at home. He said, "Lots of times my mother took me shopping in Macy's but I hate to go. I get all excited. There's so many things happening all together. All the people and all the things and I can't decide. And then my mother gets mad at me because I don't want to try things on and then everything gets all mixed up and I'm all confused." [9]

Since our children are very hard on their clothes they need a great deal by way of dresses, shirts, socks, pants, gloves, etc. But after selecting one or two items their interest lags, and we must therefore make such trips fairly often. Frequently they afford us good opportunities for meaningful contacts, although shopping

[8] Participant observer: Joan Little.
[9] Participant observer: Patty Pickett.

is always more of a surface activity than eating, or learning or bathing. Nevertheless, our children have been overpowered often enough by parents who denied them all freedom in choosing their own clothes and their resentment is often very keen. Many of them have had such unpleasant experiences around the lack of freedom to choose their clothes that quite significant experiences are sometimes had on our shopping trips.

This is particularly true of children who suffer from schizophrenic-like personality disorganization. Some of them have no clear sense about just what pertains to their bodies. Pieces of clothing are conceived of as parts of the body, reflecting in some cases its defensive armouring, in others its falling apart. In some of the latter cases, all efforts to help the children organize themselves must concentrate for a long time on helping them to keep their clothing from constantly falling apart. These children have an amazing talent for tearing new pieces of clothing to pieces, or for looking disheveled immediately after careful help in dressing.

Chris' many obsessional preoccupations included a feeling that he was going to be hurt, that his body was inadequate, and so forth. Whenever he got a new piece of clothing he tore it up immediately. At home he had been punished for this but to no avail. At the School we let him do as he liked, and he had any number of devices for destroying new clothes. Mainly, he would never wear anything until he had torn holes in it. For example, when he had just put on a new shirt he would go to a square post in the play yard, pull the shirt over the post and lean back, stretching the shirt out, with the corner of the post right in the middle. Leaning backwards he would sway back and forth with his shirt stretching more and more, until finally a big hole was torn right in the middle of the shirt. All other pieces of clothing Chris treated in similar ways.[10] Clothing that he couldn't manage to pierce, such as heavy corduroy, or sturdy woolen coats he managed to "lose" in record time, so we stopped buying them for him.

The reason that Chris could only wear clothes with holes in

[10] Participant observer: **Patty Pickett.**

them he could tell us only two years later, almost a year after he had stopped putting holes in everything he wore. Then he admitted that he used to imagine he'd been shot at, or impaled. Rather than have this done to him (as he was convinced would happen), he had done it to himself. Moreover, the holes he made in his shirts meant he had already been impaled but was still alive. Thus at home his being forced to wear clothing which were intact meant that he was going to be shot at, impaled, and so on, in the future.

At the School, his freedom to wear clothing with holes in them meant that these things had happened in the past, and that he had done it himself, thus increasing his feeling that he was now in command of his own fate, that the bad things had already happened and were no longer a threat in the future.

Being shot at or otherwise wounded was by no means Chris' only anxiety. Another fear he also connected with his clothes was that of being hemmed in, restrained, or suffocated. Anything touching his body closely intensified this fear. About his desire to wear loose-fitting clothing he was able to speak much sooner than about why he needed to put holes in them. But that, too, Chris could admit only after he was convinced that at the School he was not forced to wear clothes that fit him.

This, incidentally, is another example of how most of the time we must first do the right thing on the basis of what Freud called the "empathy of the unconscious," on vague hunches, and often long before we find out why it happened to be the right thing to do. Often we never learn why it was the thing to do, or whether it was exactly correct in a therapeutic sense. The child's general progress, or the converse, must then tell us whether or not we were ever on the right track.

It was several months before Chris had any real contact with his counselor, and this happened for the first time while they were shopping for clothes. The important factor was that he was permitted to decide on their size. Each piece of clothing he selected was several sizes larger than what was needed to fit him. Nevertheless, and to his amazement, the counselor supported him in his wishes and bought everything he selected without question, despite violent objections by the salesman.

As they left the store Chris found himself really talking to his counselor for the first time, outside of the School, as he complained to her that everything his parents had ever bought him was never loose enough, had always "squeezed him in." Wearing the over-sized pieces of clothing he had just bought himself didn't make him look any better put together, but they were the first pieces of clothing he enjoyed wearing. On subsequent shopping trips, the clothing he selected was still too large, but less so than before, until after two years he was able to select and wear clothing of his own size, and without having to tear holes in them. By that time he not only looked better put together, but also felt and acted that way.[11]

Sometimes, in less serious cases, a single chance to test the freedom to choose is enough for a child. That he can make his own choice, and that the shopping trip may be concluded without result if he cannot make up his mind is sometimes a new and unexpected experience. Frank, for example, once drove a shoe salesman to distraction because whatever the salesman brought forward was rejected. The counselor remained unperturbed, and it was not just a suffering forbearance which is just as distasteful to the child as being forced to buy something he doesn't like. She simply encouraged him to take his time and not to buy unless he really wanted the shoes. After more than an hour of asking for different sizes or different fashions of shoes, Frank suddenly relaxed, and said, "This is really an awfully nice little store." And saying that, he chose the pair of shoes he wanted and bought them.[12]

Such experiences not only cement the relationship between child and adult, they also convince the child that he is capable of making decisions. Even more important, they eventually make more and more of a child's everyday experiences enjoyable ones, and only in this way can life in general begin to seem attractive.

[11] Participant observer: Patty Pickett.
[12] Participant observer: *Idem.*

Once this stage has been reached, it also helps to soften many unavoidable hardships that a child's life outside of the School may entail.

Letting children select their clothes as they please would be pointless if we then exercised pressure about when and where to wear them. Some children go beyond reasonable limits in flaunting a new independence they have not yet integrated. They need to prove to themselves that they are not only independent of society, but even of nature, as it were, at least as far as the weather is concerned.

In a way, such behaviour is like the reactions of small children in reverse. Small children consider it a personal affront if it rains when they want it to shine, or if it gets warm when they intended to use a new sled. Severely disturbed children who otherwise, too, present psychotic-like symptoms, are particularly apt to flaunt their magic independence from, and megalomanic superiority to, the forces of nature by the way they dress.

George (but also Harry, Paul, Mary and others) showed such behaviour early in their stay at the School. It was as if now, at a later age, they had to restore their self-confidence by a testing of their own magic powers, a testing they were kept from in infancy because they were so totally overpowered. As infants or small children, they never felt free to make those magic and megalomanic assertions about the world which are the privilege of the small child and which normally disintegrate very soon under the impact of more and more realistic experiences. On hot summer days, George would as soon as not wear heavy socks and top boots, a heavy leather jacket, or a heavy raincoat with the hood drawn over his head—and these over many other pieces of heavy clothing. In winter he would run around in open sandals without socks, or with short pants, wearing only a T-shirt on top. Strangely enough, none of these children suffered adverse effects to their health from their strange clothing habits.

No efforts are made to argue the unreasonableness of their habits with them. A counselor may say on a hot day that she's glad to be wearing light clothing because it's more comfortable; or she may say on a cold and rainy day that she's glad to be wearing a coat that keeps her warm and dry. In this way we try to indicate, without directly speaking about it, that a realistic approach to the conditions of nature is more effective than a magic or a megalomanic one. But these children cannot dispense with their magical efforts to control the weather by the way they dress until after they have learned to deal with all life experiences more realistically.

Freedom in dealing with their wearing apparel must also extend to the freedom to destroy it. All children use their clothing symbolically as can be seen from the dress-up games of normal children. In emotionally disturbed children this is accentuated, of course. Runaway children, for example, will use their shoes to prevent themselves from running away, and do other things that are even less screened behind symbol.

Bob, who had been a runaway for many years made his first efforts to stay put by throwing his shoes away. One pair he threw out of a window, another over a fence. Other runaways who now want to stop truanting tear their shoes apart, manage to lose them from their feet, or just kick them off.

For each child, how he deals with his clothing and how we react to it, has specific meaning. For Bob throwing his shoes away meant being forced to stay put; but Ann lost her shoes for other reasons. Her mother had always bought her shoes that were too small for her because, as she put it, "Ann is still just a baby." While she also bought Ann other clothes that were smaller than necessary, these were not as painful to wear as the small shoes. Thus it became understandable that Ann managed to lose her shoes regularly for several months, even if they were right in size and bought by us. Shoes, to her, meant being restrained from growing up or being held back from acting her age.

The less mature a child is, the more he views clothing as part of his body, of his person. Those children in particular who have known serious deprivation, either physical or emotional, in never having been provided with adequate clothing, see as close a connection between clothing and all necessities as others do between food and all necessities. Some of Paul's remarks are very much to the point here. One day he was stirring some fudge he and his counselor were making together. As he let it fall in folds he suddenly asked her, "What does this remind you of?" The counselor couldn't guess and asked him what it reminded him of, and he replied, "It reminds me of clothes—you know the things you wear." Later he elaborated further, "It just looks like clothes being folded, doesn't it, and it's as good as nice clothing." [13]

Paul was one of the children who at the beginning of his stay at the School could never accept any service that involved direct bodily contact. He, too, could never accept food that was given to him but had to grab for it. He never permitted his counselor to touch him, and only grudgingly accepted toys. Direct body touch he could not permit. But whenever his counselor was caring for his clothes, Paul would watch her very carefully. With his eyes he followed her as she walked around the room laying out his clothes in the morning, or putting his clothes out to be sent to the laundry or the cleaner. His first signs of pleasure at being cared for appeared when he slowly began to smile as he watched his counselor taking care of his clothing, taking care of what came next after his body. Only much later did he permit her to take care of his body itself.

Paul, and many others like him, regarded the treatment of his clothing as a sort of test case once removed. He watched to see how an adult would treat something that pertained to, but was not actually part of, his body. Only after his observations had assured him of the adult's good intentions, both in granting him freedom and in taking care of his clothing, would he also permit the adult to take care of his body.

Many children—the so-called "over protected" children—have experienced careful nurturing but without freedom and without respect for their autonomy. Other children, the so-called "neglected" children, have experienced pseudo-freedom and pseudo-autonomy, but have never known adequate care. Therefore, how

[13] Participant observer: Gayle Shulenberger.

their wearing apparel is dealt with is a touchstone for many of them against which they test the intentions of adults at the School.

I have selected clothing, going on trips to buy them, and their general meaning for the child as a major focus for the child's relation to the outside world because, after the feeding schedule and the education to cleanliness, clothing habits are often one of the first social conventions to which the child is expected or forced to conform. But I had another reason for choosing clothing as an example of how relations to the outside offer opportunities for treatment and help. At the beginning of the chapter I mentioned that the University provides a more or less protecting layer between the world of the School and the world outside.

Similarly, a child's clothes seem like a layer to him, protecting his body from direct impact by the outside world, a buffer between him and the world. In this way, going shopping for clothes on the outside has a much greater impact on the child than shopping for toys, for example. The trip to the toy shop may follow the pleasure principle entirely, may be purely enjoyable. But in buying clothes, even with the freedom we permit, the child must still conform in some measure to the conventions of the world.

For example, we allow girls to buy guns and soldiers, boys to buy dolls and doll clothes, and so on. But while we let the child select whatever clothes he wants to wear as far as patterns, sizes or fashions go, we do not let a boy select girls' dresses (or vice versa) no matter how strong his transvestite tendencies may be. Thus in shopping for clothes, the child must make some compromises between his personal desires and the demands of the world. He must learn to select a protective layer for his body that will most nearly satisfy both.

But clothes are not the only things very close to his emotions or his body which the child must learn to compromise with society about. There are parts of his body about whose treatment he must eventually conform, as in the treatment of his hair, for example.

Most children dislike having their hair cut because of their general fear of having any parts of their bodies touched, not to speak of having them shortened or cut off. But there are others to whom their hair and its growth has very different and personal meanings, though still generally connected with some fear of bodily harm. Sometimes we find it necessary to let a child's hair grow for months without cutting, just as we find it necessary at times to let him dress as he likes. But we explain to the child that we feel it our obligation to protect him from the ridicule of outsiders who tend to deride boys with long hair, for example, and that he can wear his hair that way if he wants to, but then we will not take him outside the immediate vicinity of the School, or outside the protective outer layer of the University environment.

The child, of course, can go out by himself, but we will not lend ourselves to helping him make a fool of himself in society. Within the School we tell him he may run around as he likes, but if he wishes, for example, to go downtown with us, he must be ready to conform to our indeed minimal demands for conformity as regards hairdo, cleanliness, or clothing.

The freedom to avoid having his hair cut which he enjoys for some time will eventually permit a child to view it as less threatening. At the same time the desire to venture further outside with us, may mount. Then even the child most attached to his hair, or most afraid of having it trimmed, will eventually ask to have his hair fixed.

When that point is reached, then our going with a child to the barber shop or beauty shop sometimes offers deep insight into a child's reasons for avoiding a haircut or his fear of having his hair trimmed. What is even more important, it offers wide opportunities for helping him with some of these fears. So these particular contacts with the outside also have their propensities for treatment and help.

Lester insisted that he never wanted to have his hair cut. Assurances we usually give on such occasions—such as about the integrity of his body, that hair is, in a way, dead matter when compared with skin, muscles, or bones—all these fell on deaf ears. So did other less specific assurances we give children at such times, on the assumption that it is not so much damage to their hair that they fear in opposing a haircut as damage to other parts of their body.

In Lester's case the counselor's assuring remarks brought a very unexpected reaction, but only after he had already agreed to go to the barber and was on his way there. He said that he was going to let his hair grow "real long" because then he would look like a girl. Further conversation revealed that behind this desire to look like a girl lay a much deeper fear of castration than is usual even for our children. He added that once he looked like a girl he would "have his balls cut off" and then he'd really be a girl.

By this time they had reached the barber shop but in view of Lester's state of mind, he and the counselor simply walked up and down in front of the shop while they continued their talk. Finally the counselor managed to assure him that he was safe at the School, that whatever his desire might be, the kind of thing he imagined could never happen. When he really believed her promise that short hair or long hair, haircut or no haircut, his genitals would be safe, he entered the barber shop. But as soon as he was inside he complained of stomach aches and various other physical ailments.

Our barber knows our children and regardless of whether or not they show their fear of haircuts, he lets them all play for a time, exploring the instruments of the barber, investigating the barber's chair, studying its mechanism, and so on. Lester, who had often been to the barber with his mother, only now for the first time had the clippers explained to him. The barber showed him how they would not, and could not, cut his skin, although they cut off his hair. Lester tried it out, and finally his anxieties were sufficiently calmed to allow him to submit to a haircut.

Now that Lester believed that this barber shop, at least, was a safe one, he asked to have his hair shaved, to have it "all cut off." And not until this request was denied, and it was explained that he was only getting a normal haircut, did the last of his fears vanish. This rejection of his demands for the most radical cutting was much more reassuring than all the previous discussion of his fears and their origins. That even the barber, the man with the dangerous scissors, was appalled at the idea of such unnecessary cutting added considerably to Lester's feeling of security.[14]

Going to the barber, or shopping for clothing, has at least some predictable meanings for a child that we can foresee. We can plan our actions somewhat, and be prepared for at least some of the child's reactions. But help can be equally or even more important when we run into the unexpected, the hidden problems that suddenly become activated by something the child sees. Then a correct response to his emotions at the moment may be more useful to a child than the best planned activity we have decided on beforehand, or the most careful interpretations we can give in the play-room. A last example may illustrate how experiences a child can have only through contacts with the outside can become an important turning point in restoring him to emotional health, if the incident is properly handled.

Carol, who was eight, suffered from severe depressions interrupted only by violent outbursts of anger and hatred that were actually dangerous to the other children. Temper tantrums were her way of discharging her hatred of a brother who had been the preferred child. The brother had died a year earlier and Carol was convinced that her parents would have preferred it if she had died and her brother remained alive.

Carol felt that since she was the bad one in the family she

[14] Participant observer: Ronnie Dryovage.

ought to have died and that soon she would be punished by having to die; so what was the use of living, or of coming to terms with others. She hated everybody, most of all herself. When she came to the School she expected to be hated for her violent aggressions, or to be punished for them. But instead she was told that the adults liked her and tolerated her behaviour because we were convinced she had good reasons to act as she did, that though we regretted her ways, we respected what lay behind them.

Carol remained diffident toward us, but after a few months became interested enough in her environment to occasionally explore it and later test it. Then her observations about others showed her that actions which in her previous setting would have been considered "bad" and punishable, were accepted here without much ado and certainly without retaliation. She began to compare herself with other children and saw that her actions were by no means outrageous. Similar behaviour in other children was not punished, and none of them died when they misbehaved.

The experience of being accepted by her counselors, plus her own observations, slowly gave her at least enough security to come out of her depression for moments at a time. But this newly won strength she used mainly to test her fearful delusions. She now set out to find if it was true that she could be "bad" without being punished or destroyed. Through her continuous angry provocations she tested out counselors, teachers and children.

Finally, she was satisfied that nobody was going to force her to give up a behaviour pattern she needed, and that nobody expected her to be "good," to be cheerful, or to have a "good time." She now felt tolerated by others for what she was, but since she could not accept anybody, she could not feel accepted in turn. On the whole, she remained in a depressive state, which seemed to assure her against being overwhelmed by interference with her need to sulk, mourn and hate. Despite all our efforts she remained so for months. She used the protective environment of the School to keep her depression from being punctured. It remained for the uncontrolled stimulation originating in the outside world to force Carol into experiences that resulted in a positive relation to a counselor which in turn changed her outlook on life.

This began one day with a minor disaster in the park. During one of Carol's usual efforts to provoke her counselor, she slipped and fell into a pond from which her counselor "rescued" her immediately. The counselor showed great concern for Carol's well-being and made no allusion to her provocative behaviour. Both facts Carol accepted in stolid silence though the attitude of the counselor was obviously in contrast to the scolding she expected.

This incident brought no changes in Carol's immediate behaviour or in her basic outlook on life. But much later she told us that she was not so much impressed by the counselor's rescuing her, which she rightly considered to be part of a counselor's duty and no special favour. What had really meant something to her, she admitted, was that the counselor, without any scolding, gave Carol her own coat to wear, took Carol's shoes off because they were wet, and carried her back home so that her feet could stay warmly packed inside the counselor's coat. This, she said, hadn't made her like the counselor, but had convinced her she was somebody to trust.

Fortunately, not even a cold resulted from Carol's dunking in the cold water, so the incident also showed her that bad behaviour isn't punished by sickness and death, as she had always thought. This, more than what the counselor had done, made a dent in Carol's delusional fears about being destroyed in retaliation for bad behaviour. Although at the time of the incident she still was not ready to accept the relationship offered by her counselor, it made her readier for one than she had been up to then.[15]

Two days later, Carol had another important experience. During a walk in the park, she had a temper outburst in which she

[15] Participant observer: Jean O'Leary.

attacked another child. When the counselor told her that she might turn her anger against her rather than another child, she only became more provocative. A few minutes later the children found a dying squirrel and Carol became very upset. No one could persuade her to leave and at last she started to cry. The counselor spoke gently to her but to no avail. Finally the counselor suggested that they look for other squirrels who were unharmed and still roaming the trees. To this Carol agreed and when she spied a squirrel in a tree she suddenly cheered up.

In her first spontaneous gesture of affection she put her arm around the counselor and then asked the counselor to tell her all about squirrels and how they live.[16] For the first time since her depressiveness began, her autistic preoccupation gave way to real interest in another person's knowledge of the outside world. The next day Carol made a direct plea for affection from her counselor and was able to accept it. This ability to accept warm contact with others was the first break in the isolation she had been forced into by her brother's death and the attitude she felt her parents had taken.

[16] Participant observer: Jean O'Leary.

11

in the bathroom

MANY of the anxieties I will be dealing with in this chapter can be traced to the earliest days in the lives of our children.

They go back to the period of earliest infancy when the children first experienced inadequate handling in the way they were held when they were fed, changed, or bathed. For one thing, parental anxiety about the relationship to the child, and the mechanisms a parent may have used in trying to compensate for it, may have expressed themselves in little or no stimulation of the child's skin, or in a rigid and hence painful way of holding the child's body.

Parental anxiety, of course, is only one of the many emotions that speak poorly for an infant's development. But it is one of the things that may have interfered at the earliest age with a parent's relation to his child, and hence with the child's feeling about himself and the world. Disgust at the baby's excretion is another emotional attitude that may have conditioned the way a mother held her child or moved him as his diapers were being changed.

Later, when such a child is in the tub, the normally pleasant and diffuse sensations induced by a warm bath will revive in him memories of his unpleasant experience with touch. But it will also permit us to replace old and traumatic experiences with touch by new and corrective sensations. First will come those which originate in being able to enjoy a bath undisturbed. Later will come the ones having their source in being pleasantly cared for by another person.

In this connection, it should be stressed that no real trust in other people, and no real affection for them, can develop as long as an individual is convinced that being touched by this or that person will be unpleasant or even painful. Restoring a child's ability to experience touch as pleasant must of necessity precede any pleasant human relations, just as it was the earliest bodily sensation leading the normal infant to emotional security through pleasant relations to his mother.

There are many settings in which a child can learn to acquire pleasure in touch. But the child in his bath offers the most natural setting in which we can help him to enjoy it as pleasant, and to appreciate the moving of his body in the nude.

Something one of our eight-year-old girls once said showed very clearly how a mother's conscious or unconscious hostility may make her afraid to touch her own child because she is really afraid that in doing so she may harm her. For a long time this girl could not bear to have anyone touch her. After many months, in which she came to recognize that we always respected her desires, she also began to understand that in touching her our purpose was not to overpower her.

Later, after she felt more accepted and even liked, she once told her teacher: "You're not afraid of me. You like me. Touch me." And in this request the girl expressed the feeling that to be touched by another person can be pleasant only if that person is not only not afraid of one, but likes one.[1]

Unfortunately, things are complicated for us because few of our children connect taking a bath with any peaceful experience. On the contrary, bathing usually conjures up unpleasant memories, some buried, but some of them painfully recent. For many of these children the disagreeable sensations experienced in infancy, when they were touched in a hostile or anxious way,

---

[1] Participant observer: Ida Bass.

were later aggravated at bath time by painful scrubbings, as well as unpleasant scoldings or warnings about not getting so dirty or about doing a better job of cleaning themselves.

Yet while many of our children have already experienced poor handling in the crib (witness the many eating disturbances, the sensitivity to touch, disturbances of motility and feelings of inadequacy about the body), only rarely did these first steps of human development involve any clashing of wills. The infant, during his first year of life, is too dependent, too poorly integrated, has too inadequate a picture of the world and his place in it, to actually be able to fight back.

Matters are different for most children during their education to cleanliness. There an actual clashing of wills does occur very often. Even if no battle rages between parent and child over the child's having to give up the freedom to eliminate whenever and wherever he pleases, the child's mind is well developed enough by then to realize it is the will of the parent that overpowers him. Thus, to many children, the education to cleanliness which comes later is a parallel experience to their having been defeated by their parents at an earlier time, and their having had to submit the most intimate functions of the body to the will of the parent.

All this is true if the education to cleanliness has had the character of a battle of wills. Fortunately for many children, this part of their training is achieved through joint efforts by parent and child, in which case their common mastery over a difficult problem is another bond that links them together and increases the child's feeling of mastery, security, and self-respect.

For most children at the School, the freedom to go dirty if they so desire, the freedom from all pressure or control in the matter of elimination, becomes another important starting point in acquiring a fresh view of themselves as autonomous human beings. This was nicely characterized by the statement of one eight-year-old child who in all her previous life had never recognized people as human beings. Her only "achievement" in life had been her meticulous cleanliness although she was unable to function in any other respect. It took her five weeks at the School before she could see anyone except as a mortal enemy or as someone who existed only to fetch and carry for her. But at the end of her fifth week, when I asked her if she knew who I was she replied, after some hesitation, "You're Dr. B."

Up to this time she had expressed only the conviction that Dr. B. was trying to kill her, poison her, or otherwise persecute her. This time, however, to the question, "But what do I do around here?" she no longer replied by saying, "You want to kill me," but with a big grin, indicating some first human contact, she said, "You let me get dirty."

Thus with regard to the bathroom it must be realized that a major function of this area of the School is its disuse, unless the child can accept it without feeling he is submitting to something against his will.

While it is important for many children that they feel they can go dirty and use the bathtub or washbasin only sparingly, it is important for others that in terms of their preoccupations they can use the bathtub or toilet for hours without being questioned and without feeling we disapprove.

Apparently, what happens in the bathroom cannot very well be separated from what undressing in front of others means to the children, but that subject has been discussed in Chapter Nine. Here it may be repeated that in getting out of their clothes before a bath, or on other occasions when they undress in front of an adult or one another, many children show an increase of anxiety and sexual feeling. With very few exceptions, the newcomer feels uneasy and self-conscious about undressing in front of others. When he has to undress, he withdraws into the bathroom or the locker room and closes the door; or he waits until a counselor's back is turned or the adult is momentarily out of the room. Others wait to undress until the lights are out or do it under the bed covers. We assure them there is nothing to be ashamed of or afraid of, but otherwise let them do as they please. Again, as discussed in Chapter Nine, the example of the other children's casualness usually helps them to feel more natural about it in time.

But these factors are not always enough for children whose specific traumatization took place around denuding themselves or taking a bath, and this seems to have been true for a number of our children. In particular, their parents seem to have made threatening or provocative jokes, or disparaging remarks about their genitals at such moments. Sometimes we can infer this from a child's behaviour and help him accordingly. Harry, for example, used to give us the most dramatic demonstrations of his castration fears both when he was getting up in the morning and also when undressing and getting ready for his bath. At such times (as described in the context of morning), he would get hold of a mousetrap, and manage to "trap" his penis in it.

Harry's behaviour, incidentally, and its numerous meanings, may illustrate another point. Here was an act that to all appearances seemed identical in the morning and in the evening. Yet actually it had the most diversified emotional connotations, depending on the setting and the personal context. Just as all psychological phenomena are highly overdetermined, having meaning on many different levels, so any symptomatic behaviour may have a variety of meanings to a child.

The expenditure of emotional energy in thus daring to express unconscious motives, the anxiety Harry had to overcome when he used the mousetrap for the first time, the enormous relief when he found he could use it without the terrible consequences he feared, all these were so great that once used, he would use the device again to express many other pressing needs.

We would forfeit a child's trust in our ability to understand the hidden meaning of his behaviour, and hence his trust that we can help him with the anxieties that motivate his behaviour, if we were to glibly assume that the same type of behaviour in different settings had the same meaning. The child would soon recognize our analyses for what they were: an unwillingness to explore—not only for him, but with him—the unique meaning of

each of his actions, a laziness on our part in trying to understand the fears he was trying to express or to overcome.

In the morning Harry was trying mainly to test the intactness
of his body by his use of the mousetrap, hence assurance that it
was safe for the day was sufficient. But at night, even repeated
assurances that no one could deprive him of any part of his body
was not enough in itself.

From his remarks at bedtime, it became obvious that he also
felt that no woman could fail to be jealous of his male organs,
once she got a chance to look at them. Any critical attitude of
his behaviour at this moment would either have increased his
fears, or convinced him of his female counselor's jealousy.

Thus in the morning, Harry's symptomatic behaviour was an
effort to convince himself that he was strong, healthy, and intact. But at night, the unconscious meaning of what seemed to
be similar behaviour was its near opposite: he was trying to prove
to the dreaded female how willing he was to take his punishment, to be deprived of his penis. In his past life as a truant, he
had always been able to evade the threatening mother during
the day by a show of manliness, and his daring in the morning
had the partial meaning of a daring exploit. At night he would
be sleeping, and at the mercy of the feared mother. Therefore
at night he had to placate her anger, or her jealousy, by symbolically punishing himself. At night his use of the mousetrap had
the connotation: "See, I do it to myself, so you don't have to
do it," and also: "I have already lost my penis, so don't do it
to me in my sleep."

At the School his counselor's attitude of acceptance toward his
maleness slowly convinced him that she was neither jealous nor
punitive. And this attitude, conveyed to him at the proper moments, was eventually more important and more effective than
any assurance about the integrity of his body.

Another of our boys regularly had an erection whenever he got
ready to take a shower or a bath. Although we had no tangible

evidence, other indications suggested that he felt his mother used to stimulate him sexually while he was preparing to bathe, and once he was excited, he would feel she was making fun of him.

Here again it was important that this was neither overlooked nor criticized, nor yet considered freakish behaviour. It was helpful to him to experience a good relationship to a woman without direct sexual stimulation, and in exactly the situation where such a relationship had first been traumatic. When other children made fun of him his counselor explained to them that such things happen and protected him from their ridicule. This incident won the counselor a good deal of his trust.

With this child, seduction by a parent could be inferred. Other children, by direct statement, support the notion that emotional difficulties often go back to parental behaviour around the contacts of dressing and bathing which should actually have been pleasant and reassuring, but were experienced as seductive by the child.

Louis revealed his sexual excitement around dressing, undressing and bathing as soon as he entered the School. But it took much longer for him to reveal how his mother's behaviour was experienced by him as seductive and threatening.

At first, when the other children were undressing, getting ready for bed, or getting up in the morning, he would grab at the genitals of other boys. For their protection this had to be stopped, but the grabbing of other boys' genitals was only replaced by his grabbing his own penis with an anxious expression. After much reassurance he admitted that his behaviour was not so much aggressive as it was anxious: What he was afraid of, he said, was that his penis was going to be split in half or cut off.[2] He would test our assurances by trying to provoke others to poke him or hurt him in the genital region, and even when he found that nothing happened he would still show how fearful he was by hiding his penis whenever he undressed, as if to protect it. He was constantly trying to push it back between his legs.

Conversation with him while he sat in the bathtub trying to

[2] Participant observer: Ronnie Dryovage.

make his penis disappear permitted him to state for the first time how he wished he were a girl. Later, on similar occasions, he admitted he had played make-believe games in which he was a girl, and that for years he had tried to pretend to himself that he was one.

Six months after enrollment Louis had made considerable progress in relating to others. He had learned to trust us, and had begun to assert himself more. It was only then, after a Christmas visit had revived his fear of seduction, that he spoke about the original experience which he had interpreted as seduction. This was the experience he had first tried to re-enact when undressing, and the fear of which he had partly worked through with his counselor at bath time.

"I'm going to tell you a joke," he said. "No—I better not—you might not like it. It's dirty. My mom told me. It's real dirty, but she does it all the time." Then, without giving the counselor a chance to interrupt, he went on to describe a popular children's game his mother used to play with him. She would tap on his forehead, saying, "Knock on the door," then open his eyelid and say, "Peek in," then grab his nose and say, "Lift up the latch," and at this point, with his mouth open, he said, the game was supposed to continue by the mother putting her finger into his mouth, saying, "Come in." But instead of that she would grab his penis and pull it hard.[3]

Both castration fears and traumatization through seduction are often worked through best around bathing time but not only because the children have shed their clothes or because it was the setting in which fearful experiences originally took place. Since many of our children were shocked into submission during their education to cleanliness, the fear of dirt has often combined itself with their sex fears. In these and other cases, castration fears and anxieties about cleanliness become closely related.

Richard was one of the children whose castration fear, and its origin, first came to the fore in the bathroom. His compulsive

[3] Participant observer: Ronnie Dryovage.

mother had instilled in him a great fear of dirt and had insisted on frequent washings and a painful scrubbing during the daily bath. Bathing itself was such a disagreeable experience for him that for a long time we encouraged him not to bathe at all, but only to wash himself. Even so, he was too afraid to let go until his combined fear of his mother and of dirt was considerably lessened. After that he felt secure enough to take a bath or not to take one, as he pleased.

It was some time later when he was having a bath one evening, that he re-enacted what looked like a seduction by his counselor and followed that by pretending to castrate himself. But while his movements showed his penis being sawed off, what he said was, "Oh, now you cut off my arm!" So his counselor said to him matter-of-factly, "You know, Richard, I'm not your mother." There was a momentary shock, but immediately afterward Richard's reactions showed some first signs of response to her as a woman distinct from his mother, and a person who was trustworthy.[4] It was the first time he seemed to accept her even in a tentative way, and to evidence real contact for the time being. And when enough reassuring experiences had been repeated, Richard slowly became easier and more natural about taking a bath.

The connection between castration fears and the education to cleanliness is further illustrated by Priscilla's behaviour. At first, Priscilla used to sit on the toilet for hours, talking gibberish to herself. Since she was left in peace at such times, she became more courageous and began to add anal and sexual jokes to her talk. Then she took to soiling the toilet seat and later to playing with the feces under the pretext of cleaning the seat off. For her soiling she had expected severe punishment, and when it failed to come she was encouraged enough to state her fears more explicitly. She spoke repeatedly, for example, of men attacking women from the rear.[5]

But this talk was overheard in the dormitory by Lucille (then

[4] Participant observer: Patty Pickett.
[5] Participant observer: Joan Little.

a seven-year-old). When she heard these "obscenities" going on without anyone getting punished for it she felt encouraged to talk about certain of her own fears. One day after listening to Priscilla's stories, she stood naked in front of a mirror and told her counselor about having seen a man shaving in front of a mirror just as she was standing now. Then the man dropped his razor, she said, and it cut off his penis.

To begin with, the counselor assured Lucille that she was safe from harm at the School. Then to Priscilla she explained that her description of a violent or painful attack from the rear was not a true picture, that she was misinterpreting the feelings involved in an act of intercourse she seemed to have witnessed. In explaining this to Priscilla the counselor was aided by conversations she had had with the same girls when all three of them had observed dogs on the street in sex play. Without her referring to it, Priscilla said, "You mean like you explained to us about the dogs having fun when they're jumping on each other and intercoursing?" This reassurance about sex, plus the added reassurance that a man's penis cannot be cut off and that no girl ever had a penis, encouraged Lucille to repeat her story about the man cutting himself with the razor. But each time she was less excited and less certain she had seen such a thing.[6]

A few weeks later Lucille took her first steps toward working through this anxiety. She found a razor blade and tried it on her leg (supposedly to cut off some hair), and in doing so, managed to cut herself. The cut was taken care of and it was again explained to her that people don't shave with razor blades but with safety razors which can never cut them very badly. She was then allowed to experiment with a safety razor, and with her counselor's help, managed it safely. The small cut soon healed, and after the hair she had cut off began to grow back, her fear of bodily harm was no longer quite as extreme.

While some children have had traumatic experiences around the education to cleanliness, there are others for whom it was

[6] Participant observer: Joan Little.

the only rewarding handling they ever knew at the hands of their parents. Lucille, again, was a case in point. Everything in her life had been irregular if not chaotic. But her mother had insisted on the regularity and importance of elimination, and had spent a great deal of time with her during her education to cleanliness. The result was that for a long time the only chance we had to establish contact with her was when she was sitting on the toilet. Her counselor had to be with her and talk to her there, long before she was in contact with the child in other situations. Even considerably later, whenever Lucille felt perturbed she would run and sit on the toilet, and if her counselor wanted to help her in her upset, she had to talk with her there.

In Lucille's case, the parental contacts she had had around the education to cleanliness were, relatively speaking, among the most pleasant and assuring she had known. Hence, it became the situation in which she felt most secure and was first able to establish some kind of contact. But the same is not true for the majority of our children. For them, the question of cleanliness has unpleasant if not openly fearful connotations and because of this fact, any help given around the problem can become a basis for good relations.

Chris, for example, could tolerate no physical contact of any kind, and while he really wanted skin stimulation, even the softest stroking produced tremendous anxiety. Equally hated was any skin stimulation he got through his contacts with water because it awakened unpleasant memories of having been scrubbed. We found a solution to this impasse when we convinced him he could just sit and play in a tub of warm water for hours without either washing or soaping himself.

For some time he allowed no one to come close to the tub. But eventually he let his counselor sit with him, and finally let her join in his play with the boats which were his favourite toys in the tub. In this way she managed to have relatively prolonged contacts with him. After a few months of this he finally asked her to wash him, but quickly, and only when he was just about ready to leave the tub. As for letting her dry him, that was still out.

Another few months later, on an early afternoon, Chris wanted to take what he called a long bath, which meant staying in the tub for hours. With the warm water all around him, and secure from all outside interference, Chris became very relaxed with his counselor and began to talk openly about some of his phantasies. He remained in the tub as long as there was water in it, and when the plug was pulled he watched the water go down the drain. He was particularly interested in watching it swirl when it got low in the tub, stopping it now and again with his hand, and then letting it run on again. When all the water was drained he fell silent and some of the good contact was lost. But he refused to leave the tub. He curled up in it, dry as it was, and after a while said he wanted to go to sleep in it. The counselor pointed out that he might catch cold there and said she would prefer it if he curled up in his bed. As on many other occasions, she offered to dry him so he could get warm, and this time he let her; when he was dry he also let her help him into his pajamas.[7]

With this as a beginning, Chris ventured further in exploring some of his fearful preoccupations but now he began to come closer to reality. First, he got hold of a metal box which had originally been waterproof, and took it into the tub with him to play. Sometimes he would put two or three small toys in the box, close the top, and then bang the box around in the tub to see if the water would get into it or not. Other times he would put the toys on the floor and experiment with filling the box part way with water, letting it fill up gradually and then sink to the bottom. It was part of the "game" that the counselor had to rescue the box or the toys "just in time," and also assure Chris more directly about his own safety.[8]

Despite their steadily improving relation, it was a long time before Chris would permit his counselor to wash his arms, legs, back, or chest. Eventually, though, he not only let her, but asked

[7] Participant observer: Patty Pickett.
[8] Participant observer: *Idem*.

her to. But he still wouldn't allow her to touch him anywhere near his face or neck. Sometimes he would object to the way she held his wrist or his ankle, saying she held him too tightly. Actually, she made a point of handling him very lightly so that he would never get the feeling of being gripped or pressured in any way.

When Chris finally permitted her to wash his head and face he took great care to protect himself. If her hand was washing his forehead, cheeks or neck, Chris would put his hands over his ears, or hold his nose, or put a hand over his mouth to protect all bodily openings from contact.[9] It took more than another year before he would let his counselor touch him at, or near, any bodily openings. Thus his ability to permit, and later to enjoy touch, had to develop from the vague skin sensations produced by warm water, to touch on the extremities, to touch experienced as pleasant because of his relation to the person who touched him—until even touch at the more vulnerable parts of his body was experienced as pleasant instead of dangerous. It took Chris quite an additional time before his ability to enjoy closeness to a person could be transferred to other localities than the bathroom.

With his body curled up in a ball as if in the uterus, Chris had re-enacted his desire to return to the womb. Later, in the game with the box and toys, he acted out and explored how it would feel to be totally surrounded by water again, an idea which created the fear of drowning. At a much later time, when Chris was not only better able to communicate but had also established enough contact with reality to wonder about such desires, he said things that revealed more clearly what had motivated his actions in the tub.

First he teetered back and forth, pretending he was in a boat being rocked by the waves. Then he said: "I'm in a small room, but it's upside down. The floor is where the ceiling is supposed to be; water's pouring into the room . . ." and so on, with many variations, all expressing the feeling of being rocked, head down,

[9] Participant observer: Patty Pickett.

in a small room full of water.[10] From these images it also became understandable why Chris became so anxious when he saw the water whirling down the drain in the tub, and why he enjoyed so much putting his hand out to stop it from running down.

Neither before, nor at that time, did we interpret these things for Chris. It was only his general behaviour that showed us how he had had to start human relations from the uterus on, as it were. He had to learn to trust his counselor while he felt enclosed by water, curled up in it like a foetus. After he felt protected by her in this position, he could stand having her touch him, and so forth; step by step he had to establish relations as an infant would originally have established them to the outside world, and to persons representing it.

Ronnie had been brought up by a series of foster parents who proceeded on the notion that punishment and a rigid discipline were the answers to his total lack of socialization. As a result Ronnie was blocked in all his outwardly directed activities and seemed submissive to the foster parents' demands. In practice, however, he retreated to a delusional world in which he was busy destroying those he hated, which was almost everybody. Against his own aggressive wishes and the punishment that faced him if they were ever to break through, he defended himself by many compulsions, the most marked of which was a severe washing compulsion. No one recognized the child's emotional imbalance—neither his schizophrenic existence in a phantasy world, nor the absence of any human relations, nor his various compulsions—as being serious enough to require special attention. Only the fact that this seemingly intelligent boy of eleven was still trying to pass first grade work led to his placement at the School.

As in many other cases, it was the discrepancy between failures in school and the academic achievement expected of a boy of his age which at last drove society to take action in salvaging the child. Parenthetically, I might add that the seriousness of many other

[10] Participant observer: Patty Pickett.

children's disturbances would also go unrecognized if it were not for the fact that school achievement provides a relatively objective standard against which to measure the child's lack of success. If there were equally valid standards against which to measure a child's ability, or inability, to form human relations, the deviate development of many children could be recognized much sooner, with far better chances for rehabilitating them.

To return to Ronnie, he used his first days at the School defending himself against the many new temptations to a freer behaviour by spending practically all day in the bathroom, scrubbing himself. Over a period of months his compulsive washings became less frequent, to be replaced by a generalized messiness, and finally by a return to soiling. Casual remarks by his counselor about the soiling brought no reactions at first. But when she was helping him wash while he sat in the tub, the infantile care, in a setting that also reminded him of parentally enforced cleanliness, created an enormous emotional tension. By this time, however, he felt that he might be able to do something about it since the counselor's behaviour in the bathroom was so radically different from what had led to his compulsive defenses. He began tentatively by saying: "Patty, I have a trouble that bothers me." When she asked what it was, he replied: "I do it in my pants, and I've been doing it more and more." His counselor asked him why he did that instead of going to the toilet, and Ronnie replied: "Well, it makes me mad to go to the bathroom, and anyway I don't want to." There was some further friendly conversation then, and finally, when the counselor asked what made him so mad, Ronnie exclaimed in an angry and excited voice: "Nobody ever told me those things. Nobody ever taught me."

His counselor told him she could understand his feelings, that he had been living in many different places and that people had expected him to take care of himself when he was too young to know how; that probably too many things had been expected of him when he really didn't see why he should do them, but that here at the School we would try to take good care of him; that we had all the time in the world to wait till he was ready to learn what he wanted to learn and that here we would not push him.

Ronnie now spoke much more freely and without any questioning on the part of the counselor, he said: "Yeah, like when I was home. You know, Patty, every little thing had to be just so. If I dropped a comb, she'd say, 'pick it up right away' and I had to wash all the time. Every little thing I'd have to wash all the time, and then always at a certain time. And if I was ever the least little bit late, or dirty, oh boy, they were always mad."

So it was this situation—the bathroom, the washing, the handling of a child at his most vulnerable, the very situation in which he had once been severely overpowered and was now given tender care—which permitted Ronnie to understand some of his difficulties and to open up about what led him to develop his compulsive defenses.[11]

Sometimes encouragement has to be backed up by the physical proximity of the tub and the chance to get clean in a hurry, before children will drop their defenses against the impulse to dirty themselves. The knowledge that they can get clean again almost immediately will sometimes prevent their anxiety from mounting to panic when they find they have gotten too dirty.

Alice, when she first came to the School, was compulsively clean, overly compliant, and overanxious to please. Her first effort to test our requirements for cleanliness was very modest; she began with a tiny spot on her dress while she ate, later dirtying it a little more.

Despite her efforts to provoke criticism, nothing was said, but she had already gone as far as she dared. She would have liked to defy the habit of cleanliness imposed by her mother at home, but fear kept her powerless for some time.

One evening, however, her defenses broke down as her counselor was telling her it was time for her bath. Alice objected, and asked, "Do I have to?" which was very unusual for her. Her

[11] Participant observer: Patty Pickett.

counselor said no, she didn't have to, but that it might be better. "You know you can get as dirty as you want to during the day," she said, "but then I think you ought to take a bath in the evening." Then Alice asked her counselor to come to the bathroom with her, and there the whole conversation was repeated.

When the counselor came to the part about "You can get as dirty as you want to during the day," Alice said, "You mean like this?" and she rolled back and forth on the bathroom floor which was wet, and at the moment not too clean. In the space of several seconds she managed to get herself dirty all over. "Yes," her counselor said, and laughed because it was funny. After Alice felt she had gotten dirty enough, she let the counselor help her get undressed for the first time and also accepted her help in the bath.[12] Actually this was a turning point for Alice.

It didn't mean that her many problems were solved, or that she was ready to give up her overcompliance in all areas of living. But her days of tyrannizing over herself in matters of cleanliness were numbered and the restrictions she had placed on herself because of it began to loosen from this point on. So at least in one aspect of living she began to permit herself to behave more as she wanted to.

Like Alice, Andy, too, had conformed to parental demands as regarded cleanliness, but had chosen other ways to show his resentment. He was only seven years old when he came to the School, but already he had reacted to a strict and inconsistent upbringing with fire-setting and other less dramatic forms of delinquency. Reacting particularly to the harsh pressure for cleanliness, he resented anything that had to do with getting clean.

As he became more secure at the School, he got dirtier and dirtier. But one day his counselor remembered Andy's having mentioned that he liked bubble baths and she offered to give him one in an effort to counteract his aversion to bathing. This idea pleased him, although for days he had rejected the idea of

[12] Participant observer: Joan Little.

getting clean. Now, attracted by the bubbles and several new and particularly attractive bath toys, he finally got into the tub.

After playing with the boats and his other toys for a while he looked up at his counselor and asked, "Will I always have to take a bath?" So she told him more or less what Alice had been told. "Well," she said, "I want you to take a bath at night time to get clean so that the next day you can go out and get as dirty as you want to. Then at night I'll get you cleaned up again so you can get dirty all over again the next day."

Part of this answer seemed surprising to Andy and he said, "You mean, you *want* me to get dirty?" The counselor replied that that was up to him, but that sometimes it was fun to get good and dirty, though she added, "But how can you get dirty if you never get clean?" Then Andy asked her if he could "go out tomorrow in the yard and dig a great big hole and make mud pies and get myself in it and bury myself with dirt?" His counselor said yes, he could do all that as much as he wanted to and Andy concluded with an air of finality: "Good! Then I'm going to make a big hole in the tanbark [covering our playground] and get in it and bury myself in it."

Andy now felt reasonably sure that his desire to get dirty was being accepted as legitimate and a few minutes later, as his counselor was washing him, he began to talk about his other great anxieties: fear of exposing himself and castration fear. But this he approached in a roundabout way. "I like you to wash me," he said, "but I always washed myself at home, and I never had anyone in the bathroom. I want you to go out." His counselor asked him why, but he couldn't say. She told him that if he could give her some reason for wanting her to leave she would be quite willing to let him alone. At this he became flustered and fumbled a little and then he said, "You know, boys don't like to have girls see them." She asked him why not and he lowered his eyes, looking down at his penis, but wouldn't say any more and wouldn't look at her. Nevertheless, as she continued to wash him he became very relaxed. For the first time he not only did not pull away, but came closer to her. When she had finished washing him, Andy said: "Now I'm clean and I'll have to get out of the tub," but his counselor encouraged him to stay on a little longer and play with his boats.

Andy consented, but as soon as they began to play again he got very upset and told her he had broken a boat. He said it sort of challengingly as if he expected to be punished for breaking it. But his counselor shrugged her shoulders and told him boats are to play with and some of them do break sometimes, but that nothing could or would happen to his body, that it was all of one piece. Reassured again, Andy asked if she thought they could glue it together again. She told him yes, they could dry it and then fix it, and Andy was relieved. That evening marked the end of Andy's fixed resistance to bathing. With the help of his counselor he no longer fought his bath every evening and for once enjoyed some sustained and restful play.[13]

Other children must express their defiance of parentally imposed cleanliness in other ways. One of our girls used to sit on the toilet for long time periods and engage in anal talk. Generally she did that when she was sure her counselor could hear her. The counselor's presence, without her ever becoming critical, was apparently the type of assurance she needed. By neither interfering nor approving of such actions, the child's anal obsessions were brought into a social context. At the very least, her resentment of a rigid toilet training was finding social expression in obscenity instead of being discharged in solitude and in murderous phantasies.

Later she progressed from dirty talk to physical dirtiness. She managed to get her dresses and underwear very dirty and prevented their being sent out to the cleaner's by hiding them in every conceivable place. This attitude remained fixed as it applied to the clothes she received from home, or had brought to the School when she came. It was only after she had gone through a period of exaggerated dirtiness that she began to be relatively clean, and this she managed only when she wore un-

[13] Participant observer: Fae Lohn.

derwear or dresses that she and her counselor had shopped for together since her coming to the School.[14]

The importance of this freedom *not* to be clean (or the freedom to use the toilet as they please) is very critical to some children with severe anal fixations, as was best put by one of the children themselves. Lester, when his favourite counselor returned from a few days' vacation and asked how he had been, said, "I went to the toilet as soon as you left and I stayed there till you got back today." [15]

Obviously the statement was untrue, but in a way it was untrue only because he knew he could have done pretty much as he said, if he had needed to. It was the freedom to stay in the toilet, and to concentrate on elimination and what it meant to him, that permitted him, even in a time of stress, not to have to do so. In his statement, incidentally, Lester interpreted his freedom as something that had actually happened, which was very much in line with his general confusing of emotions with reality.

To certain children, at the beginning of their stay, the freedom from control over cleanliness and elimination is more important than sex freedom, for example, perhaps because the former was more heavily tabooed at home. We find many children who were dealt with overstrictly in matters of cleanliness, but who experienced parental leniency (if not conscious or unconscious seduction by parents) in sex matters. The reverse pattern is rare, at least in our experience. (In this connection it should not be overlooked that approximately two thirds of our children are middle- or upper-class in origin, and only one third of them are placed in the School by social agencies. But even the latter often come to us from homes which, although lower-class, still have middle-class aspirations which reflect in the upbringing of their children.)

Another reason for the greater importance of freedom with re-

[14] Participant observer: Joan Little.
[15] Participant observer: Ronnie Dryovage.

gard to cleanliness is the fact that we cannot go as far in granting sex freedom as we can in encouraging the child to act out his anal or urethral preoccupations.

How freedom in matters of elimination can raise a child's feeling of importance was nicely demonstrated by one of the boys. Bert, after he was convinced it was safe to use the toilet in line with his emotional needs, would excitedly ask other children to visit him or spend time with him there, rather than inviting them to play with him in his dormitory or on the playground or any other place. His stock phrase during his first two weeks at the School, and whenever he felt accepted by one of the children, was: "Come on up to our toilet and let's play there," which he would say with his eyes shining.[16]

Because it was so important for him to have freedom there, the toilet became the most important place for him; actually he behaved as if it were his realm. In his eyes, an invitation to spend time with him in the toilet seemed an incentive that no one could resist.

Before coming to the School, Bert had been a compulsively clean child who had finally reacted against his rigid education to cleanliness with violent aggression against other children. This was climaxed by a serious episode at public school in which he cut a child's face severely with a sharp piece of metal in a fight for, of all things, the drinking fountain. It was the seriousness of this attack which led to his placement in the School.

Once Bert understood that at the School he could do as he wished about elimination, he began to act out past misgivings about his toilet training. It began in the bathroom where he stuffed up the toilet as if trying to show that with the toilet unusable we could not expect him to be clean. Then he flooded the bathrooms repeatedly. In all this, he used soap as the vehicle of uncleanliness whenever he could. In trying to avoid being clean he stuffed soap into the toilets and washbowls, and then made them overflow.[17]

[16] Participant observer: Fae Lohn.
[17] Participant observer: *Idem.*

After a few weeks, this symbolic behaviour which seemed to ridicule his compulsive education to cleanliness began to occur whenever Bert had an argument with another child. Instead of screaming or hitting as he would have done before, he now stormed out of the dormitory into the bathroom where he turned on all the faucets, flooding the bathroom and making it unusable. It was as if he could wreak vengeance most directly if he aimed at a bathroom, the place of past miseries where he was forcibly taught to be clean. Later, when he had grown more contented with life and something happened to anger him, Bert was satisfied to destroy only the instruments of cleanliness: the soap bars. He would then fill all three washbasins in his bathroom with hot water and put bars of soap in each one. When the basins were full he would turn off the hot water himself and quietly return to the dormitory to play with the other children or his counselor.

His first decent relationship was established around play in the bathroom. For weeks his counselor left the washbowls unemptied whenever he stuffed them, just staying there and playing games with him in the water. When the result of his anger was thus turned into a source of pleasant contact, and was added to by the satisfactions he received in all other respects, Bert's aggressiveness was somewhat reduced. Then he was satisfied to flood the bathrooms in a more acceptable way, namely, by splashing large quantities of water out of the tub while he was bathing.

Later the counselor made efforts to socialize the splashing by bringing it into the context of his play with bathroom toys, a type of play, incidentally, which he had previously rejected. When Bert began to learn how to knock down the soldiers he lined up on the rim of the tub, and to sink human figures which he put in his boats, the splashing of the floors was reduced both in frequency and intensity. Human images then replaced the inanimate water as targets of aggression and became an important step in bringing his hostility into a personal contact, which eventually facilitated the solution of his emotional difficulties.[18]

Quite a few of our boys begin by flooding the bathrooms, often quite seriously if we do not discover it immediately. They generally select moments when they feel unobserved in the bathroom, which is not too difficult, of course, since we respect their desire for privacy at all times when we have no weighty reasons not to. Since our bathrooms are fairly large, so that the children can really move about pleasantly, and since they contain one or two tubs and two or three washbasins, the child has as many as ten faucets at his disposal. And if, as Bert and many other children have done at one time or another, they turn all these waterspouts on after first carefully stuffing all the drains up, quite a torrent of water may flow onto the floor. Soon little rivers inundate our corridors, or flow down the stairs, much to the delight (but also the secret anxiety) of the instigator.

So far we have never known a girl to do this, although they are the equals of boys in stuffing toilets and letting them overflow. To date, though, the deliberate turning on of all waterspouts for the purpose of flooding the house has been indulged in only by boys, and mainly boys who were severely and punitively overpowered by their mothers. That they also indulged in megalomanic phantasies about more literal aspects of their manliness goes without saying. But their urethral orgies in trying to flood their whole world (which is the School) was truly something to behold. Yet the feeling of near omnipotence it gave to these previously subdued boys was often worth the damage they did to the building. As always, of course, this is true provided we keep them from getting stuck in the megalomanic conceptions of their urethral powers, and use the heightened well-being they experience as a result of their behaviour to channel their energies into more constructive directions.

Incidentally, watching Bert's reactions after he had inundated the bathroom with a heavy stream of water, and his utter frustra-

[18] Participant observer: Fae Lohn.

tion when he had to be stopped from doing further damage, gave us some understanding of why his most violent assault had occurred in a fight for the use of a water fountain. To find himself deprived of control over a stream of water, and to have to see another child exercise it, created such uncontrollable rage in Bert and such a desire to get control of the water flow, that he slashed the other child's face.

Emily, with her terrible anxieties about cleanliness, was not simply preoccupied with keeping herself clean; just as compulsively as she washed her own body, she kept after her toys. When we first gave her bathroom toys, the only way she knew of to play with them was to soap them and scrub them over and over again.

Soon after she had stopped being so rigid about cleanliness, she began to see ghosts threatening her whenever she went to the toilet. As her defenses began to crumble within the freedom of the School, the infantile anxieties that originally gave rise to them came back to the fore. She was particularly afraid of the ghosts' eating her up, revealing the oral aggressions which underlay her anal anxieties.[19] In order to reassure her, she had to be given support whenever she went, or intended to go, to the toilet. Moreover, if we had limited this support to only one counselor, it would never have been effective and the anxiety about losing the only person who gave her security when she was in the toilet might have cancelled out the security of that person's presence. Besides, it was most unlikely that one person would be around every time Emily wanted to go to the toilet, a desire that for some time was very frequent, and inclined to be lengthy. After a time Emily felt sure she could always count on someone to accompany her, and she found the courage to ask them to, which facilitated matters. She would then say to various counselors, or to her teacher, "Come to the toilet with me, I'm afraid."

Later Emily began to experiment with independence. She would ask the teacher or the counselor to wait outside the toilet

[19] Participant observer: Joan Little.

for her, and still later, to wait outside of the bathroom. But she would also be cautious and say: "You'll be sure to be right here when I come out." [20]

With greater security about how others actually felt about cleanliness—and about her—her phantasies began to disintegrate very slowly. Then her delusional fear of ghosts destroying her was replaced by what had probably been an earlier form of anxiety about elimination—that it was dangerous to lose what had once been part of one's body. This anxiety she tried to attack more realistically, by trying to prevent her excreta from being flushed down the toilet, and by using her fingers to stop up the rectal vacuum that frightened her.

Her behaviour, and her reactions to assurance which for some time reached her only while eliminating, will again demonstrate the value of treatment efforts covering all moments and all places in which a child's living proceeds. It was only after repeated assurance that she was safe from ghosts when eliminating —assurance which for a long time meant nothing to her in verbal form but came across to her only through the presence of her counselor and the counselor's tone of voice—that she would speak up as she sat on the toilet. For example, she would sit there for an hour and a half eliminating at intervals, and after each elimination she would insert a finger into her rectum and keep it there for some time, saying: "When you do it you can stick your finger in." [21]

Similarly it was only by observing her as she sat on the toilet that we could understand, and later help her to understand, why she was always trying to cover her ears. To a large degree, this was due to her fear of noises, and of one noise in particular: the noise of a toilet being flushed, which to her signified the final loss of a part of her body.

After Emily had been helped to overcome her anxiety about elimination, and we had explained to her in ways she could understand that she did not lose part of her body when she ex-

[20] Participant observer: Ida Bass.
[21] Participant observer: Florence White.

creted, it became possible to further reduce her anxiety by freeing her of the terror she felt about anything that had to do with being unclean, or which took place around elimination. Her greatest feeling of security she received when she began to feel better about her counselor's acceptance of her in spite of her "uncleanliness."

One day at this time, when she was again in the bathroom with a counselor, she asked very anxiously if the counselor didn't hate the smell she was making. The counselor said no, she didn't mind. But Emily suggested she ought to hold her nose, or at least turn her head away. The counselor told her again that she didn't mind, and also insisted that she liked Emily and didn't see why she should turn her head away from anything she was doing. The worst test was over, then, and Emily seemed to let herself believe she was accepted.[22]

As she began to feel less and less fearful about elimination and less worried about cleanliness, going to the toilet became Emily's happiest experience. It was the bathroom, then, where we would find her most human, and where at least some of the time she was willing to recognize others as human. She would then talk incessantly about the topic she had never dared mention before. Over and over she would sing to herself, "Emily goes to the toilet, Emily goes to the toilet." [23]

During this time, as Emily gained security with her own counselor, she began to act out on her toy animals what had happened to her at home—where she had been whipped severely for her frequent "misbehaviour"—and what she constantly expected to happen again if she got dirty. Viciously, and for prolonged periods, she beat her teddy bear on its behind. She gave it enema after enema and because (as she announced) it was not as clean as it should have been, she tore off its eyes, saying, "You bad Teddy! You can't be your mother's girl." [24]

Now that Emily had made headway against her greatest anxi-

---

[22] Participant observer: Esther Blustein.
[23] Participant observer: Joan Little.
[24] Participant observer: *Idem.*

ety, elimination, she was ready to accept help with her next great anxiety, masturbation, but that will be discussed in Chapter Twelve. Here I will only stress that again it was only because we were with Emily at the moment and place of her greatest anxieties that she could show us something about them. But at the same time, it showed us that since she was now ready to act out her sex anxieties she was also ready to work them through.

Until then, Emily had neither reacted to, nor sidetracked, any efforts to approach her about the matter of sex differences, a topic we had carefully brought up now and then because we were aware of her acute sex fears. She simply ignored our efforts, behaved as if she didn't understand or wasn't interested in what we were talking about. But one day her counselor observed that, contrary to her usual procedure, she sat backwards on the toilet, though only when urinating. She also, on this occasion, watched herself carefully as she urinated, her whole behaviour seeming to indicate that she was trying to experiment with the way boys go about it. This was the clue that told us it was time to help her at least to understand, if not to accept, the physiological difference between boys and girls, and along with it the different ways they urinate.[25]

Stuart, as mentioned in the Introduction, had never felt adequately protected by his parents because they had given him the impression that he was stronger and more competent than they. But this had not been true for the earlier part of his life. As a matter of fact, that he had once been overpowered by the nurses who took care of him in infancy and early childhood made him still more insecure later on, when he began to think of himself as the one in command.

Stuart's education to cleanliness had been very strict. Not only was he fully trained before he was one year old, but even before that he had been given suppositories every day, and put on the toilet seat every hour. Thus during his toilet training he had experienced the total control which he later tried to impose on his

[25] Participant observer: Esther Blustein.

parents and the rest of the world. As a result of his training he was compulsively clean when he came to the School.

In acting out, and later working through, his resentment toward the world Stuart began with the more lately imposed demands for washing and bathing, long before he could work through his anger about the way he had been toilet trained. As a newcomer, Stuart's anger expressed itself in random but violent temper outbursts, and in vicious attacks on adults and children which seemed equally random in motivation.

Our first chance to help Stuart came when he was taking a bath one evening and broke a bar of soap into four pieces calling them mother, father, grandmother, and grandfather. First he let them float around in the tub for some time and then, with great glee, he drowned them and declared they had totally disappeared, had dissolved in the water.[26]

Two months later he began to indulge his great interest in the defecation that was so rigorously controlled at an early age, and began to show signs of defiance against the habits enforced at that time. He began to wipe himself with a towel instead of with toilet paper and would then hold the towel to his nose to smell it, and hang on to it for some time.[27] Shortly after that he stopped wiping himself altogether, but at first only when he knew he was going to get clean very soon afterward.

He would do this, for example, just before his bath, or would request a bath shortly after he had had a bowel movement. The fact that children can take a bath any time they like made it possible for Stuart to defy parentally imposed cleanliness without suffering too much anxiety about soiling himself or his underwear. Thus Stuart was able to free himself of some of his anxieties by finding out through experiment that no catastrophe followed from being unclean.

A month later he felt encouraged enough to become more open about his sex anxieties and to experiment with those. One might speculate as to why this was another fear he could explore

[26] Participant observer: Ronnie Dryovage.
[27] Participant observer: Calvin Axford.

only in the bathroom. It might have been because the bathroom was where he had just known a reassuring freedom in regard to cleanliness, but it might also have been because of the connection in his mind between sex and elimination. Losing something that had once been part of his body seemed to bring out some of the sex anxieties that were most acute where the fear for his penis was concerned.

Usually when Stuart was going to have a bath, he took along a model seaplane he had built for himself. One day he pointed this toward his penis and brought the propeller close to it. After some encouragement by the counselor to explain what he was doing, Stuart admitted that he was trying to see if the propeller would cut off his penis. The counselor talked reassuringly to him and he dropped the game, but was by no means fully rid of his fears.[28]

A month later his behaviour at bedtime suggested that it was probably this fear of losing part of his body, as symbolized in his mind by the loss of his feces, which induced him to reveal his castration fear in the bathroom. Stuart had just used his allowance to buy a huge pencil (nearly a foot long and quite thick). That night, as he was going to bed, he took the pencil and held one end of it to his penis, putting the other end in his mouth. In doing so, he announced very excitedly that he could now "suck the piss out of my penis" and wouldn't have to lose it.[29]

This episode may also illustrate how important it is that we grant children the greatest possible freedom of action. Without it, they would never have a chance to test out their anxieties, and those anxieties might remain hidden much longer. It was only because he knew he had absolute freedom to spend his allowance as he pleased (and because his allowance was ample) that Stuart could buy the pencil he needed in terms of his particular anxieties.

If, for example, Stuart had not been given all the candy he

[28] Participant observer: Calvin Axford.
[29] Participant observer: *Idem.*

wanted, or if he had had to use his allowance for this or other "unessential" needs, he might have felt under sufficient pressure to buy candy or to save for something else his heart was set on, and would have been unable to follow a certainly unconscious motive in buying the pencil. The pencil itself he bought on the spur of the moment, without knowing he was going to use it in the way just described. He also used it on the spur of the moment, following unconscious motives in putting it to his penis and his mouth. Thus an all-around freedom to act on spur of the moment impulses is necessary if a child is to bring out in life situations those types of behaviour which, under more restrictive circumstances, will appear not at all, or only in the protection of the treatment room removed from the child's everyday life experiences.

As always, I must add that some definite protection is also needed in permitting such freedom. Otherwise it can disintegrate into chaos, or lead to consequences that may turn it into its opposite. If, for example, Stuart had been permitted to discharge his anger in destructive temper outbursts (as at home) he would have felt little need to work through his emotional difficulties. If, on the other hand, he had not felt that the counselor would protect him against ridicule by other children, if he had had to fear that the counselor might ridicule or scold him because of his open handling of himself, or because he openly expressed what he was acting out with the pencil, then, too, Stuart would have been too afraid to behave as he did.

After another month, Stuart became more specific about his fear of losing part of his body. At bedtime he began to talk about girls having their penes cut off, and about vaginas growing in their places. When his male counselor assured him that no girl ever had a penis, that they had always had vaginas, Stuart changed his story and claimed that girls cut off their own penes. And when this, too, was discussed at length with him, including why many boys develop such ideas, Stuart finally admitted that his actual fear was that boys might have their penes cut off. When assured about this he again altered his story to say that a boy might cut his own penis off. And now, finally he accepted his male counselor's assurance, and felt considerably less anxious about the matter.[30]

But a man's assurance was not enough. In the final analysis, it had been a woman who had overpowered him during his toilet training. Therefore, Stuart had to get similar assurance from a woman. He now provoked an analogous conversation with his woman counselor, but more directly and again while he was taking a bath. He began it by saying to her, in front of another boy, "Did you know that a girl had a penis and it was cut off and now she has only a vagina left?"

The counselor gave him careful reassurance about this point and also discussed sex differences with him as well as children's anxieties about them. And this time, Stuart gave a more direct picture of the connection he had established between forbidden sex activities and his fear of being castrated. He began to masturbate, again provocatively, and while doing so he asked his counselor, "If a man's penis were cut off, would it grow on again?" But now his behaviour made it easy for his counselor to show him the connection between his castration fear and his masturbation, and she gave him much patient reassurance about both.[31]

[30] Participant observer: Calvin Axford.
[31] Participant observer: Betty Lou Pingree.

12

bedtime

ANY help we can give a child at bedtime may well be more important than whatever we can do for him during the day. Restoring him to undisturbed night rest is one of the most significant services the School can render the child, and often one of the earliest steps toward unraveling his problems. Many of our children come to us with a long history of insomnia and night terrors. If we can at least restore their ability to enjoy ten or more hours of unbroken sleep, we have gone a long way toward settling them down, making them less anxious, less tense, and in general more comfortable. This service, once achieved, then makes our work during the day very much simpler.

While undressing and bathing have their critical moments because of their potentials for erotic stimulation, bedtime, for a host of other reasons, is one of the most difficult periods of the day at an institution for emotionally disturbed children. It is not just that the children are wakeful because they have a fear of the dark or of nightmares. Fear of the next day, of perhaps not awakening again in the morning, is also strong enough to keep some of them from falling asleep.

Jack, for example, whose night fears will be taken up again later in the chapter, was one of the children who found relief from bedtime anxieties of several years' standing within a few months after coming to the School. Nevertheless, he suffered a short revival of his night fears on returning from a visit to his parents. At that time he revealed why he had always dreaded falling asleep when he told his counselor: "Josette, if I'm awake —I mean if I'm alive in the morning, I'll be lucky." [1]

But while Jack was able to state his fears with their hold still relatively strong on him, other children can do so only after their night fears have partially or wholly disappeared. They must first convince themselves of their safety at night, before they can admit they were ever frightened at all. Keith, for example, long after he had learned to sleep soundly at night, told us one day, "I used to think I was going to die if I went to sleep. Now I know if I'm asleep I'm just resting." [2]

With other children it is their separation fears that are most acutely revived at bedtime because they know that during the night the person they trust most—their favourite counselor—will not be physically present, though they know he is available if they need him. Fortunately, however, bedtime is also a period when group living exerts its reassuring qualities. The example of other children who are already more trusting about life, who can fall asleep without special fears or special efforts, is reassuring in itself. So is the presence of the other children and the fact that at least one counselor for each group lives in the house and is easily reached.

During the first days or weeks of his stay almost every child will test to see if his counselor is really there for him during the night, and it is one of his most comforting experiences to find that is so. For the most part, children come to their counselors' rooms in the middle of the night to see if an adult will spend time with them and quiet the fears that have been aroused by separation or nightmares. So it is understandable that learning to find his way to the room of his counselor is usually the child's first experience with orienting himself physically within the School. (Spatial orientation is an important step toward security, and the inhibition of exploring is first lessened when the child

---

[1] Participant observer: Josette Wingo.
[2] Participant observer: Florence White.

explores the buildings and grounds. Exploration of the School slowly extends to the block, and finally to the neighbourhood. When the children get ready to explore in this way, they are helped to visualize and master space by drawing plans of the School, then maps of the block and the neighbourhood, etc.)

The children are not only afraid of what may happen to them when they cannot be watchful, but also of what they may possibly do to others when controls are relaxed. One boy, for example, believed he might kill someone if he walked in his sleep, another that he might accidentally fall out of a window.

Ronnie's mother, from the time of her son's birth, had suffered severe depressions, had made attempts at suicide, and had even contemplated killing her children and herself. So Ronnie was taken out of his home and lived in nurseries or foster homes from infancy on. When he came to the School at the age of eleven he was totally unable to relate and lived entirely in his delusional phantasy world. His intellectual blocking was so severe that he appeared feeble-minded.

After three weeks at the School, he became able to talk about his night fears and at the same time to indicate that his intellectual blocking was no less than an avoidance of thinking; he was afraid to think because his thoughts might lead to dreams, and then in his sleep he might commit those criminal acts he only contemplated in his thoughts.

As he told the psychiatrist, "If you think about it, it makes you dream. And then you may do it—just kill." He said he was mainly afraid he might do "it" in his sleep. Ronnie admitted that it helped that the counselors were around, but added that it was too bad they didn't sleep in the same room with him. Then he decided that even that might not help because even if the counselor were in the room at night and seemed to be awake, he might actually be walking in his sleep. He continued that it would be best if somebody could be awake and watching him all the time.

Ronnie added that he thought that maybe I was always awake, but he wasn't even sure about me. He ended the conversation by saying that the main thing was "to find out first—I have to have proof;" i.e., about whether he could afford to think, and if it was true that there was no danger he might act in his sleep on the basis of his thoughts.

Ronnie must have convinced himself fairly soon about how safe it was to sleep because some four weeks later he was falling asleep relatively easily, and for the most part slept undisturbed. At about the same time he was beginning to learn in class though up to then he had never even performed on a pre-school level. This was probably not so much because the nature of his thoughts and hostile wishes had changed, as that he had convinced himself that the persons whom he hated so much were nowhere near. He may also have reasoned that even those persons he might meet if he walked in his sleep at the School were not the ones he hated so deeply.

As in Ronnie's case, the content of this kind of anxiety in children is not so much the fear that they may hurt or kill just any person in their sleep, even though that fear is the only one they are aware of and hence the only one they can talk about directly. What a child is unconsciously afraid of is that he may hurt some specific person, whether a parent or one of his siblings. Similarly, if the child fears that somebody is liable to do him injury, behind this "somebody" is always hidden a particular significant person; if he fears punishment (by castration or otherwise) for his aggressive or sexual desires, it is usually a parent rather than a sibling whom he fears.

Although the child does not consciously know who the person is he is so afraid of, or for whose safety he fears, the very fact that the School is geographically removed from that person does a great deal to quiet his night fears.

In the same way, children who suffer from insomnia because they want to be able to control their parents all the time, or at least to know what their parents are doing at night, soon realize that staying awake all night at the School is no use to them in achieving this goal. Hence it becomes understandable that the physical separation from parents and siblings, in itself, goes a long way to restoring the children to sound sleep if their insomnia or other sleeping difficulties have their roots in the mechanisms just described.

Mere physical separation, however, though it offers some protection from fear, does not automatically reduce masturbation or castration fears unless the fears were specifically concerned with what a parent might do if the child was found masturbating, or if the child thought that it was only a parent and nobody else who might threaten his genitals. The fear of some specific person is rarely the sole origin of such fears, and hence the child needs more than distance in space to reduce his anxieties.

When they first come to the School, almost all children suffer from sexual fears in some form or other. They are afraid, for example, that they may masturbate after the adult leaves the room, or that the adult will find out if they do. Even those children who masturbate conspicuously often do it out of fear, and their masturbation is a constant effort to convince themselves that their genitals are adequate.

In every group there are some children who want the light left burning, or the curtains drawn aside, so that the room will not be too dark. The reason may be that they feel less isolated while there is some light, or they may want to be able to think that someone can see them, which may help them in fighting the desire to masturbate. Other children would prefer total darkness, which would make them feel relatively safe from observation and hence free to masturbate. In practice we try to steer a middle course. The bedrooms are neither pitch dark nor really well-lighted, but all corridors and bathrooms are well-lit as additional reassurance for the children, and to help them find their way to the counselors' rooms if they should need an adult. Even more important is our removing their fear of masturbation, but that usually takes quite a time.

A child's fear of darkness is not limited merely to separation from other persons (their protection or control), or to nightmares, or the harm that may befall him, or even what he may do to others. Just as often it is a child's fear of other instinctual desires that he feels he is not supposed to satisfy.

The child's anxiety about doing something forbidden in his sleep when his ego has lost control over his actions, is typically expressed in the fear that he may wet his bed during the night. The simplest way to deal with this fear—and often with it the bedwetting—is to treat the whole thing not as something forbidden, but as by and large acceptable behaviour. This also deprives it of some of the secondary pleasure attached to it; it loses its spiteful, or daring, or provocative connotations. In short it is taken as a matter of course. The children are given to understand that the maids will change the sheets daily instead of weekly, and there the matter ends.

If other children take to teasing the bedwetter, we protect him. We make it clear that he has every right to wet his bed if he wants to, but on the other hand, when bedwetters say they cannot help wetting their beds, their remarks are accepted with some slight scepticism.

This is in line with our policy of stressing the fact that every child at the School has the right to do what he wants to if it involves no dangers to himself or to others, and does not infringe on the legitimate interests of others. So while we protect the child's "right" to wet his bed, we try to let him know that in our estimation he is well able, if he really wants to, to exercise all the controls and to master all the achievements that are in line with his developmental age. Thus, while we do not put him on the spot by openly doubting his statement that he cannot help wetting—a doubt that would fall on his ears like a threat to his self-respect and the feeling of status we wish to build up in him —our slight scepticism at least indicates that we have more faith in his ability to control himself than he has. We give him to understand that he underestimates his own powers.

In line with these considerations, the newcomer's demands that he be wakened at night to be taken to the toilet are rejected.

We just tell him not to be afraid of wetting his bed, that we don't mind a wet bed, but that under no circumstances will we break up his sleep to save the laundry the trouble of washing a few sheets. The last remark is important in convincing the child that he does not make trouble for us by wetting—a secondary gain I have already mentioned as a strong factor in the wetting of quite a few children. For them it was formerly one of the few ways in which they could satisfy the unconscious desires of parents, or make life difficult for them without being punished for it.

After a few weeks at the School, all children understand that bedwetting is a symptom like any other, neither more serious nor more obnoxious. As a matter of fact, we sometimes go far beyond this protection of the bedwetter and his "right" to wet his bed, and find it necessary to encourage a child to do so.

The gradual changes in Emily's behaviour were typical of a child fearful of bedwetting who comes to like us and trust us because of our attitude toward enuresis. One evening rather early in her stay at the School, Emily was having a hard time falling asleep. She was mumbling things to herself which her counselor could not understand, but refused to talk more clearly about what was bothering her. Nevertheless, she wanted her counselor to remain sitting close to her bed and to continue listening to her indistinct ramblings. Finally the counselor understood something about "bed" and "wet" and asked Emily if she had wet her bed.

In garbled language, Emily said she sometimes used to wet her bed, but that she never did that anymore. The counselor told her it was all right to do it now, if she wanted to, and Emily asked several questions, trying to find out if this was really so, such as what happened to her sheets if she wet, and so forth.

Her counselor tried to explain our attitude to Emily and she seemed to understand because she said that at home she had been whipped for her bedwetting. The counselor made it clear that she disapproved of such an attitude toward bedwetting and assured her again that nobody thought much of it at the School and would certainly do nothing about it. To which Emily replied, "That's why I like it here. I'm happy." And spontaneously she stood up on her bed and put her arms around her counselor.

After she had settled down under the covers again Emily mused aloud about having strange feelings about her parents. She went on to wonder about the counselor and about what the School was really like. So the acceptance of Emily's desire to wet her bed led directly to her daring to open up somewhat about her feelings about her parents. But what seemed even more important was the fact that it made the world of human beings (her counselor) and the world around her (the School) appear worth wondering about too, while before and for most of the time, she had never seemed interested enough to inquire.[3]

As bedtime approaches, we must slowly help the children to quiet down, but that is no simple task with a group of emotionally disturbed children. The warm bed quiets some of them but, as discussed in Chapter Eleven, the emotions often aroused while undressing and bathing may again prove exciting—and we cannot often dispense with the evening bath if we mean to live up to our promise that they can get as dirty as they like during the day. Therefore, quiet games, once the bathing is over, sometimes help to restore peace. Eating together is even more effective. A kitchen raid in pajamas is a great help, but we have five groups and only one kitchen. At the very least, a good night snack to be eaten in the dormitory often restores some control over excitement that arose while the children were getting undressed and bathing.

Story telling or reading is very quieting for the children and due to group pressure, it is almost always possible without friction. The children see to it themselves that it is quiet enough so that they can enjoy the story. And if a child uses this time for masturbation, it does not matter; that the room is now quiet will eventually exert its influence, and the other children's enjoyment of the story will also induce him to listen.

Nearly all children come to enjoy the stories at bedtime, and

[3] Participant observer: Jean Leer.

for more than one reason. It is one time when the whole group is doing more or less the same thing, and the counselor is performing equal services for everyone while he reads. No one can really compete for the counselor's attention and the fight for ascendancy rests. Moreover, there is little chance for provoking either the adult or other children, so that the motives for acting out are eliminated.

In general, during the reading of the story, the concentration on common phantasy material provides an additional link among those who are listening and favours reassuring personal relationships. The temporary restriction of movement makes it easier to establish contact, while many sources of personal friction are eliminated as there is less and less stimulation. The relative quietness during this interval is particularly reassuring to hyperactive children.

With the end of the reading period the children feel another step closer to the dreaded isolation at night, and night fears come again to the fore. Therefore, after the reading of the story is over, each child has to be dealt with again, but now, in accordance with his individual needs. In doing so, the counselors are helped by the fact that some children have fallen asleep during the reading thus reducing the number of children who will need their attention at the same time.

Before going to bed, all children are free to perform those rituals they depend on at night, which they find very reassuring. Some children have to arrange their clothing, others have to count their animals, still others have to be tucked in in special ways. Anxious and self-critical children have to go through the events of the day with their counselors and be given reassurance that everything was all right. Some children have to get rid of their anger by discussing all the events that annoyed them during the day. Others must be reassured about the following day pretty much along the lines of what happens in the morning. In this way, much tension is discharged that might otherwise interfere with the child's rest at night.

In helping them fall asleep, the intention is directly opposite to what it was in the morning. In the morning we wish to help the child as he tries to establish his ego control; at bedtime we want to help him relax it. In the morning we must convince the child that it is safe to meet the day and its activities; at bedtime that he is safe even when he relaxes his watchfulness.

While in the morning we must often start with non-verbal or slight verbal communications, in the evening, we must do the reverse. First we may talk about topics of specific interest to the child, such as answering questions that grew out of the story just read. Bedtime stories, incidentally, should be simple and non-threatening; they should be so simple that the child can understand them without intellectual strain (which would make him wide awake), and reassuring enough to relax his anxieties. Listening to such stories is a comfort to the child because it convinces him that his knowledge, and hence his intellectual ability, is adequate.

Short conversations are slowly replaced by more casual remarks which tend to reduce the ego's watchfulness. And finally, for those who need or enjoy it, non-verbal contacts replace verbal communication. The child is tucked in or the counselor sits beside him. We avoid back rubbing or other direct physical skin contact, although many children request it at first. We have found that such contacts usually provide too much erotic stimulation, and with it, fresh anxieties. Hence, they are not suitable for relaxing the child before falling asleep.

Sometimes individual reassurance at night is quite simple, provided the adult is already accepted as trustworthy and has not stimulated the child to anxious phantasies by reading him provocative stories. Jack, for example, had suffered from insomnia for years due to night fears. During his first weeks at the School he retained his habit of taking three cap pistols and five horror comics to bed with him every night. These he would spread out —the guns over his chest above the covers, the comics farther down.

One night, after the counselor had read the story and turned off the light, Jack, who had been quiet while the story was being read, called him over to his bed and asked if he had ever heard of the "creeper." The counselor said no, and Jack told him that the creeper came around and choked people in their sleep and killed them. The counselor asked where he had heard that, and Jack said he had seen it in a movie and also in the comics.

So the counselor talked a bit about how unrealistic some movies were, especially the "horror" ones. Jack said very little, but when the counselor had finished explaining and got up to leave, Jack called him back and asked him to take his comics away. The counselor picked them up and laid them on the dresser, but a few minutes later Jack called him back to his bed and told him about another comic book story that had frightened him.

As before, they talked for a while about how comics, like movies, are often very unreal. Then the counselor stressed how police-men were always around to protect people, how the doors were locked every night so that nobody could come in without our knowledge, and how there were always several counselors in the house to be called on at all times. Jack then relaxed in his bed and asked the counselor to put the cap pistols away saying he didn't need them any more. And a few minutes later, he was asleep.[4]

It was shortly after this, while Jack was playing with another child, that he was able to act out, and to some degree work through, his fear of persecution, and at the same time to con-nect it with his anal preoccupation and his resentment of a harsh toilet training.

During the day Jack and another boy had been acting out in play their phantasies of persecution. They pretended they were being chased by dinosaurs and they transferred this play to the pool when they went swimming. There they pretended to be escap-ing their persecutors by jumping into the pool. But they could only state this to their counselor after she had questioned them about their strange way of jumping into the water and had de-scribed what it looked like to her.[5]

[4] Participant observer: Victor De Grazia.
[5] Participant observer: Josette Wingo.

Perhaps it was the protective security of the water all around them which freed them in talking about anxieties they had formerly kept to themselves. At any rate they were led to a discussion of whether comic book stories are valid or not when they began to talk about dinosaurs' chasing men. The counselor's explanation did not impress the boys too strongly but at least they had now brought their fears to their counselor, made it part of a potentially constructive relation.

That night, when the prospect of sleep reactivated their anxieties, the two boys returned to their delusions and acted out being persecuted by animals, but now in a more personalized form. Jack took up two of the stuffed animals he had received after coming to the School, "Bambi," and his elephant "Fatty." Pushing them violently against one another, he pretended he was engineering a friendly encounter, saying, "Bambi and Fatty meet each other for the first time," and again and again he slammed them together. So with his animals he acted out his own general behaviour, i.e., making polite, friendly comments while in reality being hostile toward others.

Soon the two animals were in a big fight, with Jack again pretending everything was amicable by repeating, "Bambi and Fatty meet each other again," and at the same time slamming them violently against each other. But now some of the other children objected to the way Jack was mistreating his animals. The counselor agreed that she didn't think Jack was treating them very nicely, but she restrained the others from interfering, insisting firmly that Jack could do as he liked with his animals. She added that that was what toys are for—that we could do with them what we couldn't do with living things. So the children shifted ground and objected to the fact that Jack's animals were hitting one another without reason, and asked Jack why they were so angry at each other. Apparently this put Jack on the spot and he admitted he was really punishing his animals.

In brief, the children's positive interest and their efforts to restrain his violence were so comforting to Jack that he felt safe about showing more openly what he had previously hidden behind his violence and his fear of persecution: namely, his phantasies having to do with elimination.

Jack now dropped "Fatty" (who represented his tendencies to persecute) and concentrated on "Bambi" alone (the overpowered, the helplessly persecuted). The friendliness of the children and the support of his counselor permitted him to give up the defensive role of the violent aggressor and to revert to its origin, his feelings of being persecuted.

Jack began to slap "Bambi" around, shouting: "He's got to learn, he's got to learn! Bam, bam, he's got to learn!" With some effort, the counselor quieted Jack's excitement and asked him what it was Bambi had to learn and Jack replied: "to take his shit outside." The counselor continued to assure him by her friendly physical closeness and interest, without actually saying anything, or giving the impression of any interference. And in time, this gentle treatment of his interest in elimination made Jack see the world in a more positive light. As a result, "Bambi" seemed to learn, without any further punishment, how to behave in a socialized way as far as toilet training was concerned. Jack took the toy deer from his bed onto the floor, held him as if he were being put on the pot, and then praised him in a friendly way, saying: "Good, now you took your shit outside." [6]

This episode had extended over all of the afternoon and evening, and Jack was able to find a solution by utilizing the various opportunities lent by the various settings he needed, such as the pool. But the real ending (for that day) to Jack's resentment of his toilet training he found only at bedtime.

At night Jack wished to come to terms with the world and his anxieties before relaxing his controls in sleep. It was probably this which gave impetus to his going further in expressing himself at bedtime than during the day. But even more important was the fact that the relaxing of controls had already set in, which is typical for bedtime at School. Yet it was only after Jack

[6] Participant observer: Josette Wingo.

was in bed that he dared to act openly about what lay behind his anxieties and aggressions.

While Jack was active during the day, his very activities kept him from relaxing his controls or from giving up his defensive devices. So during the day Jack felt persecuted by extinct animals: i.e., by archaic, instinctual desires and anxieties which in terms of his age should also have been extinct by now. From these he could only escape into an even more archaic way of life —into the water, or in utero. But at night, the support of his counselor and the children's friendly interest, combined with the relaxation of control at bedtime, made it possible for Jack first to humanize his instinctual tendencies and then to make them appear more contemporary and also less dangerous.

From a preoccupation with dinosaurs he progressed to an interest in his toy animals which had more human connotations for him. At least they were contemporary, and were often experienced as friendly or even subservient, and not always as overpowering. The contradictory tendencies which had persecuted Jack during the daytime he could now separate into their two main components: the aggressive one (Fatty) and the submissive one (Bambi). The human comfort derived from children and counselor eliminated the need for aggression (Fatty) and only the more human, more childlike "Bambi" remained.

By this time Jack was in bed and the further relaxation of controls allowed him to state more directly that all his feelings of persecution and aggression had to do with matters of elimination and toilet training. He could realize then, that contrary to past experience, it was possible for the act of elimination and toilet training to be handled in a gentle way. This insight gained, Jack could fall asleep that night more at peace with the world and himself.

Here I might mention that Jack was by no means the only child who felt persecuted by extinct animals. On the contrary, this seems a rather typical anxiety with our children, particularly those who show great preoccupation with elimination. Also, the transition from huge extinct animals to friendly toy ones is

PLATE 13, FIGS. 1 and 2. *Left:* Having fun in the bath—but keeping himself to himself. The counselor satisfies his needs, plays with him, gives him toys and food, helps him without demanding anything in return. He isn't ready to let her touch him yet, he is still much too afraid of physical closeness to an adult. As yet, he cannot permit himself even to like her. Now they play separately, but eventually they will play together. *Right:* This boy has learned to trust his counselor and enjoys having her wash him. He has even asked her to wash his ears. It's all right as long as it is she who does it.

PLATE 14. Getting him to leave off playing and undress himself for bed is often quite a problem. The counselor holds out his pajamas and he has already taken off a shirt, but he turns back to the game. He is not yet through with playing. Now that he has the freedom to go to bed in peace, he frustrates the counselor as he was frustrated at home where he was put to bed not as he liked but as his parents wished.

PLATE 15. A snack at bedtime quiets down even the most overactive and anxious children.

PLATE 16, FIGS. 1, 2, 3. Night fears haunt all anxious children. Quieting them down and quieting down their worries helps them to fall asleep contentedly. They feel better, too, if they have all their prized possessions right at hand, as assurance. *Above:* He has to arrange his animals in a continuous wall against the outside world before he can go to sleep. They will keep watch for him during the night and protect him. *Below left:* The story at bedtime permits everyone to find his own way to the transition from waking to sleep. The boy in the upper bunk has built a bedside bookshelf, a mailbox, and so on. When he looks up, he can see that though he has grown accustomed to defeat, was always the "dumbbell" (although he is bright), he can do many things now. He made the picture of the *Santa Maria,* and he keeps a chart which chronicles the day's temperature. Once he didn't even know about weather changes; now he can keep track of them. Soon he will be able to keep track of his life. *Below right:* Tucking one in, while the other looks at his animals wondering if they are really placed right to assure him of companionship for the time when the lights will be turned off.

a rather typical sign of progress. But these and further steps in treatment depend mainly on our success in making them subject to the child's control. That is why the children need to live in a controlled environment for a considerable length of time, and uninterruptedly. It is the only way we can provide them with the corrective experiences which will convince them that they are in control, just as Jack came in control of "Bambi," once he was able to forget about "Fatty."

Much of the personal help given around falling asleep is based on individual considerations and the past history of the child. In Hank's case, the counselor's presence in the room seemed to be too stimulating, and as long as she was there, he remained wide awake and restless. On the basis of this observation, it was decided that for this child it would be better if the counselor left the room, despite his request that she stay there and talk to him. Therefore, when the other children fell asleep she left the dormitory. But she returned after five or ten minutes to remain for another few minutes, then left again, and so on.

Over a period of weeks, Hank convinced himself that the counselor was not permanently gone when she walked out of the room, but returned very often to make sure he was safely asleep. When that fact was securely established in his mind, his watchfulness dissolved and he would fall asleep within minutes after the counselor left the room at night. Only then did the child open up about why he could never fall asleep as long as an adult was present in the room.

"You know," he said, "at home, whenever I couldn't fall asleep, my parents did a lot more for me than you do." His counselor asked him what he meant, and he said, "Well, they explained things to me and everything." Further questioning revealed that for years his parents had overstimulated him at night. First they had told him phantastic and gruesome stories and then, with his anxieties aroused, they would try to quiet him with long explanations about sickness, its remedies, how it felt to die, etc. The result was that the presence of an adult, to this child, meant the temptation to begin fearful discussions—while the return of the adult without verbal communication proved very reassuring.[7]

The desire to masturbate and the fear of its consequences are both typical for our children, and in most cases reach their climax at bedtime. Therefore reassurance about masturbation given at this critical time is more effective than at any other. In this instance, Emily's case may again serve to illustrate.

Some time before the events I speak about, Emily had gotten some old batteries out of her flashlight. (All children are given flashlights of all forms and makes, and the bigger they are the better they like them. The combination of their form plus their ability to penetrate the dark makes them most desirable toys for all children.)

One evening Emily was using one of her old flashlight batteries to masturbate with, but it was obviously painful and seemed to frighten her a little. Her counselor told her she didn't want her to be poking herself with an old battery, that if she wanted to touch herself between her legs it would be better to use her fingers which wouldn't harm her body. In the talk that followed, the counselor managed to convey to Emily that she did not want her to punish herself for her desire to masturbate by doing it in such a way that she would almost certainly hurt herself.[8]

The conversation was apparently effective because Emily no longer actually hurt herself when she masturbated, but only imagined she might. This was observed a few nights later at bedtime when Emily complained to her counselor that she was afraid to fall asleep. She said she had had a bad dream in which a lady fell off a chair and got hurt very badly. (Emily masturbated so violently that she fell off whatever she was sitting on or lying on at the time.) A little later she began to say to herself, as if ordering herself around, "Don't cut yourself, don't cut yourself." The counselor told her that no harm would come to her if she touched herself between her legs, and that her doing

[7] Participant observer: Fae Lohn.
[8] Participant observer: Joan Little.

so didn't make the counselor angry. She suggested that Emily try to go to sleep now and this time Emily said, "All right, I won't cut myself," and shortly afterward fell asleep.[9]

Eleven days later Emily was able to go beyond this in stating her fears. She was again finding it hard to fall asleep, giggled nervously, and otherwise showed considerable anxiety. Her counselor sat down at her bed and asked what was wrong. Emily said she had a funny feeling down there; it tickled, she said, but she was afraid to scratch herself.

Offhand, this sounded strange coming from a child who openly and excessively practiced anal and genital masturbation day in and day out, night in and night out. Most probably the reason was that her counselor had by now become very important to her. While the counselor still "becared" her, Emily had truly begun to love her, and perhaps feared that her attachment to the counselor might have changed her into a loving mother, i.e., a person who also interdicts instinctual pleasures. But this she had to test.

What apparently worried Emily now, was what her counselor's attitude toward masturbation might be, whereas before what her counselor approved of or didn't approve of had been less important to her. The counselor assured her repeatedly and in unvarying terms that masturbation was not harmful, until one night her talk had an unusual sequel.

Emily had been lying on her face as she listened, when suddenly she turned over and shouted at her counselor, "No mother and daddy in the world would do that." Despite the counselor's efforts to quiet her down and assure her in all possible ways, Emily screamed steadily, "No mother and daddy in America would say that. No American would do that," and she continued in this vein for an hour and a half.

Finally she became calm enough for her counselor (who had been holding her on her lap all this time) to put her back in her bed. For several hours, then, she sat with Emily, talking quietly about various things until the child seemed restored to some

[9] Participant observer: Joan Little.

calm. Eventually, though, Emily herself came back, in a very indirect way, to her desire for and fear of genital masturbation, and her counselor again assured her it was all right. Then Emily put her arms around the counselor's neck, hugged her, and said, "You'll always like me whatever I do, won't you. You'll always be nice to me and let me tickle there, won't you?" The counselor assured her again and the panic was apparently over for the night as Emily fell sound asleep.[10]

In addition to fears about masturbation, the time just before falling asleep is often selected by the children for stating other sex fears and also their confused notions about sex—notions which they keep much more to themselves during the day, even in individual sessions, because the ego has much more control at such times. Ann, for example, after the lights had been turned out one night, said aloud to herself, "Babies come out of penises. If women die they die all over, but if a man dies, his penis is still alive." Here, as in similar instances, her remarks gave the counselor an opportunity to straighten out some of her fearful sex phantasies.[11]

Ann, incidentally, had a long history of enuresis, night terrors, insomnia, rocking, and head banging that lasted for hours. On her first day at the School she sought advance reassurance about some of her night fears by telling her counselor "You know I cry at night—sometimes all night. But I know your door. It's the one with the butterfly. I might come and call you." She insisted that she wanted to be wakened at night and taken to the toilet so as not to wet her bed, but we told her there was nothing wrong with wetting at night, that she needn't be afraid of it, that many children wet their beds, and so on.

This, of course, she subjected to testing. When she was reasonably sure there were really no recriminations or even joking remarks about bedwetting, she allowed herself to wet her bed, but for the first time in years slept peacefully through the night.

[10] Participant observer: Joan Little.
[11] Participant observer: *Idem.*

Within two weeks her difficulties in falling asleep at night were reduced considerably. The night fears, head banging, rocking, etc., also disappeared in a relatively short space of time, to be replaced by a more socialized jumping on her bed which persisted for some time. But for a long time, after each home visit, she needed reassurance all over again before she could sleep well. Without it she would return to her hour-long rocking on the bed, to her desperate attempts to fight off sleep, and would again suffer night fears. And again, all these symptoms would disappear as soon as she felt safe about wetting her bed if she wanted to, and secure enough to do it now and then.

Incidentally, when her night rest was more or less restored to normalcy, she was able for the first time to verbalize, and later to gain insight into why she ran all the time as if possessed. Then it appeared that in her case, the difficulties of falling asleep at night were closely connected with anal, urethral, and sex fears, all of them revived while undressing, bathing, and eliminating before bedtime, and the whole picture aggravated by her underlying fear of enuresis. Such a combination of anxieties is behind the wakefulness of most of our children and accounts for most of their difficulties in falling asleep.

Those first months, Ann was forever on the go, as she had been for years previously. Particularly dangerous was her tendency to dart out into the street in front of oncoming cars. After convincing herself that we never wakened her to put her on the toilet during the night, she made one last attempt to provoke her counselor into chasing her, but to no avail. This time, however, she was willing to answer when asked why she was always on the run. "I thought you were going to catch me," she said, "and make me go to the toilet." We kept assuring her that no one wanted to force her to go to the toilet and that it was all right if she wet her bed at night, until eventually she was able to reveal anxieties which were more deeply hidden than the one of being forcefully taken to the toilet but which also accounted for her rushing around all the time.[12]

[12] Participant observer: Joan Little.

One day, during the showing of a science movie, Ann watched a squirrel running, and remarked, "He runs fast like me—he won't get killed." At about the same time she also showed the degree to which she interpreted being taken to the toilet as an aggressive act, and the new ability to verbalize her feelings gave rise to a new and spontaneously devised threat. To those whom she wished to intimidate she would now call out, "If you don't do that, I'll pull your pants down." [13]

Here again, the disappearance of the symptomatic behaviour was only a necessary step toward the working through of its less conscious motivation. It took many more months before Ann was able to begin to work through her resentment of being a girl, and also the castration fear which lay behind her hyperactivity, her insomnia, and her enuresis. But without restoring her ability to enjoy proper night rest Ann would not have been able so soon (if ever) to deal with her unconscious feelings and resentments.

While Ann reacted with bedwetting to her resentment of being a girl, Lucille had to re-enact a ritual with her favourite doll every night before falling asleep. The symbolic meaning of the ritual was that the doll (which personified herself) would keep watch over her during the night; but it also symbolized the fact that she—through her doll—possessed the male characteristics which she lacked in reality and without which she felt so severely deprived that she could not sleep restfully. Her doll was set up very carefully at the head of her bed, the doll's legs spread apart and a small toy animal placed between them to represent the male genitals. Only after she had thus provided herself with male characteristics and a male protector could Lucille fall asleep.[14]

As she grew more secure and began to accept herself as she was, the symbolism of the ritual became less obvious. Instead of the doll, then, three toy animals were arranged in a certain way to protect her sleep. Later the ritual disappeared and any cuddly toy animal, now used in a non-ritualistic way, seemed to be ade-

[13] Participant observer: Joan Little.
[14] Participant observer: *Idem*.

quate. Thus in her change of bedtime ritual Lucille acted out her own progress until ritual was replaced by free and flexible companionship.

Incidentally, the clearing up of Lucille's difficulties gave us another example of how compulsive rituals may first be changed into more socially acceptable compulsions before they disappear entirely. First she became compulsively neat about putting away her toys and clothing, a task she had been very negligent about as long as she had clung to the bedtime ritual. But this compulsive orderliness we could bring into a social context much more easily, and discuss more realistically, until it was reduced to what might be considered a normal show of orderliness for a child of her age.[15]

Mary's behaviour one evening, to cite another instance, shows how sexual fears that are aroused during the day, come to the fore at night when there are no other activities to distract the child or to give him outlet for tension. It also shows how familiarity with the children's experiences during the day make it easier for us to comfort their fears before falling asleep.

One day two boys were wrestling on the play field and one of them fell in such a way that he chipped one of his teeth. That evening Mary, who used to masturbate extensively before falling asleep, did not masturbate at all. She was restless and wakeful and seemed very anxious about something. The counselor connected her being upset with the accident, and began to talk with her about it.

Although Mary had been given reassurance about the accident immediately after it happened, she had reacted rather casually at the time. Now, as the counselor talked to her about the mishap and thus showed her that somebody understood her unspoken anxiety, Mary could afford to express her fears at least symbolically.

She put one finger of the hand she usually masturbated with into her mouth, and bit it very hard. Thus the fact that her counselor comforted her at this critical moment encouraged her

[15] Participant observer: Joan Little.

to show how in her own mind she interpreted the accident as the boy's punishment for masturbating, and how she was now trying to avert similar punishment for her own masturbation by inflicting it beforehand on herself. Her counselor assured her that the accident had nothing to do with masturbation, that masturbation was not dangerous and would bring no harm to her body nor any punishment by accident, and in a little while Mary fell quietly asleep.[16]

In general, it happens very often that children do not react immediately to things they see or hear that upset them. They behave as if they were either uninterested or untouched by the experience and seem hardly to listen when the conversation takes place. The memory may be repressed on the spot, but at night, often weeks later, when the ego control lifts and the repressed returns to consciousness, the experience may come to light in full force.

The children themselves are quite aware of the decrease in ego control which takes place before falling asleep, although it goes without saying that my way of putting it has no place in their thinking. They also recognize how the withdrawal of interest from the outer world weakens the ego's power of control over anxious or instinctual pressure because vital energy is no longer directed (or needed) for dealing with the outside, and nearly all of it is directed toward the inner world. One evening at bedtime two girls initiated a conversation with their counselor about whether or not it was possible to shrink heads, and spoke of the pygmies they had heard about who did such things. The counselor commented on the odd subjects they brought up at bedtime and asked why they rarely spoke about such things during the day. To which one of the girls replied, "Because in the day time we're busy and don't have time to think about it." [17]

Mary, for example, was one of the children who had been present at the conversation between Lucille and Priscilla (reported on page 319). At that time, she had seemed totally disinterested in

[16] Participant observer: Joan Little.
[17] Participant observer: *Idem.*

their talk about sex, intercourse, being cut by a razor and so forth. Three months later, however, on a day when her sex curiosity and anxiety had been stirred up by her sister's wedding, they attached themselves to the forgotten conversation which suddenly attained personal meaning. Recalling the conversation at bedtime gave her an outlet for verbalizing in a general way about her preoccupation with the sex life of her sister whose wedding she had attended the day before.

Mary waited until the lights were off and then started out by asking her married counselor about her (the counselor's) sex relations with her husband. Mary's anxiety at that time was mostly connected with separation fears. She was afraid that the sex relationship might keep her counselor away from her, as she feared that the marital relationship would make her sister lose interest in her.

Her questions revolved around whether her counselor enjoyed intercourse, and when the counselor said she did, Mary wanted to know if the counselor, having had intercourse on the preceding night, would be on duty the next morning? When she was assured about that, she wondered if the counselor would have a baby and then stop working with (and for) her. The counselor told her that she did not plan to have a baby for two or more years, and again Mary was reassured.[18]

Nevertheless, six days later and again at bedtime, she resumed the conversation, but this time with greater emphasis on sex relations than on separation fear. Probably, too, she was prompted by the unconscious desire to find out if she could have any part in her sister's sex life, i.e., share her sister's husband with her.

This became clear several weeks after the incidents described here, and again at bed time when her sex fears and sex desires were strongest. She then asked her counselor in great detail about whether brothers (brothers-in-law) and sisters could marry, have intercourse, have babies, etc. She started out by saying she had heard a song about King Solomon and his many wives. Then she asked her counselor how he could have had intercourse with so

[18] Participant observer: Dorothy Flapan.

many wives and when it was suggested that they probably took turns, she was satisfied and returned to more primitive sexual interests.

She wondered about the counselor's breasts, asked to be cuddled and then carried, and commented on a little pin the counselor was wearing on her dress. The pin was in the form of a bird, and she said the bird was drinking from the counselor's breast. Then she leaned up against her, saying, "I'm leaning against your breast," and made sucking noises. She wanted to be babied and in every possible way to be indulged.[19]

Next, she switched her bedtime talks to her other counselor whom she had known much longer. Since this counselor was unmarried she seemed more suitable to Mary as a person to be discussing non-heterosexual problems with, while heterosexual matters she still preferred to discuss with her married counselor. Mary asked what would happen if she were to make a doll and put a penis on it; would anybody be angry? When her counselor replied that nobody at the School would be angry about it and that it would be perfectly all right, she asked specifically whether I would be mad. Her counselor said she was sure I wouldn't be mad and why did she think I might, but Mary just reassured herself by saying, "He has a penis, doesn't he?" Her counselor said, yes, and Mary said, "Well, then he knows about them," and with that she switched to her observations of men.

She remarked that our swimming coach, whom she had carefully watched in the pool that afternoon, had large sex organs. This led to the explanation that sex organs develop like any other part of the body, that small boys have smaller penes than grown men, etc. Then Mary asked if boys ever have emissions at night, and when told yes, she wanted to know about the difference between that and bedwetting.[20]

The next evening, immediately before going to bed, she carried out what she had only thought about on the previous night. She took one of her dolls, and using clay, she provided it with

[19] Participant observer: Dorothy Flapan.
[20] Participant observer: Joan Little.

male genitals. A while later, when she was already in bed, she told her counselor that she had once cut herself with a razor, and she held up her finger to show the mark.

The counselor pointed out that the cut was all healed, and now Mary admitted that some time before she had also tried to cut her hair with a razor. When asked why, she admitted further that she had overheard the story about the razor, and had then tried to cut her pubic hair. And now, finally, she recalled the episode in the bathroom between Lucille and Priscilla referred to above. Further conversation revealed more about the nature of Mary's sex anxieties and her misinformation about sex, her belief that she had had a penis which had been cut off, etc., and this permitted her counselor to give her correct information.[21]

The various steps needed in dealing with sex anxieties always stretch over a long period of time. Dealing with this particular one of Mary's extended over several weeks. She brought them up only at bedtime, although she spent considerable time during the day with the same counselors, and although she saw another person twice weekly in individual sessions.

During the day she maintained relationships on a noncommittal, even keel, learning, playing, and never broaching sexual matters or material that was otherwise threatening. It was as if she had to preserve the various "safe" relationships all through the day, to be able to talk about her worrisome thoughts and emotions to some significant person at night. This, incidentally, shows how useful it is for the child to have a variety of meaningful relationships available to him at any one time. It leaves him free to bring what he considers risky material into one particular relationship, buttressed in his daring by a feeling of security in many others.

This is also one of many examples in which the most significant material came to light in a relationship to a counselor who functioned in a maternal role, rather than with a person who, traditionally speaking, was more similar in function to a therapist since she saw Mary regularly in individual play sessions. In her

[21] Participant observer: Joan Little.

play interviews Mary maintained a relationship all during this time which to her represented her relation to her older sister. She needed such a sister-figure at that time because her sister's marriage had revived both her separation anxiety and her sexual emotions—there was good reason to believe that at one time there had been intimate sex play between the sisters.

By maintaining a stable relationship to someone who stood in place of her sister she could discount, somewhat, her acute separation fears; she could also, by the same token, say to herself that realizing or even talking about her wish to arrogate her sister's husband would not interfere with her relation to her sister, since her sex talks with her counselor at night did not interfere with her relation to the sister-figure who saw her in individual sessions. And finally, her interest in men remained separated from the lesbian relationship to her sister which at that time she had transferred to the counselor who saw her individually.

This separation of roles and feelings paralleled the split in her "day" view and "night" view of herself and of the world. During the day she was the well-functioning girl, happy at least in her relation to her sister (her only close relative since both parents were dead); at night she was her sister's rival. All these feelings could be worked through only much later, when her ego was strong enough for her to deal consciously with this material without disastrous consequences for her integration. Then all these feelings had to become subject to the control of Mary's ego. But this had to be done during the day and hence does not belong to this chapter on night and sleep.

At night, as in the morning, the child's anxiety about the integrity of his body is very close to the surface. Many children have to check up on all parts of their body to make sure they are all intact before they can relax ego control and fall asleep.

Ann's sex anxieties and her fear of bedwetting have already been mentioned. These, and other factors, had made her a sex delinquent, and had prevented her from learning or growing up, although her mother's unconscious desires contributed heavily to her deviate development. After these anxieties had been dealt with and considerably relieved, if not resolved, much more primitive anxieties appeared and these, too, made their first appearance at bedtime.

In February, St. Valentine's day became a red-letter day for Ann because expecting nothing, she had received many Valentines from other children, and a Valentine present from her counselor which she particularly cherished. All this permitted her to let down a few more of her defenses—particularly those against being unclean—and also permitted her to show us what fears she was trying to defend herself from by being so excessively clean.

Ann had been meticulously clean and tidy when she came to the School. Her contacts with her mother and her various foster parents had consisted mainly in the trouble they had taken with her external appearance (she is a very pretty child), by giving her permanents and elaborate hair-dos in addition to keeping her ritualistically clean. Ann always flushed the toilet several times after using it and also cleaned herself elaborately afterwards.

On the evening of St. Valentine's day, she omitted for the first time to flush the toilet and did not even wipe herself. At bedtime her counselor heard her saying to herself, "Two eyes, one nose, two ears, one mouth, two cheeks," and so on, enumerating all the parts of her body. The counselor asked her what she was doing and she said, "I'm counting my parts. What if I was all here except one?" The counselor assured her she was decidedly all there and then Ann became more specific. "What if one leg wasn't there?" she asked.

The counselor assured her that both legs were there and so were both arms, that she had a very nice body and that every part was just the way a small girl's ought to be. But Ann continued, "I wonder if part of me is missing." So her counselor assured her again that girls never had a penis, that they have a bodily opening instead, and she described it.

Ann listened carefully and then she said, "Do boys have more fun than girls? I don't have any fun." When asked what sort of fun she thought boys had that she couldn't have, Ann was unable to specify. Her counselor pointed out that she could play with the same toys the boys used, and the same games, and only then did Ann connect her counselor's statement about being a girl with her own general feelings of inferiority, and also with her inability to learn. "I'm Mr. Nobody," she said, "in this dormitory there are five girls and one dumbbell."

Her counselor reminded her that that very day she had written many Valentine letters, and said how pleased she had been because Ann had learned to write all the names she had never been able to write out before. Ann brightened up immediately, jumped out of bed, got her flashlight and the Valentines, looked at those she had written herself and asked if the spelling and writing were correct. Contrary to fact, her counselor said they were. (Most of the letters were correct.) Then Ann remembered that she had been given a new work book in school, her first primer, and decided she would like to start it now.

Ann, who until then had been utterly disinterested in learning about the world now asked, "How is paint made? How are waste baskets made?" She was looking around the room at the moment, and wondering about objects she should have been very familiar with by then. From these questions, she moved on to questions that were obviously bothering her much more. She asked, "What would happen if my mother died?" (her father had died when she was four years old) and, "If I was left all alone, who would take care of me?"

By her questions Ann showed how from a fear for the integrity of her body she had gone on to fears about her intellectual endowment, and from that to fears about her security within society. After receiving assurance in each case, she became interested for the first time in exploring and understanding the world. She also loosened up for the first time on some of her bedtime rituals. The stuffed animal which she had always had to place in the bed with her, she now put on a stool close to her bed and after that, in a matter of seconds she was asleep.[22]

[22] Participant observer: Joan Little.

Sex fears are not the only ones that come to the fore at bed-time—many others which are not so easily classified also seem to emerge as soon as the ego relaxes its control, and the child needs help with all of them before he can sleep. Sometimes at bed-time, we must restore a child's security by assuring him about his status within the group.

Bert, who at first felt quite isolated in the group and not too sure if the others accepted him, felt particularly low at night. The counselor was aware of this and one night she suggested that all the boys get into bed and that instead of her distributing night snacks (this time cookies and candy), Bert ought to do it. He would be the mailman and hand out the mail (the snacks). At first, Bert rejected the idea shyly, though he was obviously pleased. But after some urging by his counselor and the assur-ance of the children that they liked the idea, Bert accepted his role.

As he went on his rounds from bed to bed, he grew more sure of himself; the children seemed pleased when he gave them their snacks, and when he was through with the group of five, Bert, who had always been afraid to go to bed now simply got under the covers without any further ado. He seemed quite free of fear, and when one of the boys commented that it was nice that the mailman got a package, too, and a big one, he smiled, turned over into a comfortable position and fell asleep.[23]

Charles' difficulty in falling asleep had more than one origin. His fear of his own destructive powers getting out of control has been described in Chapter Eight. But Charles had many other anxieties to haunt him and prevent him from falling asleep. Very often the only way he could show us what was bothering him in particular on any one night was to invent stories which then made it possible for the counselor to help him. One evening, for example, he told his counselor he was going to tell her a story about Donald Duck and the hiccups. (Hiccups, throat clearing, and tooth grinding were among Charles' many symp-toms.)

[23] Participant observer: Gayle Shulenberger.

The story revolved around Donald Duck's getting the hiccups and going to his mother for some medicine. But instead of the right medicine, she gave him pepper, and he only got sicker and very angry at "that woman who gave it to him." Then Charles began to act strangely and when asked what he meant by his behaviour he said, "I act as if I were out of my mind." Then he said, "I don't understand women. They're so funny."

This led to a conversation of how he had taken his mother's efforts at having him lose weight as attempts to poison him. The counselor helped him to understand that while he had many good reasons for being angry at his mother, he had also exaggerated and misinterpreted some of her actions as being far more hostile than they actually were. This acceptance of his anger as being justified, while at the same time being helped to see his mother as less threatening than he believed her to be was what helped him, on this particular evening, to fall asleep. But this did not mean that by the next night there would not be some fresh anxiety for Charles and his counselor to deal with together.[24]

I have dwelt at length on the specific fears we encounter in the children at bedtime, but most frequently it is the non-specific fears we are faced with. Here again, reassurance given in a variety of ways will slowly give anxieties a chance to take on more concrete forms and eventually allow us to get at them.

While Mary's biting of her finger (mentioned above) was a punitive system, an expression of retaliatory and incorporative tendencies, as a symptom it was still the expression of some integration. But with the lapse of ego control before falling asleep, self-destructive tendencies that are less integrated and also far less specific may also come to the fore and must be eased by the counselor. This was true of Eddie when he first came to the School. As soon as the lights were turned off, he would start to chew his hands, to bite them, and then to bite his toenails and other parts of his body if he wasn't stopped.

[24] Participant observer: Gayle Shulenberger.

Neither verbal assurance nor any efforts at non-verbal comfort (such as tucking him in) were of permanent help. He would stop for as long as the non-verbal comfort lasted, but would only return to more violent efforts at biting and chewing himself. When his counselor offered him cookies to chew, he ate them up but inevitably returned to biting himself. Only after the cookies had been fed to him continuously, for a long time, did his oral aggressiveness seem to be pacified enough for the time being to permit him to relax. Then he was able to accept his stuffed toy elephant as a companion and to curl up with it, quite relaxed and content. After that, when he was tucked in, he would fall asleep almost immediately. But similar diversion of his aggressive tendencies had to be continued every night for many weeks.[25]

As at all other times of the day, the primitive assurance of food is always some relief. Some children, particularly at the beginning of their stay, really need an incredible amount of food before they can settle down; they must also be provided with cookies and candy on their beds so that they can know that if they wake up at night there will always be food within hand's reach.

George, for example, used to say at bed time, "I want hundreds of snacks." Actually he ate enormous quantities of candy in the evening, more so than at any other time during the day. Even after he had eaten a pound of candy and cookies, and had stored another twenty or thirty cookies in his bed as provision for the night, he was afraid the supply might be limited and would inquire anxiously, "Do we have any more cookies?" And we had to assure him about the quantities remaining in the store room before he could fall asleep.[26]

That all the children are finally asleep does not mean no anxieties will crop up to be dealt with during the night. Middle-of-the-night contacts are not too frequent, and are hard on staff

[25] Participant observer: Josette Wingo.
[26] Participant observer: Gayle Shulenberger.

members, but they are terribly important to the child. And they, too, must be handled as well as we know how. Very often, at such times, the child's ego has so little control over the unconscious which conditions his behaviour that non-verbal contacts and assurances are likely to be most effective. But precisely because the unconscious is so predominant in a child when he wakes up from dreams, the content of anxieties that are hidden during the day come to the fore much more readily, and can be dealt with much sooner than they can when the ego is more in control and defenses are more or less fully at work.

It was in the middle of the night, for example, that Mary revealed the connection between her nightmares and her mother's illness, as well as her desire to return to the security of infancy. Interestingly enough, she insisted that her counselor, too, had to be in a more relaxed (a less ego-controlled) frame of mind before she would talk about what lay in her own mind.

Late one night she came crying to her counselor's room. All she would say was that she had had a bad dream about an operation but beyond that she was silent. After some reassurance from her counselor she stopped crying and agreed to go back to bed. Her counselor took her to her room, put her to bed, tucked her in and then sat talking quietly with her. After a while Mary asked her counselor to get undressed and get all ready for bed and then come back and stay a while longer with her. (The counselor had been up and fully dressed when Mary came to her room.) When the counselor returned Mary was relaxed and much more in contact than she ever was during the day; above all she was much less defensive.

She asked her counselor how come she was still up and around so late at night and the counselor told her she had just returned from saying good-bye to some friends who were leaving Chicago. The fact that the counselor was being left by persons dear to her started Mary talking about her night terrors which had to do with having lost her mother, with the mother's long and painful illness, and with Mary's fear that her own fate would be identical with her mother's. A little later, and as if talking in a dream, she spoke about how she had been overeating for some time and had been walking around with her stomach protruding because she wanted to look like a baby, wanted to be one again.[27]

None of these things were matters she would have permitted herself to say, at that point of her stay at the School, if she had been fully awake.

But experiences at night need not only be due to the breaking through of the unconscious. The actions of a child may be quite purposeful and ego controlled even at such hours, although the deeper motives may pertain to the unconscious. Sometimes a child seeks assurance in the middle of the night about what to him are realistic and conscious preoccupations.

For many weeks after she first came to the school Lucille would wake up in the middle of the night, or sometimes force herself to stay awake after she had insisted that her counselor leave the dormitory without waiting for her to fall asleep. Behind this lay her desire to know what went on at the School in the middle of the night.

Lucille would pretend to be asleep and watch to see what the counselor was doing in the room. More often she would wait until she thought we believed her sound asleep, or would wake up late at night and quietly roam around the School, looking into the dormitories where the other children slept or trying to find out what went on in the rooms of the counselors who live in the house. If she ran into an adult she would claim she was frightened and was looking for somebody to comfort her. Actually she was trying to find out if exciting or threatening events took place at the School at night, as she had observed them taking place between her mother and her mother's men friends at home.

It took a long time before Lucille was convinced that life proceeded on an even keel at the School, even at night, before she could give up her night time investigations. But it may be that we speeded up the process because we sometimes encouraged her by walking with her all through the house to show

[27] Participant observer: Joan Little.

there was nothing untoward to be found going on there at night.

I would like to go on with my story of the School, but in a manner of speaking it is past midnight and all the children are asleep. Since I began with Lucille in introducing our children at the start of the book she may also end the last chapter.

Here, at the conclusion, I should like to say once more that we cannot expect to change our children in toto, to make them over into perfect human beings, notwithstanding the fact that the idea of perfection is a contradiction in terms to the all too human shortcomings in all of us. We can only try to bring out the best in all of them. They need not all go to college or become leaders in the business world, but if Harry becomes a truck driver, as he plans, we want to have helped him be a good truck driver who enjoys his life and makes it worth living to those he will be able to love. We try—and in this we succeed oftener than not—to teach our children to be able to live successfully, not only in regard to what society expects of them, but also as to what they enjoy and what will one day make life meaningful to them. Most of all we try to help them make their peace with themselves and with one another.[28]

[28] Understandably, the reader will wish to know how successful we are in our work with the children, how well equipped they are when we send them back into the world, and how well they stand up later on under emotional difficulties. But for that we must ask the reader's patience. The School, in its present organization, has been in operation since 1944, which means that no more than two or four years have elapsed since any one child has been "graduated." This period is far too short for us to feel sure about the permanency of our successes. Still we have now sent out into life some forty children, many of whom, for example, up to the age of ten and over, were unable to maintain themselves in school and had never learned even the rudiments of reading or writing. Nearly all of them left the School having reached their grade level in academic achievement and are doing well in public or private school. This provides at least an objective indication, however inadequate, that the efforts of the staff are expended to some purpose. No systematic follow-up studies have thus far been possible because no funds for them were made available to the School. On the basis of casual rather than systematic follow-ups it appears that better than eighty percent of our former students have been doing very

Learning how to live a useful and satisfying life has until recently been vested in the home, or in institutions like the church. It was taught to children mainly by example, by the unspoken values of the adults who raised them. Often it was not even obvious to adults that it was this they were teaching their children, nor did many of them think it at all necessary to teach the skills of living. That they were learned, often went without saying.

But it is only in a society where the desirable way of living and of living together is commonly accepted by the vast majority (and therefore conveyed to the child by his parents) that the school can restrict itself to the teaching of academic skills and knowledge. The most important of all skills, that of living well with oneself and with others, can be acquired only by living in an emotionally stable and satisfying human environment. If too many families no longer provide it, a vicious circle is created because parents cannot convey to their children what they have never learned themselves. This vicious circle must be broken. Experience gained from deviate cases in a School such as ours may well prove useful to parents and to normal schools, and eventually be of help to all children in acquiring that greatest art of all: how to live a socially useful and emotionally satisfying life.

---

well during the years since they left the School, sometimes far better than we dared to expect in view of the severity of their initial difficulties. In the meantime a book of case histories is in preparation. One such case (see Publications on the School, no. 9) has been printed separately and provides at least a first example of what the School has been able to achieve in rehabilitating a difficult child. Suffice it to say here that while every child who has thus far left the School was in many ways better equipped to meet life than when he entered the institution, we cannot claim that all of these children who were so severely damaged on entering will be able to maintain themselves successfully within society. On the other hand, since most children are normal and only a small minority so severely disturbed as the ones at the School, this book, with its emphasis on everyday activities and their implications for the rearing of normal children, has taken precedence over the publication of case histories or a more concise statement of our treatment philosophy.

publications on the school

BY THE AUTHOR AND EMMY SYLVESTER, M.D., PH.D.

1. Therapeutic Influence of the Group on the Individual
   The American Journal of Orthopsychiatry, XVII (1947) 684-92
2. A Therapeutic Milieu
   The American Journal of Orthopsychiatry, XVIII (1948) 191-206
3. Milieu Therapy—Indications and Illustrations
   The Psychoanalytic Review, XXXVI (1949) 54-68
4. Physical Symptoms in Emotionally Disturbed Children
   The Psychoanalytic Study of the Child, III/IV (New York: International Universities Press, 1949) 353-68

BY THE AUTHOR

5. The Special School for Emotionally Disturbed Children
   Forty-seventh Yearbook of the National Society for the Study of Education, Part I (Chicago, 1948) 145-71
6. Closed Institutions for Children?
   Bulletin of the Menninger Clinic, XII (1948) 135-42
7. Somatic Symptoms in Superego Formation
   The American Journal of Orthopsychiatry, XVIII (1948) 649-58
8. A Psychiatric School
   The Quarterly Journal of Child Behavior, I (1949) 86-95
9. Harry—A Study in Rehabilitation
   The Journal of Abnormal and Social Psychology, XLIV (1949) 231-65

index

body (Cont.)
  aversion to, 103, 252, 302, 310 ff., 320-3
  coordination
    and play, 219-21, 223, 225, 228
    and sessions, 252-3
    anxious testing of, 108-10
    learning to master, 219-26
  inspection of, on awakening, 105-6, 109-12
  megalomanic illusions about the, 227-8
boredom, and tension of waiting, 120-9
Buhler, 22
buildings: see Orthogenic School (setting, physical)
Burlingham, Dorothy, 66
Buxbaum, E., 241

castration fears
  acted out, 338-9
  and bathing, 327-8
  and elimination, 334, 338-40
  and fear of dirt, 317-8
  and fear of parental seduction, 316-8
  and feelings of persecution, 72
  and haircuts, 304-6
  and hyperactivity, 360
  and masturbation, 340
  and night fears, 344-5, 364-5, 367-8
  and sex differences, 319, 336, 339-40
  and truancy, 315
  symbolic testing of, 314-5
censorship, extent of, 286
child analysis, 67, 244-5
child-rearing, difficulties of
  and concomitant emotions, 7-14
  and urban living conditions, 3-5, 7
choice-making
  and shopping for clothing, 296-301, 303
  during "unplanned" periods, 124-6, 131-2
  within pre-planned activities, 280
chores, reasons for absence of, 43-5
classes, value of ungraded, 163-6
classroom
  see also learning
  and independence, 135, 154
  and play, 164
  and regressive behaviour, 148 ff.
  as standard of objectivity, 166-7
  choice of subject matter in, 154

discharge of tension in, 147, 154
disturbed reactions to subject matter in, 156-8
fear of competition in, 139-40
freedom to be absent from, 135
grouping, 164-6
group interaction in, 163-5
hours, 167
need for privacy in, 162-3
negativism in, 155, 158-9
personalized help in, 162
protection against failures in, 164-5
  self-set tasks, 147, 153-4, 158
steps in adjustment to, 149-50
truancy from, 140 ff.
classroom teaching
  character of, 140-1
  treatment role of, 166-7
cleanliness
  see also elimination; bathing
  and clothing, 328
  and retaliatory fears, 323
  and sex fears, 317-8
  and the conflicted adult, 7-11
  effects of rigid education to, 323-38
  freedom from pressure for, 312-3
  parental pressure for, 312
  testing demands for, 57 ff., 325-6
clothing
  see also hairdo
  and personality structure, 297
  and transvestite tendencies, 303
  as symbol of conformity, 303
  desire for oversized, 298-9, 301
  freedom to select, 296-301, 303
  need to wear dirty, 328
  shopping for, 296-7, 303
  symbolic destruction of, 297-8, 301
  viewed as part of body, 297-8, 301 ff.
Comenius, Johann, 22
comics, 31, 275, 350-1
communication, morning level of: see also "bad" language; non-verbal contact; symbol, language as, 93, 102-3, 105
competition
  and learning fears, 139-40
  and the general setting, 31
  desire to win in, 82
  mother-daughter, 182
  mother-son, 71-2, 79
coordination, physical: see motor disturbances

counselor
see also staff
access to, 177
as ego support, 86-8, 93-5
as protection from the group, 101-2
effect of departure by, 192, 259-60
rivalry for, 248 ff.
craft shops, 117, 279

daring
and father-identification, 138-39
and protective restraint, 125, 235-6
and status fears, 234
to relieve tension of waiting, 120-1, 125
Davis, Myron H., xi
death
of animal, 309
of brother, 306 ff.
of father, 138 ff.
of mother, 134-5, 259, 373
De Grazia, Victor, 288, 292
delinquency
see also truancy
and deprivation, 171-2
and grouping, 266
fire-setting, 55-6, 326
sexual, 25
stealing, 171-2, 174-5
delusions
see also phantasies
mutual re-enforcement of, 264-6
depression, and leisure-time choice-making, 124-5
deprivation, feelings of, and food, 170-2, 185-6
destructiveness, symbolic, 229, 297-8, 301
Dewey, John, 22
director, 30, 161, 245, 313, 343, 364
dirt: see cleanliness
dirtiness, fear of, 323-30, 333-5
doll play
and castration fear, 360, 364-5
and child analysis, 67
and separation fears, 259-60
and waking up, 104-5
dreams
and night fears, 356, 372
examination dream, 230
realistic appraisal of, 87-8
telling of, on awakening, 83-8

dress: see clothing
dressing, morning help in, 101-2
"dress-up" play, 176-8
Dryovage, Ronnie, 20, 63, 64, 200, 205, 306, 316-7, 329, 337

eating
before bedtime, 348, 371
between meals, 170
overeating, 59-60, 176, 178, 185-6, 199, 208, 211, 218, 373
eating disturbances
see also baby bottle; feeding; food; greed; meals; somatic symptoms
and early deprivation, 172, 176, 180-6
and early trauma, 192-8
and obesity, 176, 199
and personality formation, 180
and poisoning fears, 187-91
and starvation fears, 170, 176-8, 180-1, 185-6, 188
education to cleanliness: see cleanliness
ego, strengthening of the, 35-6, 86-8, 152
ego control, relaxing of, at bedtime, 350, 353-4, 362
ego distance, 17-20, 240-3
ego formation: see personality formation
ego strength
based on choice-making, 126, 131-2
gained through insight, 152
in service of hostility, 198, 216-7
elimination
see also toilet; toilet training
and fear of losing excreta, 334, 338
and fear of noises, 334
and sex differences, 336
and soiling, 318, 324, 337-8
and urethral phantasies, 332
fears about, 333-5, 338
preoccupation with, 198-200, 337-8, 353-4
empathy, between children, 210
enuresis
and money, 257
and the newcomer, 60-1
fear of, 346-8, 358-60
handling of, 7-8, 346-8
Escalona, S., 69
exhibitionism, on awakening, 111
exploration: see learning inhibition